Rwanda

THE BRADT TRAVEL GUIDE

Second edition

Janice Booth and Philip Briggs

Bradt Travel Guides, UK
The Globe Pequot Press Inc, USA

Second edition published 2004

First published 2001

Bradt Travel Guides Ltd
19 High Street, Chalfont St Peter, Bucks SL9 9QE, England
www.bradt-travelguides.com
Published in the USA by The Globe Pequot Press Inc, 246 Goose Lane,
PO Box 480, Guilford, Connecticut 06437-0480

British Library Cataloguing in Publication Data
A catalogue record for this book is available from the British Library

ISBN 1 84162 088 2

Photographs
Ariadne Van Zandbergen

Illustrations Annabel Milne
Maps Alan Whitaker

Typeset from the author's disc by Wakewing
Printed and bound in Italy by Legoprint SpA, Trento

Authors

JANICE BOOTH

Janice's career has encompassed professional stage management, amateur archaeological excavation, charity work, writing short stories, poetry, newsletters and articles, selling haberdashery in Harrods, translating documents about African agriculture, travelling whenever possible, and compiling logic problems for puzzle magazines. She started editing Bradt travel guides after meeting Hilary Bradt on a bus in the Seychelles in 1996, and since first visiting Rwanda in 2000 – and co-writing the first edition of this guide – has contributed articles on Rwanda to various magazines and websites.

PHILIP BRIGGS

Philip is a travel writer and tour leader specialising in East and southern Africa. Born in Britain and raised in South Africa, he started travelling in East Africa in 1986, and his first book *Guide to South Africa* was published by Bradt in 1991. Since then, Philip has divided his time between exploring and writing about the highways and byways of Africa. In addition to authoring the Bradt travel guides to Tanzania, Uganda, Ghana, Ethiopia, Malawi, Mozambique and East & Southern Africa, he has contributed to numerous other books and contributes regularly to *Africa Geographic*, *Travel Africa*, *Africa Birds & Birding* and other magazines.

DIVISION OF LABOUR

Philip has written everything connected with natural history: geography, wildlife, and the national parks and reserves and other lakes/forests, together with their surroundings and access towns.

Janice has written Chapters 1, 5 and 6 (except where otherwise attributed) and Appendix 1, and co-ordinated all chapters.

The rest, unless specifically attributed, is a joint effort – except that Janice has done all of the updating for this new edition.

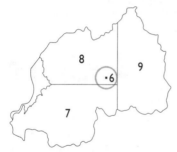

Contents

PUBLISHER'S FOREWORD

Rwanda has been one of our most heart-warming success stories. It was published because the authors wanted to highlight the fact that the Rwandan government has put its tainted past aside and the country is now a safe and fascinating tourist destination. Janice Booth and I went to Kigali to launch the first edition in July 2001. I was bowled over by the enthusiasm for the guide shown by Rwandans, from the president down to small hotel owners and tour operators. It has unquestionably helped the country re-launch tourism and put the economy on a sounder footing. I am hugely proud of it and welcome this second edition, which reflects the many changes that have taken place in the last few years.

Hilary Bradt

Hilary Bradt

LIST OF MAPS

Acknowledgements

Janice Booth

Making this list is always daunting, because I'm indebted to so many people! Patricia Kanyiginya has been as quietly and efficiently available for this edition as she has been from the very beginning. At ORTPN, Mrs Rosette Rugamba and Emmanuel Werabe have helped readily despite their busy workload. Malik Fal and Patrick Masumbuko of On the Frontier have been generous with information, as have Dr Liz Williamson and Michael Grosspietsch. Augustin Mutera, Patrick Sebudandi and Fidel Akili went off researching on my behalf, as did Marie Chantal Uwimana, who also found time to answer my last-minute pleas for forgotten details. Katot Meyer infected me with his enthusiasm for unusual corners of Rwanda and has been a staunch correspondent, as has Chris Frean. Chiel Lijdsman of the Ikirezi bookshop dealt patiently with my flood of emails and Ian Munanura helpfully updated wildlife information. I have sorely missed the warm, enthusiastic and efficient presence of the late Florence Nkera, who was so supportive of the travel guide and sadly will never see this new edition. The names of other contributors appear with their contributions. Finally, my thanks to the people of Rwanda as a whole, whose smiles and friendliness made my research trips around their beautiful country so enjoyable.

DEDICATION

To the memory of Florence Nkera, who helped in so many ways

Introduction

Janice Booth

When I first visited Rwanda, four years ago, it was to search for any surviving family of a long-time Rwandan friend who – I assumed, from his silence since 1994 – had died in the genocide. The media still portrayed a violent, damaged and dangerous country, and I did not expect to enjoy my visit.

In fact I was captivated. The beauty, safety, friendliness and accessibility – not to mention the amazing mountain gorillas, which I visited – all combined to make me fax Hilary Bradt then and there from Kigali saying she should consider a Bradt guide to Rwanda. She agreed, Philip Briggs was (to my great relief) available to cover the wildlife, and so the first edition was born.

Five visits later, I've seen for myself the extraordinary regrowth of Rwanda's tourism sector, which is already back to its pre-genocide peak. More than that, I've seen the whole country transform itself from a shell-shocked ruin, site of appalling horrors, into a vibrant, prosperous, safe and energetic nation, well able to tackle the demands of the 21st century and to welcome tourists. Its progress, in only nine years, has been astonishing.

Of course there is still great sadness. Not a family was untouched by the genocide, and no-one forgets. Memorials honour the dead and underline Rwanda's message to the world – which is 'Never again'. But it is the courage, beauty, energy and determination of Rwanda and its people that make the greatest impression on the visitor.

It is a truly stunning country, this 'land of a thousand hills': the ancient forest of Nyungwe, the lakes and rolling savanna of Akagera, the hillside roads twisting among tea plantations and banana groves, sunsets over the silver water of Lake Kivu, colourful local markets, intriguing handicrafts, thrilling displays of traditional dance, rich culture, museums and old royal palaces – and of course the unmissable mountain gorillas up there 'in the mist' among the Virunga volcanoes. And all of this is crammed into an area less than half the size of Scotland, so that nowhere is more than a day's drive from anywhere else. Tourists are spoilt for choice.

Before the genocide, Rwanda's three main earners of foreign exchange were coffee, tea and tourism, and this is still the case – with tourism seeming likely to far outstrip the other two and help to rebuild the economy. For now, it's still an unspoilt country, with no crowds and no queue for gorilla-viewing permits. This is sure to change, just because it's such a terrific tourist destination – so don't delay! Start planning your visit...

Part One

Practical Information

THE REPUBLIC OF RWANDA AT A GLANCE

Geography

Land area 26,340 km² (less than half the land area of Scotland)
Location 120km south of the Equator in the Tropic of Capricorn
Capital Kigali
Rainfall Annual average 900–1,600mm; rainy seasons March–May and October–December
Average temperature 24.6–27.6°C; hottest August and September
Altitude From 1,000 to 4,500m above sea level; highest point is Mt Kalisimbi (4,507m)
Terrain Mostly grassy uplands and hills; relief is mountainous with altitude declining from west to east
Vegetation Ranges from dense equatorial forest in the northwest to tropical savanna in the east
Land use 47% cropland, 22% forest, 18% pasture, 13% other
Natural resources Some tin, gold and natural gas
Main exports Coffee and tea
National parks Volcanoes Park (northwest); Nyungwe Forest (southwest); Akagera Park (east)

Human statistics

Population Approximately 8.2 million; 53.8% female, 46.2% male
Life expectancy at birth Women 50.1 years, men 48.1 years
Religion Roman Catholic (majority), Protestant, Muslim, traditional
Official languages Kinyarwanda, French, English. Some Swahili is also spoken.
Education Primary, secondary, technical/vocational, higher/university
GDP per capita US$260

Politics/administration

Government The broad-based Government of National Unity, with three branches: executive, legislative and judicial.
President Paul Kagame
Prime Minister Bernard Makuza
National flag Blue, yellow and green, with a sun in the top right-hand corner
Administrative divisions 12 provinces, divided into 92 districts

Practical details

Time GMT + 2 hours
Currency Rwandan franc
Main health risk Malaria
Electricity 230/240 volts at 50Hz
International telephone country code 250
Airport Kigali International Airport
Nearest seaports Mombasa (1,760km); Dar es Salaam (1,528km)

Background Information

Rwanda is a land-locked country in Central Africa. Also known as the 'Land of a Thousand Hills', Rwanda has five volcanoes, 23 lakes and numerous rivers. The country lies 1,270km west of the Indian Ocean and 2,000km east of the Atlantic – literally in the heart of Africa.

NATURAL HISTORY
Philip Briggs
Geography

Rwanda's mountainous topography is a product of its position on the eastern rim of the Albertine Rift Valley, part of the Great Rift Valley which cuts through Africa from the Red Sea to Mozambique. The country's largest freshwater body, Lake Kivu, which forms the border with the Democratic Republic of the Congo (DRC), is effectively a large sump hemmed in by the Rift Valley walls, while its highest peaks – in the volcanic Virunga chain – are a result of the same geological process which formed the Rift Valley 20 million years ago. The Rift Valley escarpment running through western Rwanda also serves as a watershed between Africa's two largest drainage systems: the Nile and the Congo.

Western and central Rwanda are characterised by a seemingly endless vista of steep mountains, interspersed with several substantial lakes whose irregular shape follows the mountains that surround them. Much of this part of the country lies at elevations of between 1,500 and 2,500m. Only in the far east of the country, along the Tanzania border, do the steep mountains give way to the lower-lying, flatter terrain of the Lake Victoria Basin. The dominant geographical feature of this part of the country is the Akagera River and associated network of swamps and small lakes running along the Tanzania border. Much of this ecosystem is protected within Akagera National Park.

Vegetation

In prehistoric times, as much as a third of what is now Rwanda was covered in montane rainforest, with the remainder of the highlands supporting open grassland. Since the advent of Iron-Age technology and agriculture some 2,000 years ago, much of Rwanda's natural vegetation has been replaced by agriculture, a process that has accelerated dramatically in the last 100 years. The only large stand of forest left in Rwanda today is Nyungwe, in the southwest, though several other small relic forest patches are dotted around

3

the country, notably Cyamudongo and Mukura Forests. Patches of true forest still occur on the Virungas, though most of the natural vegetation on this range consists of bamboo forest and open moorland. Outside of Nyungwe (soon to be designated a national park) and the Virungas, practically no montane grassland is left in Rwanda; the highlands are instead dominated by the terraced agriculture that gives the Rwandan countryside much of its distinctive character. The far east of Rwanda supports an altogether different vegetation: the characteristic African 'bush', a mosaic of savanna woodland and grassland dominated by thorny acacia trees.

Fauna

Rwanda naturally supports a widely varied fauna, but the rapid human population growth in recent decades, with its by-products of habitat loss and poaching, has resulted in the extirpation of most large mammal species outside of a few designated conservation areas. Rwanda today has three main conservation areas: the Volcanoes Park, Akagera Park and Nyungwe Forest. Each of these protects a very different ecosystem and combination of large mammals, for which reason greater detail on the fauna of each reserve is given under the appropriate regional section. Broadly speaking, however, Akagera supports a typical savanna fauna dominated by a variety of antelope, other grazers such as zebra, buffalo and giraffe, the aquatic hippopotamus, and plains predators such as lion, leopard and spotted hyena.

Nyungwe Forest and the Volcanoes Park probably supported a similar range of large mammals 500 years ago. Today, however, the faunas differ, mostly as a result of extensive deforestation on the lower slopes of the Virungas. The volcanoes today support bamboo specialists such as golden monkey and mountain gorilla, as well as relic populations of habitat-tolerant species such as buffalo and elephant. The latter two species are probably extinct in Nyungwe (buffalo were hunted out 25 years ago, while elephant spoor has not been detected since a dead elephant was found in late 1999), but this vast forest still supports one of Africa's richest varieties of forest specialists, ranging from 13 types of primate to golden cat, duiker and giant forest hog. Despite the retreat of most large mammals into reserves, Rwanda remains a rewarding destination for game viewing: the Volcanoes Park is the best place in the world to track mountain gorillas, while Nyungwe offers visitors a good chance of seeing chimpanzees and 400-strong troops of colobus monkeys – the largest arboreal primate troops in Africa today.

Rwanda is a wonderful destination for birdwatchers, with an incredible 670 species recorded in an area which is smaller than Belgium and has less than half the land surface of Scotland. Once again, greater detail is supplied in regional chapters, but prime birdwatching destinations include Nyungwe (280 species including numerous forest rarities and 26 Albertine Rift endemics) and Akagera (savanna birds, raptors and waterbirds). Almost anywhere in the country can, however, prove rewarding to birders: an hour in the garden of one of the capital's larger hotels is likely to throw up a variety of colourful robin-chats, weavers, finches, flycatchers and sunbirds.

HISTORY
Earliest times

Even back in the **ice age**, Rwanda was showing its typically green and fertile face; a part of the Nyungwe Forest remained uncovered by ice, so that animal and plant life could survive there. Excavations undertaken from the 1940s onwards identified several **early Iron-Age** sites in Rwanda and neighbouring Burundi, yielding fragments of typical 'dimpled' pottery (see *Africa in the Iron Age*, Roland Oliver & Brian M Fagan, Cambridge University Press, 1975). At Nyirankuba in what is now Butare province, a site of **late Stone-Age** occupation (without pottery) underlay a later occupation level containing both pottery and iron slag. Iron-smelting furnaces at two other sites in southern Rwanda (Ndora and Cyamakusa) gave radio-carbon datings of around AD200–300. Oliver & Fagan (above) describe these furnaces as being some 5ft in diameter, built of wedge-shaped bricks. Other sites in the area of Rwanda, Burundi and Kivu show late Stone-Age occupation sites underlying early Iron-Age occupation. The early Iron-Age pottery was later succeeded by a different and coarser type, apparently made by newcomers from the north who were cattle raisers – but archaeological investigation in Rwanda has been sparse, and there must be much still awaiting discovery. Some artefacts are displayed in the National Museum in Butare.

Rwanda's earliest inhabitants were pygmoid **hunter-gatherers**, ancestors of the *Twa* (the name means, roughly, 'indigenous hunter-gatherers'), who still form part of the population today and are still known for their skill as potters. Gradually – the dates are uncertain, but probably before about 700BC – they were joined by Bantu-speaking **farmers**, who were spreading throughout Central Africa seeking good land on which to settle. Fertile Rwanda was a promising site. The arrival of these incomers, known as *Hutus,* was bad news for the Twa; now a minority, they saw some of their traditional hunting grounds cleared to make way for farming, and retreated further into the forests. Then Iron-Age technology developed tools – such as hoes – which enabled the farmers to grow more crops than were needed for subsistence and thus to trade.

Next came the **cattle raisers**, taller and lankier people than either the pygmoid Twa or the sturdy farmers, who may have come from either the north or the northeast. With only oral tradition to guide us, there's no hard historic evidence for the timing of their arrival – some say before the 10th century AD, others after the 14th. Gradually, whether by conquest or by natural assimilation, a hierarchy emerged in which the cattle raisers (known as *Tutsis,* meaning 'owners of cattle') were superior to the farmers and a master–client relationship known as *ubuhake* developed. Then most of Rwanda was a monarchy ruled by a Tutsi king or *Mwami* – although there remained outlying areas where the farming groups did not accept his authority.

Note The three groups are more correctly called Batwa, Bahutu and Batutsi, while individuals are a Mutwa, a Muhutu and a Mututsi. However, we have opted for the forms Twa, Hutu and Tutsi because outside Rwanda they are commonly used. The plural of Mwami (sometimes spelt Mwaami) is Bami. The language spoken by all three groups is Kinyarwanda.

The kingdoms of Rwanda

Rwanda has a rich oral history, which was maintained primarily by members of the Rwandan royal court. According to this history the founder of Rwanda's ruling dynasty, Abanyiginya, was not born naturally like other humans, but was born from an earthenware jar of milk. The grandmother of Rwandans lived in heaven with Nkuba (thunder) who was given the secret of creating life. He made a small man out of clay, coated him with his saliva, and placed him in a wooden jar filled with milk and the heart of a slaughtered bull. The jar was constantly refilled with fresh milk. At the end of nine months the man took on the image of Sabizeze. When Sabizeze learned of his origin, he was angry that his mother had revealed the secret and decided to leave heaven and come to earth. He brought with him his sister Nyampundu, his brother Mututsi, and a couple of Batwa. Sabizeze was welcomed by Kabeja who was of the Abazigaba clan and king of the region (in the present-day Akagera National Park). Sabizeze then had a son named Gihanga who was to found the Kingdom of Rwanda. A Rwandan historian, Alexis Kagame, estimates that Gihanga ruled as King of Rwanda in the late 10th or early 11th century.

Before the arrival of Europeans, Rwandans believed they were the centre of the world, with the grandest monarchy, the greatest power and the highest civilisation. Their king or *mwami* was the supreme authority and was magically identified with Rwanda. There was a strong belief that if the ruling monarch was not the true king, the people of Rwanda would be in danger. The well-being of Rwanda was directly linked to the health of the king. When he grew old, Rwanda's prosperity was compromised. Only when the ageing ruler died and a new, stronger king was enthroned did the country re-stabilise.

The centralised control by the king was balanced by a very powerful queen mother and a group of dynastic ritualists: the *abiiru*. Queen mothers could never come from the same family clan as the king and rotated among four different family clans. The *abiiru*, who were also drawn from four different clans, could reverse the king's decisions if they conflicted with the magical Esoteric Code, protected and interpreted by the *abiiru*. They also governed the selection and installation of a new king. Any member of the *abiiru* who forgot any part of his assigned portion of the Esoteric Code was punished severely. Members of the *abiiru* and other custodians of state secrets who revealed the secrets of the royal court were forced to drink *igihango*, a mixture containing a magical power to kill traitors or anyone who failed in his duty. While the king could order the death of a disloyal member of the *abiiru*, he was required to replace the traitor with a member from the same family clan.

Rwanda's dynastic drums, which could be made only by members of one family clan from very specific trees with magical elements, had the same dignity as the king. The genitals of the enemies of Rwanda killed by the king hung from the drum. The capture of a dynastic drum from an enemy country normally signified annexation, with the group whose drum was stolen losing all faith in itself. This tradition is shared among all Bantu-speaking peoples in Africa. When Rwanda's royal drum *Rwoga* was lost to a neighbouring kingdom by King Ndahiro II Cyaamatare in the late 15th century, Rwanda was devastated. *Rwoga* was eventually replaced by *Karinga*, the last dynastic drum, when King Ruganzu II Ndori regained Rwanda's pride through his military exploits. The fate of *Karinga* is unknown. It is reported to have survived the colonial period, but disappeared soon after Rwanda's independence.

The origin of the division between Tutsis and Hutus is still being debated, but oral history portrays a feudal society with one group, the Tutsis or cattle herders, occupying a superior status within the social and political structure, and the other group, the Hutus or peasant farmers, serving as the serfs or clients of a Tutsi chief. The hunter-gatherer Twa were potters and had various functions at the royal court – for example, as dancers and music makers.

The complex system known as *ubuhake* provided for protection by the superior partner in exchange for services from the inferior: *ubuhake* agreements were made either between two Tutsis, or between a Tutsi and a Hutu. While *ubuhake* was a voluntary and revocable private contract between two individuals, with subjects able to switch loyalty from one chief to another, a peasant could not easily survive without a patron. Cattle could be acquired through *ubuhake* as well as by purchase, fighting in a war, or marriage. A Hutu who acquired enough cattle could thus become a Tutsi and might take a Tutsi wife, while a Tutsi who lost his herds or otherwise fell on hard times might become a Hutu and marry accordingly. A patron had no authority over a client who had gained cattle, whether Hutu, Tutsi or Twa. Whereas Hutus and Tutsis could and did sometimes switch status, a Twa seldom became a Tutsi or Hutu. In the rare instances when this did occur, it would be because the king rewarded a Twa for some act of bravery by granting him the status of a Tutsi. He would then be given a Tutsi wife and a political post within the royal court. Meanwhile the three groups spoke the same language (Kinyarwanda, a language in the Bantu group), lived within the same culture and shared the same recent history.

Rwandan nobles were experts in cattle breeding and an entire category of poetry was devoted to the praises of famous cows. Cattle were bred for their beauty, rather than utility. Between AD1000 and 1450 herders in the Great Lakes region invented no fewer than 19 words for the colourful patterns of their animals' hides. As elsewhere in Africa, cattle were closely associated with wealth and status.

AD1000–1894

Whatever the exact timespan may have been, Rwanda (or the larger part of it) was ruled over by a sequence of Tutsi monarchs, each with his various political skirmishes, battles and conquests. Oral tradition shows us a colourful bunch of characters: for example, Ndahiro II Cyaamatare who catastrophically lost the royal drum; Mibambwe II who organised a system of milk distribution to the poor, ordering his chiefs to provide jugs of milk three times a day; and Yuhi III Mazimpaka, the only king to compose poetry – and to go mad. From the 17th century onwards the rulers seem to have become more organised and ambitious, using their armies to subjugate fringe areas. The royal palace was by then at Nyanza – and can still be seen, carefully reconstructed, today.

The *Mwami* was an absolute monarch, deeply revered and seen to embody Rwanda physically. The hierarchy beneath him was complex and tight-knit, with different categories of chief in charge of different aspects of administration. His power covered most of Rwanda, although some Hutu enclaves in the north, northwest and southwest of the country clung to their independence until the 20th century. The country was divided into a pyramid of administrative areas: in ascending order of size, from base to apex, these were the immediate neighbourhood, the hill, the district and the province. (These are echoed in today's administrative pyramid of Commune, Sector, District and Province.) And through this intricate structure ran the practice and spirit of *ubuhake*, the master–client relationship in which an inferior receives help and protection in return for services and allegiance to a superior.

Beneath the *mwami*, power was exercised by various chiefs, each with specific responsibilities: *land chiefs* (responsible for land allocation, agriculture and agricultural taxation), *cattle chiefs* (stock-raising and associated taxes), *army chiefs* (security) and so on. While Hutus might take charge at neighbourhood level, most of the power at higher administrative levels was in the hands of Tutsis.

Since our only source of information about these early days is oral tradition, which by its nature favours the holders of power, we cannot be certain to what extent the power structure was accepted by those lower down the ladder, to what extent they resented it and to what extent they were exploited by it. But, whether harsh, benevolent or exploitative (or possibly all three), it survived, and is what the Europeans found when they entered this previously unknown country.

Rwanda had remained untouched by events unfolding elsewhere in Africa. Tucked away in the centre of the continent, the tiny kingdom was ignored by slave traders; consequently Rwanda is one of the few African countries that never sold its people, or its enemies, into slavery. There is no record of Arab traders or Asian merchants, numerous in other parts of East and Central Africa, having penetrated its borders, with the result that no written language was introduced and oral tradition remained the norm until the very end of the 19th century.

The Kingdom of Rwanda was isolationist and closed to foreigners (also to many Africans) until the 1890s. The famous American explorer, Henry Stanley, attempted to enter several times and did penetrate as far as Lake Ihema in 1874, but was then forced to retreat under arrow attack. Trade with neighbouring countries was extremely limited and Rwanda had no monetary system.

German East Africa

Unlike most African states, Rwanda and Burundi were not given artificial borders by their colonisers – they had both been established kingdoms for many centuries. At the Berlin Conference of 1885, they – under the name of Ruanda-Urundi – were assigned to Germany as a part of German East Africa, although at that stage no European had officially set foot there. The first to do so formally was the German Count Gustav Adolf von Götzen on May 4 1894 (an Austrian, Oscar Baumann, had previously entered privately from Burundi in 1892 and spent several days in the south of the country). Von Götzen entered Rwanda by the Rusumo Falls in the southeast and crossed the country to reach the eastern shore of Lake Kivu. En route he stopped off at Nyanza where he met the *mwami*, King Rwabugiri – apparently causing consternation among the watching nobles when he, a mere mortal, shook the sovereign by the hand. They feared that such an affront might cause disaster for the kingdom. At this stage the *mwami* had no idea that his country had officially been under German control for the past nine years.

Von Götzen subsequently became Governor of German East Africa, into which Ruanda-Urundi was formally absorbed in 1898. At this time the kingdom was larger, stretching as far as Lake Edward in the north and beyond Lake Kivu in the west; it was reduced to its present area at the Conference of Brussels in 1910. The Germans were surprised to find that their new colony was a highly organised country, with tight, effective power structures and administrative divisions. They left these in place and ruled through them, believing that support for the traditional chiefs would render them and their henchmen loyal to Germany. Meanwhile various religious missions, Roman Catholic at first and then Protestant, began setting up bases in Ruanda-Urundi and establishing schools, farms and medical centres. In 1907 the colonisers opened a 'School for the Sons of Chiefs' in Nyanza, as well as providing military training.

Allowing for the blurring caused by intermarriage and the switching of status between Tutsi and Hutu, the power structures encountered by the colonisers were linked – and this proved to be a matter of great anthropological fascination – to three very visibly different groups of inhabitants: the tall, lanky Tutsi chiefs and nobles; the shorter, stockier Hutu farmers (who formed the majority); and the very much smaller Twa. The Duke of Mecklenburg, visiting the country in 1907, noted:

> The population is divided into three classes – the Watussi, the Wahutu, and a pygmy tribe, the Batwa, who dwell chiefly in the bamboo forests of Bugoie, the swamps of Lake Bolero, and on the island of Kwidschwi on Lake Kiwu.

> The Watussi are a tall, well-made people. Heights of 1.80, 2.00 and even 2.20 metres are of quite common occurrence, yet the perfect proportion of their bodies is in no wise detracted from... The primitive inhabitants are the Wahutu, an agricultural Bantu tribe, who look after the digging and tilling and agricultural economy of the country in general. They are a medium-sized type of people...

> Ruanda is certainly the most interesting country in the German East African Protectorate – in fact in all Central Africa – chiefly on account of its ethnographical and geographical position. Its interest

is further increased by the fact that it is one of the last negro kingdoms governed autocratically by a sovereign sultan, for German supremacy is only recognised to a very limited extent. Added to this, it is a land flowing with milk and honey, where the breeding of cattle and bee-culture flourish, and the cultivated soil bears rich crops of fruit. A hilly country, thickly populated, full of beautiful scenery, and possessing a climate incomparably fresh and healthy; a land of great fertility, with watercourses which might be termed perennial streams; a land which offers the brightest of prospects to the white settler.

In 1911–12 the Germans joined with the Tutsi monarchy to subjugate some independent Hutu principalities in the north of the country which had not previously been dominated. Their inhabitants, who had always been proud of their independence, resisted vigorously, overrunning much of what are now Ruhengeri and Byumba provinces before they were defeated and brought under the *mwami*'s control. Their resentment and deep sense of grievance were to endure for the next half-century.

Germany had little time to make its mark in the colonies; in 1916 Belgium invaded Ruanda-Urundi and occupied the territories until the end of World War I; Belgium was subsequently officially entrusted with their administration under a League of Nations mandate in 1919, to be confirmed in 1923.

The Belgian era

In its adjoining colony of the Congo, Belgium had full control, but for Ruanda-Urundi it remained responsible first to the League of Nations and then (after 1945) to the United Nations Organisation. Annual reports had to be submitted and no important changes could be made without agreement from above. Despite these constraints, and despite the fact that Ruanda-Urundi had far less potential wealth than the Congo, Belgium took its charge seriously, and by the time of independence some 40 years later its material achievements (in terms of increased production; public services such as roads, schools and hospitals; and buildings and administrative infrastructures) were considerable. In terms of human beings it did far less well, as later events demonstrated.

Priorities

Rwanda had always been subject to periodic famines, to such an extent that some were named and absorbed into history as milestones of time: such-and-such a child was born 'just after the Ruyaga famine' (1897), or a man died 'just before the Kimwaramwara famine' (1906). Most had climatic origins, but some which occurred around the time of the Belgian takeover (in 1916/17 and 1917/18) could also be blamed on World War I, as precious foodstuffs were shipped overseas to feed the troops. At the same time the new Belgian authorities commented that the local chiefs made little attempt to prevent the famines recurring, or to get emergency relief to the worst-hit areas. They therefore set about implementing a strict overall food strategy to make supplies less precarious.

The peasant farmers were first of all encouraged (by field workers) to maximise their production using traditional methods. They were then given help to improve their existing techniques, for example by using higher-yielding varieties of their normal crops. From 1924 the cultivation of food crops was made compulsory, including foreign species such as manioc and sweet potatoes. Next the distribution channels were upgraded, with a new road network and the development of markets and co-operatives. Storage facilities were set up; high-grade seed was distributed; the use of manure and fertiliser was promoted; the problem of erosion (caused by overuse of vulnerable land) was tackled; farmers were required to set aside a small emergency hoard of beans, peas or cereals each year; and various new types of stock breeding were initiated. Factories and processing plants were built. Finally, the farmers were encouraged to grow crops (especially coffee) for export, so that they could earn cash with which to buy extra food in times of hardship.

These measures – not easily implemented, because of the farmers' understandable initial resentment and resistance to change – proved more or less successful, helped by a regulated but controversial and sometimes harsh policy of forced labour (*uburetwa*). Famine did recur in 1942–44 and resulted in thousands of deaths, but this could be blamed partly on the appropriation of manpower and the lack of efficient machinery caused by World War II. By the time of independence, large areas of farmland had been better protected against erosion and per-hectare crop yields had risen substantially. The scale of the anti-erosion works was massive, and many remain in the terracing visible today. Horizontal ditches were dug on the hillsides, following the contours; directly below these, hedges were planted. Water running down the slope of the hillside was trapped by the ditch, and then seeped through it to irrigate the hedge on the lower side; while the roots of the hedge contributed by securing the soil and strengthening first the ditch and then the hillside.

The agricultural improvements, together with extensive physical provisions such as roads, schools, hospitals and all the associated construction work, were probably colonisation's most helpful input to Rwanda. Its contribution to the relationship between the country's long-term inhabitants was less positive.

Power structures

Like the Germans before them, the Belgians decided to retain and use the existing power structures, but unlike their predecessors they then proceeded to undermine the authority of the *mwami* and his chiefs and to forbid some of their traditional practices, introducing their own Belgian experts and administrators at every level. This interference did not make for easy collaboration. In any case the *mwami* in power at the time of Belgian accession, Mwami Musinga, was hostile to colonisation and also resented the missionaries, since their innovations undermined the established order and worked against the subjugation of Hutus. In 1931 he was forced by the Belgians to abdicate in favour of his son, the more amenable and Westernised Mwami Mutara Rudahigwa. Until well into the 1950s, although the traditional structures keeping them in a subservient position were somewhat weakened, the Hutus still got a bad deal and remained 'second-class citizens' in almost all respects. So both Hutus and Tutsis – and indeed the minority Twas too, because they received virtually no recognition or privilege – reacted to colonisation with varying degrees of grievance.

Education

The Germans had established a few government schools in Rwanda and the Belgians followed suit, but the main source of education was always the Church. In the 1930s, the Catholic Bishop Léon Classé, who had arrived in Rwanda almost 30 years earlier as a priest and worked his way up through the hierarchy, entered into an agreement with the Belgian administration by which the Catholic Church took over full responsibility for the educational system. He may not have been entirely without financial motive: the government then subsidised the church to the tune of 47 francs per pupil and 600 francs per qualified teacher.

The Church broadened its curriculum to cover more secular subjects such as agronomy, medicine and administration; however, the main beneficiaries of the increased educational possibilities were still largely Tutsis, although Hutus were not entirely neglected and many attended primary school. Some did make good use of the limited educational openings available to them but could not easily progress beyond a certain level. Of those who trained in the Catholic seminaries (which they could enter more easily than secular educational institutions) some went on to become priests, while others switched back to secular careers. Less than one-fifth of the students attending the Groupe Scolaire in Butare from 1945 to 1957 – and emerging as agronomists, doctors, vets and administrators – were Hutus. The School for the Sons of Chiefs originally opened by the Germans in Nyanza had a minimum height requirement which effectively reserved it for Tutsis.

In 1955, there were some 2,400 schools of various types and levels (the majority were primary) in Rwanda, with around 215,000 pupils. Of the 5,500-odd teachers, over 5,000 were Rwandan.

Categorisation

Size mattered. Like the Germans before them, the Belgians were intrigued by the sharply differing physical characteristics of their colony's inhabitants, and enthusiastically measured, recorded, compared and commented on the facial and bodily proportions of Rwanda's three indigenous groups. For the more timid of the Rwandans, this 'attack' with calipers, measuring tapes, scales and other paraphernalia proved a fearsome ordeal. So man dehumanises his brothers…

Most tellingly, in the early 1930s the Belgians embarked on a census to identify all indigenous inhabitants, on the basis of these physical characteristics, as either Hutu, Tutsi or Twa, and in 1935 issued them with identity cards on which these categories ('ethnic groups' or, in French, 'ethnies', although the accuracy of this term is debatable) were recorded. If, even after strenuous measuring, someone's ethnie was not immediately clear, having been blurred by intermarriage or a change of status, those who were reasonably wealthy and/or had more than ten cattle were generally recorded as Tutsis. Identity cards – and the habit of classification they engendered – were still in use at the time of the genocide in 1994, providing an extra pointer (if one were needed) as to who should or should not die.

In 1945 the United Nations Organisation was created, with its charter promising the colonised peoples of the world justice, protection and freedom. Formerly a League of Nations mandate, Ruanda-Urundi now became a UN Trust Territory and Belgium was responsible to the UN's trusteeship council, which was to preside over all colonies' transition to independence. In 1948 a UN mission visited Ruanda-Urundi, and its report was critical of the administration, particularly regarding the inferior status of the Hutus and Twa by comparison with the Tutsis. All too often, compulsory labour was harshly enforced, and the educational system remained heavily biased in favour of Tutsis, although many priests and missions were starting to veer more towards the Hutus.

At the same time, the observers were surprised by the completeness and intricacy of the social and political hierarchy which, if used properly, would offer a sound framework for democratic development. All the necessary command structures were in place, but badly oriented.

Subsequent visits gave rise to similarly critical reports. The Belgians introduced elections at local and administrative levels – which Tutsis won, except in the far north where resentment still smouldered after the 1912 defeat. Throughout Africa, colonies were becoming restless and the scent of independence was in the air, but in Ruanda-Urundi far too little preparation had yet been made, in terms both of political awareness and practical training. Nothing was ready.

The run-up to independence

From about 1950, as the numbers of educated Hutus increased, the Hutu voice grew stronger. Hutu leaders such as Grégoire Kayibanda began to demand recognition for the majority. In 1954 the system of *ubuhake* was officially abolished, although in reality it lingered for a few more years. In 1957 the Superior Council of Rwanda (which had a huge Tutsi majority) called for independence preparations to be speeded up.

In 1956, Mwami Rudahigwa had called for total independence and an end to Belgian occupation. Just before another UN visit in 1957, a *Hutu Manifesto* drawn up by a group of Hutu intellectuals was presented to the Vice-Governor-General, Jean-Paul Harroy. It challenged the whole structure of Rwanda's administration, called for political power to be placed in the hands of the Hutu majority, pointed out injustices and inequalities, and proposed solutions. Little official action was taken.

The Catholic Church, now pro-Hutu, encouraged Grégoire Kayibanda and his associates to form political parties: APROSOMA (*Association pour la Promotion Sociale des Masses*) was openly sectarian, championing Hutu interests strongly, while RADER (*Rassemblement Démocratique Rwandais*) was more moderate. Whereas Tutsis, comfortably in a position of power, were calling for immediate independence without any changes to the system, Hutus wanted change first (to a more democratic system, recognising the fact that they were the majority) and *then* independence. For whatever reasons and after whatever deliberations, Belgium, having supported the powerful Tutsi minority throughout colonisation, now switched its allegience to the Hutu majority, ostensibly in the name of fairness and democracy.

The wind of independence was blowing strongly in colonial Africa. More political parties sprang up. UNAR (*Union Nationale Rwandaise*) was formed by the proponents of immediate independence under the Rwandan monarchy, while PARMEHUTU (*Parti du Mouvement de l'Emancipation Hutu*) was established under the guidance of the Catholic Church by those favouring delayed independence. MSM (*Mouvement Social Muhutu*) was created by Grégoire Kayibanda to support Hutu interests, while UNAR (*Union Nationale Rwandaise*) was a pro-monarchy and anti-Belgian party.

In July 1959 the Mwami Rudahigwa died in hospital, in circumstances that may or may not have been suspicious. Rumours of Belgian involvement were rife and tension grew. He was succeeded by one of his brothers. There were arrests and some sporadic small-scale violence – which erupted on a larger scale on November 1, when a Hutu sub-chief belonging to the PARMEHUTU party was attacked and beaten in Gitarama by young members of UNAR. Within 24 hours, highly organised Hutu gangs were out on the streets of towns and villages throughout the country, burning, looting and killing. Then Tutsis began to retaliate. Within about a fortnight things were calm again – around 300 had died, and 1,231 (919 Tutsis and 312 Hutus) were arrested by the Belgian authorities. The country was placed under military rule headed by the Belgian Colonel Guy Logiest, who quickly began replacing Tutsi chiefs with Hutus. He was strongly pro-Hutu, claiming to be righting the injustices of colonisation, and played a virtually unconcealed part in anti-Tutsi attacks.

It is worth remembering that this was the first organised violence between the two groups, and it happened little more than 40 years ago. Those who speak of a long-drawn-out feud originating before colonisation are mistaken. But the revolution had begun, Tutsis started to flee the country in large numbers, and outbursts of violence continued.

The PARMEHUTU party won hastily manipulated elections in 1960. Belgium, the reins of power slipping rapidly from its grasp, organised a referendum on the monarchy under the auspices of the United Nations. In January 1961, Rwanda's elected local administrators were called to a public meeting in Gitarama, Grégoire Kayibanda's birthplace. They and a massed crowd of some 25,000 declared Rwanda a republic – and the United Nations had little option but to accept this ultimatum. However, the 1960 elections were not recognised by the UN so more were held in September 1961, under UN supervision. Again they were won by PARMEHUTU, with Grégoire Kayibanda at its head. Later that year, some 150 Tutsis were killed in the Butare area, 5,000 homes were burned and 22,000 people were displaced. In July 1962 Rwanda's independence was finally confirmed with Kayibanda as its new president, heading a republican government. The university town of Astrida, so named after Queen Astrid of Belgium, reverted to its local name

Butare. Violence against Tutsis continued; by now about 135,000 had fled as refugees to neighbouring countries and the number was growing. Among those who left in 1960 was a three-year-old child named Paul Kagame, of whom much more was to be heard later.

It is true that Belgium emerged from the fiasco with little credit. But it is equally true that, even without colonisation, some kind of revolution would inevitably have occurred sooner or later, for the tightly stratified hierarchy of the 19th century could not have held firm indefinitely against the pressures, promises and potentials of the modern world.

The trend today in Rwanda is to hold the colonisers – through their behaviour during colonisation – responsible for the eventual genocide. Indeed, without colonisation the explosion might well, as a Rwandan friend said to me, 'have happened differently', and perhaps after something as inexplicable as a genocide there is a need to apportion blame as part of the recovery process. But to claim – as is also the trend today – that before the arrival of the Europeans all was peace and harmony may simply reflect the fact that oral tradition tends to favour those in power.

1962–1994

The situation became yet more tangled and yet more sensitive. Since this is a guidebook rather than a historical treatise, readers who want a fuller picture than is given below will find several good sources in *Appendix 3*, page 237. John Reader's *Africa* (Penguin, 1998) is particularly recommended, as is Gérard Prunier's *The Rwanda Crisis – History of a Genocide* (Hurst, 1998). They (among others) have been used as sources in this chapter.

Once in power, the government sought to reinforce its supremacy. 'Quotas' were introduced, giving the Tutsi (who were a minority of about 9% of the population) a right to only 9% of school places, 9% of jobs in the workforce and so on. Small groups of Tutsi exiles in neighbouring countries made sporadic commando-style raids into Rwanda, leading to severe reprisals. In late 1963, up to 10,000 Tutsis were killed. The pattern of violence continued.

In 1964 the Fabian Society (London) published a report entitled *Massacre in Rwanda*, commenting on events since 1959. Also – chillingly, in view of what happened 30 years later – a report entitled *Attempted Genocide in Rwanda* appeared in the March 1964 issue of *The World Today* (vol 20, no 3).

In 1965 Kayibanda was re-elected president and Juvenal Habyarimana was appointed Minister of Defence. In 1969 Kayibanda was again re-elected and PARMEHUTU was renamed the MDR (*Mouvement Démocratique Républicain*). But Kayibanda's regime was becoming increasingly dictatorial and corrupt. The 'quotas' and other 'cleansing' measures began to be enforced so rigidly that even Hutus became uneasy. In 1973, ostensibly to quell violence following a purge of Tutsis from virtually all educational establishments, Major General Juvenal Habyarimana toppled Grégoire Kayibanda in a military coup.

In 1975, a single party, the MRND (*Mouvement Révolutionnaire et National pour le Développement*), was formed. For a while, there were signs of improvement, although this tends to be forgotten in the light of subsequent events. Despite initial optimism and a period of relative stability, however, the regime eventually proved little better than its predecessor. Some educational reforms were undertaken, with the object of 'Rwandanisation' – revaluing Kinyarwanda and Rwandan culture. Habyarimana was reconfirmed as president in 1978, 1983 and 1988 – unsurprisingly, since he was the only candidate. The Hutu–Tutsi conflict was to some extent replaced by conflict between Hutus from the south and those from the north (Habyarimana was a northerner, so was accused of favouring 'his own'). Meanwhile, in the international sphere, rising oil prices and falling commodity prices were bringing the country's economy close to collapse and, among all but the privileged elite, dissatisfaction grew.

In 1979 a group of Rwandan exiles in Uganda established the RRWF (Rwandan Refugee Welfare Foundation) which in 1980 became RANU (Rwandan Alliance for National Unity), whose name explains its aim. In 1981, in Uganda, one Yoweri Museveni, later to become Uganda's president, started a guerrilla war against the oppressive regime of Dr Milton Obote – among his men were two Rwandan refugees, Paul Kagame and Fred Rwigima. Obote was hostile to the Rwandan refugees in Uganda and political youth groups were encouraged to attack them and their property. As a result of such attacks in 1982–83, there was massive displacement of the refugees in southern Uganda and large numbers tried (or were forced) to return to Rwanda. The Rwandan government quickly closed its borders with Uganda and confined those who had already entered to a small and inhospitable area in the north, where many of the young and the old died of hunger and disease.

In 1986, in Uganda, Yoweri Museveni's National Resistance Army (which contained a number of Rwandan refugees) overthrew Obote, and Museveni assumed power. In 1987 RANU was renamed the RPF (Rwandan Patriotic Front), and was supported not only by exiled Tutsis but also by a few prominent Hutus opposed to Habyarimana's regime.

In 1987/8, a military coup in Burundi and consequent ethnic tensions caused a wave of Burundian refugees to flood into Rwanda. In 1989 the price of coffee, Rwanda's main export, collapsed, causing severe economic problems. Censorship rules were flouted, new politically oriented publications emerged and reports of corruption and mismanagement appeared openly. In July 1990, under pressure from Western aid donors, Habyarimana conceded the principle of multi-party democracy and agreed to allow free debate on the country's future. In practice, little changed.

Then, on October 1 1990, the RPF (led by Major General Fred Rwigyema), invaded the northeast of Rwanda from Uganda, with the stated objective of ending the political stalemate once and for all and restoring democracy. French, German and Zairean troops were called in to support the Rwandan national army and the incursion was soon suppressed; but the government now took the RPF threat seriously. Habyarimana enlarged the Rwandan army from around 5,000 in 1990 to about 24,000 in 1991 and 35,000 in 1993. Various overseas countries (France, South Africa, the US) provided arms. Additionally, the 1990 RPF invasion was followed by severe reprisals: thousands of Tutsi and southern Hutu were arrested and held in prison for some months. Several were tried and sentenced to death but the sentences were not carried out, although, as one of those arrested later wrote, 'many died of the hunger and the beatings'. Sporadic unrest continued throughout the country.

Political solutions were sought, both nationally and internationally, with several Western countries now involved. In November 1990 Habyarimana agreed to the introduction of multi-partyism and the abolition of 'ethnic' identity cards, but nothing was implemented. The Rwandan army began to train and arm civilian militias known as *interahamwe* ('those who stand together'). It was later estimated that up to 2,000 Rwandans (Tutsis or anti-government Hutus) were killed by their government between October 1990 and December 1992.

The RPF – now led by Major Paul Kagame, since the charismatic Rwigema had died in the October 1990 invasion – continued its guerrilla raids, striking at targets countrywide. By the end of 1992 it had expanded to a force of almost 12,000 and was growing rapidly. Its stated aim was always to bring democracy to Rwanda rather than to claim supremacy. Meanwhile, French troops were supporting the government forces. In the face of increasing violence, international pressure was applied more strongly and the Arusha Agreement (so named because it was drawn up in Arusha, Tanzania) committed Habyarimana to a number of reforms, including the establishment of the rule of law, political power-sharing, the repatriation and resettlement of refugees, and the integration of the armed forces to include the RPF. A 70-member Transitional National Assembly was to be established. The Agreement was signed in August 1993 and should have been implemented within 37 days, overseen by a United Nations force. But the process, unpalatable to both Tutsi and Hutu hardliners, stalled. Hostilities deepened. Radio stations poured forth inflammatory propaganda. Rwanda's *Radio-Télévision Libre des Mille Collines*, in particular, insistently and viciously identified Tutsis as 'the enemy', in dehumanising and vilifying terms. Scattered outbursts of violence rumbled on.

On October 21, the Hutu president of neighbouring Burundi, Melchior Ndadaye, elected only a few months previously, was killed in a military coup, fuelling ethnic tensions in Rwanda. The UN began sending UNAMIR (UN Assistance Mission for Rwanda) forces to the country. Politics were deadlocked. A sense of impending danger grew and, by March 1994, vulnerable (or well-informed) citizens were starting to evacuate their families from Kigali.

On April 6 1994, a plane carrying Rwanda's President Habyarimana and Burundi's new President Cyprien Ntaryamira was shot down by rocket fire near Kigali airport. Both men died. The source of the attack has never been confirmed. Within hours, the killing began.

The genocide
It had been well planned, over a long period. Roadblocks were quickly erected and the army and *interahamwe* went into action, on a rampage of death, torture, looting and destruction. Tutsis and moderate Hutus were targeted. Weapons of every sort were used, from slick, military arms to rustic machetes. Orders were passed briskly downward from *préfecture* to *commune* to *secteur* to *cellule* – and the gist of every order was: 'These are the enemy. Kill.'

A painfully detailed account, which includes many eyewitness testimonies and brings home the full horror of the slaughter, is given in the 1,200 pages of *Rwanda – Death, Despair and Defiance* (African Rights, London, 1995). In *A People Betrayed*, L R Melvern analyses the political and international background (Zed Books, London & New York, 2000), as does Gérard Prunier in *The Rwanda Crisis* (see *Appendix 3*). A condensed overview of events is given below.

In three months, up to a million people were killed, violently and cruelly. Barely a family was untouched. The international media suddenly found Rwanda newsworthy. Chilling images filled our TV screens and the scale of the massacre was too great for many of us to grasp. Amid the immensity came tiny tales of heroism: villagers who flatly disobeyed the order to kill; Hutus who hid their Tutsi neighbours, at great (often fatal) risk to their own lives, or who, while feigning to round them up for the killers, furtively led some to safety. But these glimpses of humanity were engulfed and lost in the great, surging tide of slaughter that spread across the country.

On April 8, just two days after the plane crash, the Rwandan Patriotic Front (RPF) launched a major offensive to end the genocide. As they advanced, they rescued and liberated Tutsis still hiding in terror from the killers. Meanwhile, however, a new Hutu government, based on the MRND and supporting parties, was formed in Kigali and later shifted to Gitarama.

The United Nations' UNAMIR force was around 2,500 strong at the time. They watched helplessly, technically unable to intervene as this would breach their 'monitoring' mandate. After the murder of ten Belgian soldiers the force

AFTER THE GENOCIDE...

A report produced in July 2000 by the Statistics Department of Rwanda's Ministry of Finance and Economic Planning concludes that the horrors of the 1994 genocide have left large segments of the population with severe mental health problems that cannot in fact be expressed in statistics. Many people have lost family members, and/or have witnessed, experienced (or participated in) massacres or rapes. A National Trauma Survey by UNICEF in 1995, quoted in the same report, estimated the percentages of children affected by the genocide as follows:

- 99.9% witnessed violence
- 79.6% experienced death in the family
- 69.5% witnessed someone being killed or injured
- 61.5% were threatened with death
- 90.6% believed they would die
- 57.7% witnessed killings or injuries with machete
- 31.4% witnessed rape or sexual assault
- 87.5% saw dead bodies or parts of bodies

Does it make you look at the streetkids in Kigali and Butare a little differently?

was cut to 250. On April 30 the UN Security Council spent eight hours discussing the Rwandan crisis – without ever using the word 'genocide'. Had this term been used, they would have been legally obliged to 'prevent and punish' the perpetrators. Meanwhile tens of thousands of refugees were fleeing the country. In May the UN agreed to send 6,800 troops and police to Rwanda to defend civilians, but implementation was delayed by arguments over who would cover costs and provide equipment. The RPF army had taken control of Kigali airport and Kanombe barracks and was gaining ground elsewhere. In June, France announced that it would deploy 2,500 peacekeeping troops to Rwanda (*Opération Turquoise*) until the UN force arrived. These created a controversial 'safe zone' in the southwest.

On July 4 the RPF captured Kigali and set up an interim government. The remnants of the Hutu government fled to Zaire, followed by a further tide of refugees. The RPF continued its advance westward and northward. Many thousands of refugees streamed into the French 'safe zone' and still more headed towards Zaire, cramming into makeshift camps on the inhospitable terrain around Goma. The humanitarian crisis was acute, later to be exacerbated by disease and a cholera outbreak which claimed tens of thousands of lives.

On July 18 1994, the RPF announced that the war had been won, declared a ceasefire, established a broad-based Government of National Unity and named Pasteur Bizimungu as president. Faustin Twagiramungu was appointed prime minister. The following day, the new president and prime minister were sworn in, and RPF commander Major General Paul Kagame was appointed defence minister and vice president. By the end of July, the UN Security Council had reached a final agreement about sending an international force to Rwanda. By the end of August *Opération Turquoise* was terminated and UN forces had replaced the French. Internationally, it had now been accepted that a 'genocide' had indeed taken place – and it was over. At sites of some of the worst massacres, memorials now commemorate the dead and remind the world that such an atrocity must never, never be allowed to occur again.

The aftermath

The 70-member Transitional National Assembly provided for in the Arusha Agreement of 1993 finally became operational in December 1994. In November 1994, the UN Security Commission set up the International Criminal Tribunal for Rwanda (ICTR), whose brief is to prosecute those who were guilty, between January 1 and December 31 1994, of genocide and other violations of international humanitarian law; by the end of 1996 suspects were being brought to trial.

Sporadic bursts of violence were to continue for a further three years or so, with killings on both sides, as tensions in and around refugee settlements persisted and hardline Hutus who had fled across the border mounted guerrilla raids. But the RPF army and the new government remained in control. UN forces left the country in March 1996. Refugees returned home, in massive numbers. Problems of insecurity posed by former Rwanda

GACACA

The traditional system of 'Gacaca' courts has been revived in Rwanda in order to clear the prisons of the throng of genocide suspects – still about 85,000, at the time of writing – who have been held captive (awaiting trial) for up to eight years. It was estimated that the regular justice system, lacking adequate facilities and qualified personnel, could take almost 100 years to clear the backlog – clearly impossible – whereas Gacaca offers the hope of a solution within five years or so. The system was originally due to start in 2001, but was postponed so that further preparatory work could be carried out.

Around 250,000 local judges, men and women, were elected by and within their local communities in 2001, and in 2002 received brief training in such subjects as law, conflict resolution and judicial ethics. They receive no salaries but are entitled to free schooling and medical fees for their families. Throughout Rwanda up to 11,000 Gacaca courts are operating (with a panel of 19 judges per court, and requiring the presence of at least 15 judges and 100 witnesses to be valid) in different administrative areas.

First, the courts identify victims of the genocide. Next, suspects are identified and categorised, according to the extent of their crime. They attend courts in their home areas, where local witnesses speak for or against them. Suspects who confess fully and plead guilty can expect lighter sentences, as can those who agree to community service in atonement for their crimes. The courts are authorised to try, and then to sentence, anyone suspected of carrying out (or being an accomplice to) killing, serious assault or property crimes during the genocide. The more serious 'Category 1' suspects, those who allegedly organised, instigated, led or played a particularly zealous part in the violence, continue to be tried and sentenced in the formal judicial system. Gacaca courts cannot impose the death penalty, nor can they try army personnel.

For the witnesses, confronting the *génocidaires* and re-living the events of 1994 can be both traumatic and cathartic. No-one claims that the Gacaca courts are a perfect solution, just that they are the best solution under the circumstances – and at least they offer a very visible form of justice in which the villagers have a voice. Observers monitor their progress and so far they seem to be relatively uncorrupt. Once again, as they have done in so many ways since the genocide, Rwandans are playing a very personal role in solving their country's problems.

government forces and *interahamwe* troops caused Rwanda to become militarily involved with the Democratic Republic of the Congo (DRC).

In 1999, local elections were held at sector and cellule level, and the Lusaka Agreement, to end the war in the DRC, was signed.

In March 2000, President Pasteur Bizimungu resigned and in April Major

General Paul Kagame was sworn in as the fifth president of Rwanda, exactly four decades after his flight as a three-year-old refugee.

In July 2000, the Organisation of African Unity (OAU) recommended that the international community should make payments to the government and people of Rwanda in reparation for the genocide. Later the same year, the Rwandan government launched a census to determine the true and total number of genocide victims – irrespective of whether they were Hutus, Tutsis, Twa or foreigners.

In June 2002, with some 115,000 genocide suspects still in gaol after eight years and the country's regular courts unable to clear the backlog, the *Gacaca* Judicial System was launched. *Gacaca* (pronounced Ga-cha-cha, with a hard g) means 'grass', and is based on the traditional form of Rwandan justice where villagers used to gather together on a patch of grass to resolve conflicts between families, with heads of household acting as judges. See box opposite. In the first half of 2003, around 30,000 genocide suspects were released from prison and, after a spell of 're-education', returned to their villages, in an amnesty aimed at those who were aged 14–18 at the time of the genocide, the old and sick, and those accused of lesser crimes.

In June 2003, the UK's former International Development Secretary, Clare Short, spoke on the popular BBC Radio 4 *Today* programme about a recent trip she had made to Rwanda. This extract appeared on the *Today* website, www.bbc.co.uk/radio4/today.

> We rarely hear stories of hope from Africa but Rwanda is a story of hope despite its terrible history. Only nine years ago it suffered a terrible genocide with nearly one million of its eight million people slaughtered, under orders, by machete, whilst the world looked away and ignored the obligations we had signed up to under the Genocide Convention. Following the killing, the forces of the genocide were driven out of office and established themselves in Zaire – now the Democratic Republic of Congo – from where they plot and arm themselves to return to Rwanda and complete the genocide. But despite all of this, Rwanda has been rebuilding. There is now peace and order across the whole country.
>
> Rwanda has qualified for debt relief under the Highly Indebted Poor Countries Initiative and has economic reform and development programmes supported by the World Bank and the IMF. Identity cards labelling each Rwandan a Hutu, Tutsi or Twa have been thrown away. There are more children in school than ever in the history of the country. And a start has been made in using a traditional system of village justice – known as Gacaca – to return those charged with lesser offences during the genocide to their villages where they can be sentenced to make restitution to those that they have harmed…
>
> Much remains to be done to secure a safe and dignified future for the long-suffering people of this beautiful country – not least the implementation of Congo's peace agreement and the disarmament of

GOAL!

Chris Frean (October 2003)

Rwandan football reached a zenith in 2003 with the national team's qualification for the finals of the 2004 African Nations Cup. Not to be outdone, one of the leading club sides, APR FC, won through to the semi-finals of the African Cup Winners' Cup.

The national team, in traditional African fashion, have a nickname. Rwanda are known as Amavubi, which translates as 'wasps' – and they duly stung Uganda (the Cranes) and group favourites Ghana (the Black Stars) to qualify for Tunisia 2004 for the first time in their history. The wasps were slow to wake up to the task and began with defeat in Ghana and an unsatisfactory 0-0 draw at home to Uganda, but then turned things around when a victory away to Uganda in Kampala sent the country crazy; the Ugandans were not best pleased at this defeat to their lowly, smaller, lower-ranked, and less developed neighbour, and blamed the defeat on witchcraft. It was said that a chicken had been killed before the match and the remains placed in the Rwandan goalmouth. This put a hex on the Ugandan players who would not be able to put the ball in the net. Rwanda won 1–0. Protests and disagreements followed but the result stood.

Then came the final match versus Ghana. Only a win would do. But did anyone expect Rwanda to overcome a nation who has produced players renowned throughout the continent, like Abedi Pele and Anthony Yeboah, and has one of the best records in the finals? It happened. Rwanda took the game 1–0 and qualified. President Kagame, attending the match, was impressed and awarded the players substantial financial rewards for their victory. Next stop, Tunisia.

the forces of the genocide. But if Rwanda continues to make progress in reconciliation, economic and social development as it has in the last six years, then there is real hope of a future without strife and genocidal killing. And if Rwanda can emerge from hell and make such progress then there is hope for the 20% of Africa's people suffering injury, displacement and impoverishment as a result of bitter history, poor leadership and endless conflict.

Also in June 2003, Rwanda's new Constitution was signed, marking the end of the transition period that followed the genocide and replacing various documents referred to as the Fundamental Law. Finally, the presidential elections held – entirely peacefully – in August 2003 saw Paul Kagame returned as president for a term of seven years, with 3,544,777 votes or 95.05% of the total. Parliamentary elections followed in September 2003.

Rwanda has received huge amounts of foreign aid – and the fact that this has been ongoing since the genocide demonstrates international satisfaction about how the money is used. Donors renew their contracts. As an example, in

Meanwhile, at least one club side has begun to prove itself in a club tournament. The African Football Federation runs a Champions League which has replaced the old Champions' Cup, as well as a Cup Winners' Cup and CAF Cup. In 2003, League Champions Rayon Sport failed to reach the group stages of the Champions League, managing a win in the preliminary round but then losing, expectedly, to one of the best teams in Africa – Esperance of Tunis; and CAF Cup entrants Kiyovu Sport bowed out fairly early to a Zimbabwean club in the second round.

So it is APR FC which has done the business. Led by Rwanda's key player, Jimmy Gatete, the club, originally built around the army, has reached the last four. Victims along the way have included US Kenya of Lubumbashi, beaten 10–1 on aggregate; Etoile of Congo, again beaten both home and away; and in the Quarter Finals, more Ghanaians: Ashanti Kotoko, a renowned African club side, leaders of the Ghanaian League at the time, and losing finalists in 2002. Kotoko beat APR 2–1 with a very late goal in Ghana, but then succumbed to a 1–0 defeat in Kigali which saw the Rwandans through on away goals. The semi-final brings Julius Berger, a Nigerian side, and the toughest examination so far.

What is not yet known is whether the players have come under the scrutiny of European coaches. A good showing at the Nations Cup in January/February 2004 could make the difference. Rwanda, ranked 25th out of 52 in Africa, have an almost impossible opening match, versus Tunisia (ranked 7th), but could well spring a surprise in their other two group matches, versus DRC (9th) – an interesting match-up given recent history – and Guinea (27th). Two teams will qualify for the quarter-finals. Rwanda must go into the tournament hoping to finish group runners-up to Tunisia.

September 2003 three new grants were agreed: US$30 million from the World Bank for the HIV/AIDS programme; US$19.9 million from the EU Mission in Rwanda for the repair and rehabilitation of roads; and US$29.9 million from the African Development Bank for the improved supply of water and energy to Kigali, the management of natural resources and, again, HIV/AIDS. The world is no longer turning its back on Rwanda.

A small and unexpected sign of the country's progress is the prowess of its football team. One of Africa's smallest countries, only nine years away from a genocide that wiped out up to a million of its people, and Rwanda qualifies for the finals of the 2004 African Nations Cup! See box above.

Of course tensions still exist; of course the government has its critics; of course poverty persists; of course there are complaints of 'discrimination'; and of course many Rwandans – particularly in rural areas – still struggle in conditions that are far from ideal. Human rights organisations point to some abuses. The budget is seriously overstretched and the neediest still do not always benefit enough from the reforms. But this is Africa!

Considering the size and resources of Rwanda, considering what happened

RWANDA'S NATIONAL SYMBOLS

Rwanda's new flag, coat of arms and national anthem were launched on December 31 2001, to replace the old ones designed in 1962, at a time when Rwanda was shaken by ethnic violence, human-rights violations and bad governance.

The old flag contained red, symbolising the blood shed for independence, but in today's peaceful Rwanda this is seen as inappropriate. The new flag is blue, yellow and green: blue to signify peace and tranquillity; yellow to signify wealth as the country strives for economic growth; green to symbolise agriculture, productivity and prosperity. There is a sun in the top right-hand corner, against a blue background, representing new hope for the country and its people. The flag was designed by Alphonse Kirimobenecyo, a Rwandan artist and engineer.

The coat of arms consists of a green ring with a knot tied at the upper end, representing industrial development through hard work. Inscriptions read *Repubulika Y'U Rwanda* and the national motto *Ubumwe, Umurimo, Gukunda Igihugu* (Unity, Work, Patriotism). Other features are the sun, sorghum and coffee, a basket, a cog wheel – and two shields, representing defence of national sovereignty and integrity and justice.

The national anthem, *Rwanda Nziza*, has four verses and highlights heroism, the Rwandan culture and the people's patriotism. The words are by Faustin Murigo of Karubanda prison in Butare Province. The music is by Captain Jean-Bosco Hashkaimana of the army brass band.

there in 1994 and considering the inherent problems faced by almost *all* countries in sub-Saharan Africa, even without the aftermath of a genocide, the achievements of the past eight years have been amazing, and based on a huge amount of energy, courage, goodwill and sheer hard work. Progress has been dramatic. Rwanda today is a vibrant and forward-looking country, well able to cope with the demands and technologies of the 21st century.

It deserves respect.

Planning and Preparation

WHEN TO VISIT

Rwanda can be visited at any time of year. The long dry season, June to September, is the best time for tracking gorillas in the Volcanoes Park and hiking in Nyungwe Forest, since the ground should be dry underfoot and the odds of being drenched are minimal. The dry season is also the best time for travelling on dirt roads, and is when the risk of malaria should be lowest.

There are two annual rainy seasons: the big rains which last from mid-February to the beginning of June, and the small rains from mid-September to mid-December. Rainfall, especially over the mountains, is heavy during these two periods – particularly from March to May, although it is still perfectly feasible to travel during this period.

As for the two dry seasons, the major one lasts from June to September and the shorter from December to February. However, the climate is not uniform throughout the country: it is generally dryer in the east than in the west and north. On occasion, the volcanoes of the north may be capped by snow, and evenings in Kigali can call for a sweater. Nevertheless, every season is good for swimming and tanning on the banks of Lake Kivu.

An advantage of travelling during the rainy season is that the scenery is greener, and the sky less hazy (at least when it isn't overcast), a factor that will be of particular significance to photographers. The wet season is also the best time to track chimps in Nyungwe (in the dry season they may wander further off in search of scarce food), while the months of November to March will hold the greatest appeal for birders, as resident birds are supplemented by flocks of Palaearctic migrants.

GETTING THERE AND AWAY
By air

Rwanda's new airline Rwandair Express flies directly to Kigali from Entebbe (Uganda), Johannesburg (South Africa), Nairobi (Kenya) and Dubai. A link with Kilimanjaro is also planned. Tel: (Kigali office) 575757; email: rwandair@rwandair.com; web: www.rwandair.com.

Other direct flights to Kigali are run by Brussels SN from Brussels, Kenya Airways from Nairobi, Ethiopian Airlines from Addis Ababa, Air Tanzania from Dar es Salaam, and Air Burundi from Bujumbura. The Kenya Airways Nairobi flights link up with connections (some good, some bad) to/from

London. At the time of writing there's talk of a merger between Air France and KLM, which may possibly lead to a renewal of flights from Paris.

Travellers from the Americas, Australasia and the rest of Europe will do best to aim for the connections via London, Brussels, Johannesburg, Nairobi and Entebbe.

The international airport lies 10km from central Kigali, and taxis are available to/from the city centre. See *Chapter 6*, page 94. The departure tax that used to be payable at the airport is now included in your ticket – but check when you book, in case this changes again.

On no account neglect to **confirm your return flight at least three days in advance**, via an airline office or travel agent in Kigali. Unless you do this, there is – at least with some airlines – a serious risk of being 'bumped' at the last minute.

Air tickets

A number of travel companies are good sources of **cut-price tickets**, as well as offering various other services. Both authors agree that London is THE place for cheap fares, hence the bias of the list below! It isn't exhaustive but should give you a start. As shown on their websites, most of the companies listed also have offices in other countries.

UK (London)

Africa Travel Centre 4 Medway Court, Leigh St, London WC1H 9QX; tel: 0845 450 1520; email: info@africatravel.co.uk; web: www.africatravel.co.uk

Flight Centre Tel: (booking) 0870499 0040; web: www.flightcentre.com. Flight Centre has several offices in London and elsewhere in UK. It offers cut-price airfares, visa and insurance services. Also in Australia, New Zealand, South Africa, USA.

STA Travel Tel: (sales) 0870 1 600599; email: enquiries@statravel.co.uk; web (very comprehensive): www.statravel.co.uk. Has 65 branches in UK and over 450 worldwide.

Trailfinders Tel: 020 7938 3939; web (very comprehensive): www.trailfinders.com; one-stop travel shop 194 Kensington High St, London W8 7RG. Also in Ireland, Australia, etc.

WEXAS 45–49 Brompton Rd, Knightsbridge, London SW3 1DE; tel: 020 7838 7901; web: www.wexas.com. There is an annual subscription to WEXAS (for current details email: mship@wexas.com or phone 020 7589 3315) but it gives you access to a whole range of useful services (good rates for hotels and airport parking, use of airport lounges, visas...) as well as an excellent quarterly travel magazine, *Traveller*.

Overland

Four countries border Rwanda: Burundi to the south, the Democratic Republic of Congo (DRC) to the west, Uganda to the north and Tanzania to the east. Assuming peaceful conditions, frontier formalities aren't too much of a hassle – but nor are they standardised. Most frontier offices open at 08.00; they may close at 17.00 or 18.00. See page 30 for details of which nationalities don't require visas; for others, to buy a visa at the border costs around US$60. (But, for safety, check with your nearest embassy beforehand that it's still possible.) Don't count on official exchange facilities being available; there are likely to be 'black-market' money-changers around, but you should decide in advance what rate you're prepared to accept.

At the time of writing, although there are still buses running between Kigali and Bujumbura in **Burundi**, it's a volatile area and the route isn't advisable for tourists. There's every hope that things will improve during the lifetime of this guide; but meanwhile, air travel is safer.

The **DRC** seems to be settling down now and travel is becoming safer. Day trips from Rwanda to Goma and Bukavu (via Gisenyi and Cyangugu) have been possible for some time, and there are regular minibuses to/from Kigali. Lake transport is starting up again too; see page 154 in *Chapter 7* and page 201 in *Chapter 8*. But peace doesn't become widespread overnight; so do check current conditions and follow local advice. On both sides of each border there is accommodation reasonably close by – in the case of Cyangugu and Gisenyi, only a few minutes away, but further for Bukavu.

Crossing to and from **Uganda** is simple. Direct buses and minibus-taxis connect Kampala and Kigali, taking 10–12 hours and costing around US$15. There are plenty of local minibus-taxis along the roughly 50km road between Kisoro in southwest Uganda and Ruhengeri in northwest Rwanda (an hour's trip, not allowing for changing vehicles and other delays at the Cyanika border post, which might add another hour to the journey). It is also easy to travel by minibus-taxi between Kabale, the largest town in southwest Uganda, and Kigali, though once again you might have to change vehicles at the border – this trip should take about five hours in total. There are bars and other facilities at the border.

Crossing between Rwanda and **Tanzania** is something of a slog, due to the poor state of roads and lack of large towns in northwest Tanzania. The Rusumo border post lies about 160km from Kigali, roughly a four-hour trip by minibus-taxi, with the possibility of staying the night en route at the town of Kibungo (see page 214), 60km from the border. Or there is a restaurant with basic accommodation at Rusumo itself, on the Rwandan side (page 214). The closest Tanzanian town to the border is Ngara, which is connected to Rusumo by occasional minibus-taxis taking about six hours, and has a few small guesthouses. From Ngara, daily buses to Mwanza on Lake Victoria take

12–18 hours depending on the condition of the road. Mwanza is a large port with a full range of accommodation and other facilities, including thrice-weekly rail links to Dar es Salaam on the coast and daily buses to Arusha in northeast Tanzania. A rail link between Rwanda and Tanzania is planned, but don't count on it being up and running in the near future.

International tour operators

All those listed below will arrange gorilla visits plus international travel. Most offer both scheduled tours and tailor-made trips. More will start to cover the rest of Rwanda during the life of this guide. The many operators in neighbouring countries (Uganda etc) are deliberately not all listed, because readers in those countries are less likely to need them. The Rwandan tour operators listed on pages 120–1 can also arrange international travel.

United Kingdom (national code +44)

Aardvark Safaris Tel: 01980 849160; email: mail@aardvarksafaris.com; web: www.aardvarksafaris.com. Include Rwanda/Uganda/Tanzania itineraries.

Absolute Africa Tel: 020 8742 0226; email: absa@absoluteafrica.co.uk; web: www.absoluteafrica.com. Overland truck/camping safaris.

Africa Travel Centre Tel: 020 7387 1211; email: sales@africatravel.co.uk; web: www.africatravel.co.uk. See advertisement on page 90.

Alpha Travel Tel: 020 8423 643333; email: info@arpsafaris.com; web: www.arpsafaris.com

Discovery Initiatives The Travel House, 51 Castle St, Cirencester, Glos GL7 1QD; tel: 01285 643333; fax: 01285 885888; email: enquiry@discoveryinitiatives.com; www.discoveryinitiatives.com. Regular 'conservation in action' trips to Volcanoes Park and Lake Kivu. See advertisment on page 24.

Exodus Tel: 020 8772 3807; email: wo@exodus.co.uk; web: www.exodus.co.uk.

Footprint Adventures Tel: 01522 804929; email: sales@footprint-adventures.co.uk; web: www.footprint-adventures.co.uk

Rainbow Tours Tel: 020 7226 1004; fax: 020 7226 2621; email: info@rainbowtours.co.uk; www.rainbowtours.co.uk. See advertisement on page 52.

Reef & Rainforest Tours Tel: 01803 866965; fax: 01803 865916; email: mail@reefandrainforest.co.uk; web: www.reefandrainforest.co.uk. See advertisement on page 51.

Safari Consultants Ltd Tel: 01787 228494; email: bill@safariconsultantuk.com; web: www.safari-consultants.co.uk

Sunvil Africa Tel: 020 8232 9777; email: africa@sunvil.co.uk; web: www.sunvil.co.uk

Vintage Africa Ltd Tel: 01451 850803; email: vintageafrica@yahoo.com; web: www.vintageafrica.com

Volcanoes Safaris (offices in UK, US, Uganda and Rwanda) – see also details under Kigali operators (page 121). UK office: tel: 0870 870 8480; fax: 0870 870 8481; email: salesug@volcanoessafaris.com; web: www.volcanoessafaris.com

Wildlife Worldwide Tel: 020 8667 9158; fax: 020 8667 1960; email: sales@wildlifeworldwide.com; web: www.wildlifeworldwide.com

USA (national code +1)
Africa Adventure Company Tel: 954 491 8877; email: info@africa-adventure.com; web: www.africa-adventure.com
Ker & Downey Tel: 713 917 0048; email: info@kerdowney.com; web: www.kerdowney.com
Volcanoes Safaris (see details under UK, above) Tel: 770 730 0960; email: salesus@volcanoessafaris.com; web: www.volcanoessafaris.com

Belgium (national code +32)
Continents Insolites Tel: 2218 2484; fax: 2218 2488; email: info@insolites.be; web: www.insolites.be

Canada (national code +1)
Leisure Connection Tours Ltd Tel: 800 364 5104 (North America toll-free); email info@lcadventuretravel.com; web: www.lcadventuretravel.com. Scheduled and tailor-made tours including Lake Kivu, Nyungwe Forest, etc.

France (national code +33)
Explorator Tel: 153 458585; email: explorator@explo.com; web: www.explo.com
Terra Incognita Paris office tel: 155 428103; email: af@terra-incognita.fr; Lyon office tel: 472 532490; email: ti@terra-incognita.fr; web: www.terra-incognita.fr

Germany (national code +49)
Globetrotter Select Tel: 8171 997272; email: info@globetrotter-select.de; web: www.globetrotter-select.de. Three itineraries: gorillas only; gorillas+Nyungwe Forest; gorillas+Nyungwe+Lake Kivu.

Kenya (national code +254) **and Uganda** (national code +256)
Magic Safaris (Uganda) Tel: (+256) 41 342926; email: info@magic-safaris.com; web: www.magic-safaris.com. Include combined Uganda/Rwanda tours.
The Far Horizon (Uganda) Tel: (+256) 41 343468/235168; email: info@thefarhorizons.com; web: www.thefarhorizons.com. See advertisement on page 72.
Origins Safaris (Kenya) tel: (+254) 20 331191, 222075; email: info@originsafaris.info; web: www.originsafaris.info. Include combined Tanzania/Rwanda tours and birding in Akagera Park.

South Africa (national code +27)
Unusual Destinations 12 George St, Bryanston, PO Box 97508, Petervale 2151; tel: 11 706 1991; fax: 11 463 1469; email: info@unusualdestinations.com; web: www.unusualdestinations.com. Four-day and 8-day trips including Lake Kivu and/or Nyungwe Forest, tailor-made itineraries and business travel.
Wild Frontiers Tel: 11 702 2035; email: wildfront@icon.co.za; web: www.wildfrontiers.com. Tailor-made and escorted trips to all parts of Rwanda.

Spain (national code +34)
Kananga Travel Tel: 93 268 7795; email: info@kananga.com; web: www.kananga.com. Two-week combined Rwanda/Uganda tour starting 2004.

RED TAPE

Check well in advance that you have a valid **passport**, and that it won't expire within six months of the date you intend to leave Rwanda. Should your passport be lost or stolen, it will generally be easier to get a replacement if you travel with a photocopy of the important pages.

Visas are required by all visitors except (for stays of less than three months) by nationals of the UK, Germany, Sweden, Canada, USA, Hong Kong, Burundi, DRC, Kenya, Mauritius, South Africa, Tanzania and Uganda. For all others they cost around US$60, depending on the place of issue. For air travellers, visas are now issued at Kigali airport on arrival, but check via an embassy that this is still the case when you travel. Details of Rwandan embassies abroad are given below. Nationals of countries without an embassy can also obtain a visa on arrival by prior arrangement with their hosts, who can arrange a *facilité d'entrée*.

If there is any possibility that you'll want to drive or hire a vehicle while you're in the country, do organise an **international driving licence** (any AA office in a country in which you're licensed to drive will do this for a nominal fee), which you may be asked to produce together with your original licence. You may sometimes be asked at borders for an **international health certificate** showing you've had a yellow fever shot.

For **security** reasons, it's advisable to detail all your important information on one sheet of paper, photocopy it, and distribute a few copies in your luggage, your money-belt, and amongst relatives or friends at home: the sort of things you want to include on this are travellers' cheque numbers and refund information, travel insurance policy details and 24-hour emergency contact number, passport number, details of relatives or friends to be contacted in an emergency, bank and credit card details, camera and lens serial numbers, etc. We also email this information to ourselves immediately before we leave, so it is stored in our in-tray throughout our travels. It's also handy to carry a photo of your suitcase or other luggage, to save trying to describe it if it's misplaced by an airline.

Rwandan embassies and consulates abroad

Belgium 1 Av des Fleurs, 1150 Brussels; tel: (+32) 02 771 2127; fax: 02 763 0753; email: ambabruxelles@minaffet.gov.rw

Burundi 24 Av de la République Démocratique du Congo, BP 400 Bujumbura; tel: (+257) 223255; fax: 223254; email: ambuja@minaffet.gov.rw

China Hsieu Shaouei Bei Yie, Beijing; tel: (+861) 065 321820; fax: 065 322006; email: ambabeijing@minaffet.gov.rw

Ethiopia Africa Av, H 17k-20 No 001, PO Box 5618 Addis Ababa; tel: (+251) 161 0300; fax: 161 0411; email: ambaddis@minaffet.gov.rw

Germany Beethovenallee 72, 53173 Bonn; tel: (+49) 228 3670238; fax: 228 351922; email: ambabonn@minaffet.gov.rw

India B 112 Neet Bash, New Delhi 110016; tel: (+91) 11 656 8083; fax: 11 656 8085; email: ambadelhi@minaffet.gov.rw

Kenya Kilimani, Kahahwe Rd, PO Box 30.619, Nairobi; tel: (+254) 257 5977; fax: 257 5976; email: ambanairobi@minaffet.gov.rw

South Africa 35 Marais St, Brooklyn, Pretoria; tel: (+27) 12 460 0709; fax: 12 460 0708; email: ambapretoria@minaffet.gov.rw

Switzerland Rue de la Serviette 93, CH-1202 Geneva; tel: (+41) 22 919 1000; fax: 22 919 1001; email: ambageneve@minaffet.gov.rw

Tanzania 32 Ali Hassan Mwinyi Rd, PO Box 2918 Dar es Salaam; tel: (+255) 222 115889; fax: 222 115888; email: ambadsm@minaffet.gov.rw

Uganda 2 Nakaima Rd, PO Box 2446 Kampala; tel: (+256) 41 344045; fax: 41 258854; email: ambakampala@minaffet.gov.rw

United Kingdom 120–122 Seymour Place, London W1H 1NR; tel: (+44) 020 7224 9832; fax: 020 7724 8642; email: uk@ambarwanda.org.uk

United States 124 East 39th St, **New York**, NY 10016; tel: (+1) 212 679 9010; fax: 212 679 9133; email: ambanewyork@minaffet.gov.rw. *Also* 1724 New Hampshire Av NW, **Washington, DC** 20009; tel: (+1) 202 232 2882; fax: 202 232 4544; email: ambawashington@minaffet.gov.rw

Details provided by the Ministry of Foreign Affairs, Kigali. For updates and additions, refer to website www.rwandatourism.com.

PACKING

In 1907, when the Duke of Mecklenburg set off on an expedition through Rwanda with a group of scientific researchers, he carried (or rather his team of bearers carried) numerous cases of soap, candles, rope and cigars, as well as such items as salt, wire, beads and woollen blankets to barter with the natives. You could probably cut down on this a little.

In fact Rwanda is a relatively well-stocked little country, in terms of clothing, toiletries, stationery, batteries and so forth. Unless you have particularly exotic tastes (or your schedule is too crowded to allow you time for shopping), you should be able to find most of the everyday items a traveller needs, even if the brands are unfamiliar. Obviously you should bring a supply of any personal medication (and some extra, in case your return home is delayed); also bring a stock of whatever type of film you like to use, as well as enough sunscreen. Otherwise, unless you plan to go way off the beaten track (or you need camping/trekking gear, which is in shorter supply), don't feel that you must fill your bag up with a lot of semi-useful items 'just in case'. Buying things locally helps Rwanda's economy!

The comments below (by Philip) apply as much to any neighbouring African countries you may pass through or visit as they do to Rwanda.

Carrying your luggage

Visitors who are unlikely to be carrying their luggage for any significant distance will probably want to pack most of it in a conventional suitcase. Make sure it is tough and durable, and that it seals well, so that its contents will survive bumpy drives and boisterous baggage handlers at airports. A lock is a good idea, not only for flights but for when you leave your case in a hotel room – in our experience, any theft from upmarket hotels in Africa is likely to be casual, and a locked suitcase is unlikely to be tampered with.

If you are likely to use public transport, then a backpack is the most practical solution. An internal frame is more flexible than an external one. Again, ensure your pack is durable and that it has several pockets. If you intend doing a lot of hiking, you definitely want a backpack designed for this purpose. On the other hand, if you'll be staying at places where it might be a good idea to shake off the sometimes negative image attached to backpackers, then there would be advantages in using a suitcase that converts into a backpack.

Before I started travelling with piles of my wife's camera equipment, my preference was a robust 35cl daypack. The advantages of keeping luggage as light and compact as possible are manifold. For starters, you can rest it on your lap on bus trips, avoiding complications such as extra charges for luggage, arguments about where your bag should be stored, and the slight but real risk of theft or damage if your luggage ends up on the roof. A compact bag also makes for greater mobility, whether you're hiking or looking for a hotel in town. The sacrifice? Leave behind camping equipment and a sleeping bag. Do this, and it's quite possible to fit everything you truly need into a 35cl daypack, and possibly even a few luxuries – I refuse to travel without binoculars, a bird field guide and at least five novels, and was still able to keep the weight down to around 8kg. If your luggage won't squeeze into a daypack, a sensible compromise is to carry a large daypack in your rucksack. That way, you can carry a tent and other camping equipment when you need it, but at other times reduce your luggage to fit into a daypack and leave what you're not using in storage.

Travellers carrying a lot of valuable items should look for a pack that can be easily padlocked. A locked bag can, of course, be slashed open, but in Rwanda you are more likely to encounter casual theft of the sort to which a lock would be real deterrent.

However you travel, a small daypack will be useful for gorilla-tracking and other walks, and to stow any breakable goods on your lap during long drives – anything like a Walkman or camera will suffer heavily from vibrations on rutted roads.

Camping equipment

There are only a few opportunities for camping in Rwanda, and the financial advantages are limited since affordable accommodation is generally available. Balanced against that, for those without transport the campsite at Nyungwe is a far more convenient base for walks than the resthouse, and a tent is essential for hiking in off-the-beaten-track areas. Also, although there is now accommodation in Akagera Park, camping there gets you closest to the wildlife.

For backpackers who decide to carry camping equipment, the key is to look for the lightest available gear. It is now possible to buy a lightweight tent weighing little more than 2kg, but make sure that the one you choose is mosquito proof. Other essentials for camping include a sleeping bag and a roll-mat, which will serve as both insulation and padding. You might want to carry a stove and Camping Gaz cylinders (not readily available in Rwanda). A box of firelighter blocks will get a fire going in the most unpromising conditions. It would also be advisable to carry a pot, plate, cup and cutlery.

Clothes

Try to keep your clothes to a minimum, especially if you are travelling with everything on your back. Bear in mind that you can easily and cheaply replace worn items in markets. In my opinion, the minimum is one or possibly two pairs of trousers and/or skirts, one pair of shorts, three shirts or T-shirts, one light sweater or similar, one heavy sweater or similar, a waterproof jacket during the rainy season, enough socks and underwear to last five to seven days, one solid pair of shoes or boots for walking, and one pair of sandals, thongs or other light shoes.

When you select your clothes, remember that jeans are heavy to carry, hot to wear, and slow to dry – but excellent wear for gorilla-tracking and other forest walks. In other situations, light cotton trousers are preferable. Skirts are best made of a light natural fabric such as cotton. T-shirts are lighter and less bulky than proper shirts, though the top pocket of a shirt (particularly if it buttons up) is a good place to carry spending money in markets and bus stations, since it's easier to keep an eye on than a trouser pocket. A couple of sweaters or sweatshirts will be necessary in places such as Nyungwe, which get chilly at night.

Socks and underwear *must* be made from natural fabrics. Bear in mind that re-using sweaty undergarments will encourage fungal infections such as athlete's foot, as well as prickly heat in the groin region. Socks and underpants are light and compact enough that it's worth bringing a week's supply. As for footwear, only if you're a serious off-road hiker should you consider genuine hiking boots, since they are very heavy whether on your feet or in your pack. A good pair of walking shoes, preferably made of leather with good ankle support, is a good compromise. For gorilla-tracking, a pair of old gardening gloves can be handy when you're grabbing for handholds in thorny vegetation.

Another factor in selecting your travel wardrobe is local sensibilities. In Rwanda, which is predominantly Christian, this isn't the concern it is in several other parts of Africa, but travellers are nevertheless advised to dress relatively modestly. For women, the ideal garment is a knee-length skirt, though long trousers – while unconventional female wear in rural Rwanda – are most unlikely to give offence. For men, shorts are not unacceptable, but few local men wear them and it is considered more respectable to wear trousers. Walking around in a public place without a shirt is dodgy.

Many Africans think it is insulting for Westerners to wear scruffy or dirty clothes in their country, reasoning that we wouldn't dress like that at home. It is difficult to explain that at home you also wouldn't spend a morning slithering around the muddy Virungas in your last clean outfit! If you're travelling rough, you're bound to look a mess at times, but it's worth trying to look as spruce as possible, particularly since many Rwandans dress well.

Other useful items

Most backpackers, even those with no intention of camping, carry a **sleeping bag**. I've never seen the necessity for this, particularly in Rwanda. You might meet travellers who, when they stay in local lodgings, habitually place their own sleeping bag on top of the bedding provided. Nutters, in my opinion: I'd imagine that a sleeping bag placed on a flea-ridden bed would be unlikely to provide significant protection – it would be more likely to become flea-infested itself.

I wouldn't leave home without **binoculars**, which some might say makes *me* the nutter. Seriously, though, if you're interested in natural history, it's difficult to imagine anything that will give you such value-for-weight entertainment as a pair of light, compact binoculars, which these days needn't be much heavier or bulkier than a pack of cards. Binoculars are essential if you want to get a good look at birds (Africa boasts a remarkably colourful avifauna even if you've no desire to put a name to everything that flaps) or to watch distant mammals in game reserves. For most purposes, 7x21 compact binoculars will be fine, though some might prefer 7x35 traditional binoculars for their larger field of vision. Serious birdwatchers will find a 10x magnification more useful.

Some travellers like to carry their own **padlock**. This is useful if you have a pack that is lockable, and in remote parts of the country might be necessary for rooms where no lock is provided. If you are uneasy about security in a particular guesthouse, you may like to use your own lock instead of, or in addition to, the one provided. Although combination locks are reputedly easier to pick than conventional padlocks, I think you'd be safer with a combination lock in Rwanda, because potential thieves will have far more experience of breaking through locks with keys

Your **toilet bag** should at the very minimum include soap (secured in a plastic bag or soap holder unless you enjoy a soapy toothbrush!), shampoo, toothbrush and toothpaste. This sort of stuff is easy to replace as you go along, so there's no need to bring family-sized packs. Men will probably want a **razor**. Women should carry enough **tampons** and/or **sanitary pads** to see them through at least one heavy period, since these items may not always be immediately available. If you wear **contact lenses**, be aware that the various fluids are not readily available in Rwanda, and, since many people find the intense sun and dust irritate their eyes, you might consider reverting to glasses. Nobody should forget to bring a **towel**, or to keep handy a roll of **loo paper**, which although widely available at shops and kiosks cannot always be relied upon to be present where it's most urgently needed. A lot of washbasins in Rwanda are plugless, so one of those 'universal' rubber plugs that fit all sizes of plughole can be useful.

Other essentials include a **torch**, a **penknife** and a compact **alarm clock** for those early morning starts. If you're interested in what's happening in the world, you might also think about taking a **short-wave radio**. Some travellers carry **games** – most commonly a pack of cards, less often chess or draughts or travel Scrabble. A light plastic **orange-squeezing device** gives you fresh orange juice as an alternative to fizzy drinks and water.

You should carry a small **medical kit**, the contents of which are discussed in the chapter on health, as are **mosquito nets**. For those who wear **glasses**, it's worth bringing a spare pair, though in an emergency a new pair can be made up cheaply (around US$10) and quickly in most Rwandan towns, provided that you have your prescription available.

MONEY
Organising your finances
Normally there are three ways of carrying money: hard cash, travellers' cheques and credit cards. However, at the time of writing credit cards are accepted in very few places in Rwanda. There is a scheme under way to introduce Visa countrywide and this should be done by the end of 2004 – meanwhile it is theoretically possible to draw money against a credit card at the Bank of Kigali (near the post office in central Kigali), and Visa is accepted in some (but not all, so check when you book) of the larger hotels.

As for travellers' cheques (it's best if they're in US dollars) – again, theoretically they are encashable in all Kigali banks, but in practice this can fall apart, as it did for a while in 2002/3 because a lot of forgeries were circulating and banks wouldn't take the risk. When cashing them, you must generally show the sales advice slip that you got when you obtained them – that's the slip of paper that one is supposed never to keep in proximity to the cheques!

That leaves cash. The preferred foreign currency is the dollar, but all main currencies should be exchangeable, whether in banks, in forex bureaux or on the 'black market', which for the moment seems to be legal or at least tolerated. Think of it in terms of 'independent money-changers' rather than shady, back-room deals! But you should keep your wits about you. The black-market rate is generally slightly better than the forex rate which is slightly better than the bank rate (and you'll get a much better rate everywhere for cash than you will for travellers' cheques). Black-market dealers may also offer a better rate for larger-denomination notes, which anyway are less bulky for you to carry.

So – it's a changing scene. Conditions regarding credit cards and travellers' cheques may be different – and better – by the time you travel. But do have enough cash in case of glitches. If you don't want to carry too much, arrange for a friend to send it to you from home when necessary, via Western Union – there are offices in Kigali and all the main towns. It isn't cheap – the cost depends on the amount being transferred – but it's quick and secure. Any Rwandan francs left over at the end of your trip can be changed back into dollars, euros or whatever by banks, forex bureaux or money-changers.

Your biggest outlay is likely to be for your gorilla-viewing permit, which costs US$250 (cash) if you buy it in Rwanda. Some Kigali tour operators may add an extra US$25 if they arrange it for you; ORTPN (the tourist board; see page 53) doesn't. If you pre-book your permit independently from ORTPN before you leave home, you should be able to transfer the cost from your bank account to ORTPN's – ask them for details at the time. If a tour operator has arranged your trip, the cost of the permit has probably been included.

Budget planning
Any budget will depend so greatly on how and where you travel that it is almost impossible to give sensible advice in a general travel guide. As a rule, readers who are travelling at the middle to upper end of the price range will have pre-booked most of their trip, which means that they will have a good idea of what the holiday will cost them before they set foot in the country. Pre-

booked packages do vary in terms of what is included in the price, and you are advised to check the exact conditions in advance, but generally the price quoted will cover everything but drinks, tips and perhaps some meals.

For budget travellers, Rwanda is not the cheapest country in Africa, but it's damn close to it – and after Ghana it offers the best value for money of any country I've visited in the last couple of years. Throughout the country, a soft drink will cost you around US$0.40 and a 700ml beer less than US$1 in a local bar, more in a hotel or restaurant that caters primarily to Westerners. A meal in a local restaurant will cost US$1–2 while a meal in a proper restaurant might cost US$4 upwards (see pages 104–8). Budget accommodation can average out at about US$5 per head, quite often for a self-contained room (two people) with a hot shower or bath. Public transport is cheap – typically about US$1 per 50km – and distances are relatively small. Taking the above figures into account I think that budget travellers could scrape by in most parts of Rwanda on around US$10–15 per day for one person or US$20 per day for two. Double this amount, and within reason you can eat and stay where you like. The above prices assume an exchange rate of around **500 Rwandan francs per dollar**. They will increase if the franc grows stronger, as may well happen.

The above calculations don't allow for more expensive one-off activities, such as gorilla-tracking or visiting the other national parks (not expensive unless you hire a vehicle). If you want to keep to a particular budget and plan on undertaking such activities, you would be well advised to treat your day-to-day budget separately from one-off expenses.

ITINERARY PLANNING

Rwanda is so small, and all parts of it are so easily accessible from Kigali, that you needn't engage in any complicated planning. Your first port of call should be Kigali, to gather information and to get your **gorilla-viewing permits** from the ORTPN (see page 53). It's sensible not to rush off to the gorillas immediately; take a few days to get the feel of the country and to acclimatise, because the trek can be quite strenuous and the altitude can take you unawares.

The best **map** available outside Rwanda is currently Rwanda and Burundi, scale 1:400,000, published in Canada by International Travel Maps (www.itmb.com). There is also *Tanzania, Rwanda and Burundi*, scale 1:1,500,000, published by Nelles Guides & Maps (www.nelles-verlag.de). ORTPN sells a tourist map of Rwanda.

Useful **websites** for information on Rwanda are www.rwandemb/org (of the Rwandan Embassy in Washington), www.rwandatourism.com, and www.ambarwanda.org.uk (run by the Rwandan Embassy in London), all of which give relevant addresses and contact details and have numerous links. A good site for current news is www.allafrica.com. Also see *Appendix 2*, page 235.

The international country telephone code for Rwanda is 250.

Health and Safety

HEALTH
With thanks to Dr Jane Wilson-Howarth and Dr Felicity Nicholson

Rwanda itself isn't a particularly unhealthy country for tourists and you'll never be far from some kind of medical help. The main towns have hospitals (for anything serious you'll be more comfortable in Kigali) and all towns of any size have a pharmacy, although the range of medicines on sale may be limited. In Kigali, the pharmacy in Boulevard de la Révolution is open 24 hours.

Rwanda is divided into 11 health provinces, and further into 39 health districts, with almost one hospital per district. There are 365 health centres, each covering an average of 23,000 people. A centre is generally staffed by one or two nurses, supported by medical assistants. In rural areas traditional medicine is also widely used. The above figures look promising, but in fact the severe shortage of qualified personnel caused by the targeting of professionals during the genocide has not yet been remedied: there is an average of only one doctor per 50,000 people. The incidence of HIV/AIDS is approximately 14% but hard to estimate accurately.

The guidelines below relate to tropical Africa in general, since travellers may well want to spend time in more than one country.

Before you go

As you should for any trip to a tropical or remote area, visit your doctor about eight weeks before leaving for Rwanda to discuss your plans and requirements. Preparations to ensure a healthy trip to anywhere in Africa should include checks on your immunisation status: it is wise to be up to date on tetanus (ten-yearly), polio (ten-yearly), diphtheria (ten-yearly), hepatitis A and typhoid. For many parts of Africa, immunisations against yellow fever, meningococcal meningitis and rabies are also needed.

In Rwanda, as with some other countries in Africa, yellow fever vaccination is required for all travellers over one year old. You are advised to carry the certificate as proof of vaccination as you may need to show it on arrival. This also applies if you arrive from another country where yellow fever is a risk. The certificate is not valid until ten days after your vaccination, so be sure to have this done in good time. This potentially lethal virus (its mortality rate can be up to 50%) is spread by mosquito bites and is currently on the increase worldwide, so keep your vaccination up to date. If you are unable to have the yellow fever vaccination (eg: if you are immuno-compromised, or are allergic to eggs) then you will need to obtain an exemption certificate. This will usually allow you entry into one country, so if you are planning to visit more than one country you will need to check with each embassy as to whether an exemption certificate will be accepted.

Certain countries in sub-Saharan Africa also require a certificate of vaccination for cholera. In the UK this vaccine is no longer given as it is ineffective, but certificates of exemption can be acquired from immunisation centres. Currently this is not necessary for Rwanda, but seek up-to-date information before you travel.

It is wise to be immunised against hepatitis A (eg: with Havrix Monodose or Avaxim). One dose of vaccine lasts for one year and can be boosted to give protection for up to ten years. The course of two injections costs about £100. The vaccine can be used even close to the time of departure. Gamma globulin is no longer used as protection for hepatitis A in travellers, since there is a theoretical risk of CJD (the human form of mad cow disease) with this blood-derived product.

The newer typhoid vaccines last for three years and are about 75% effective. They are advisable unless you are leaving within a few days for a trip of a week or less, when the vaccination would not be effective in time.

Vaccinations for rabies are advised for travellers visiting more remote areas. Ideally three injections should be taken over a period of four weeks, at 0, 7 and 28 days. The timing of these doses does not have to be exact and a schedule can be arranged to suit you (see *Rabies*, below).

Hepatitis B vaccination should be considered for longer trips (two months or more), or if you'll be working with children or in situations where contact with blood is increased. Three injections are ideal: they can be given at 0, 4 and 8 weeks prior to travel or, if there is insufficient time, then on days 0, 7–14, then 21–28. At the time of writing, the only vaccine licensed for the latter more rapid course is Engerix B. The longer course is always to be preferred as immunity is likely to be longer lasting.

A BCG vaccination against tuberculosis (TB) is also advisable for trips of two months or more. This should be taken at least six weeks before travel.

Malaria prevention

Malaria is probably the greatest health risk to travellers in Rwanda, although it is less prevalent there than in some other African countries. There is no vaccine against malaria, but using prophylactic drugs and preventing mosquito bites will considerably reduce the risk of contracting it. Seek professional advice to ascertain the preferred anti-malarial drugs for Rwanda at the time you travel. Mefloquine (Lariam) is still the most effective prophylactic agent for most countries in sub-Saharan Africa. If this drug is suggested then you should start taking it at least two and a half weeks before departure to check that it suits you. Stop immediately if it seems to cause depression or anxiety, visual or hearing disturbances, fits, severe headaches or changes in heart rhythm. Anyone who is pregnant, has been treated for depression or psychiatric problems, has diabetes controlled by oral therapy, or who is epileptic (or has suffered fits in the past) or has a close blood relative who is epileptic should not take mefloquine. Malarone is another very effective alternative if mefloquine is not recommended, but it is quite expensive and therefore is more suited to shorter trips. It is currently licensed in the UK for trips of up to three months. It is taken once a day, starting two days before arriving into a malarial area, whilst you are there and for seven days after leaving (unlike other regimes, which need to be continued for four weeks after leaving). It is well tolerated and, unlike mefloquine, can be used by people with depression and/or epilepsy. There is also a paediatric form of Malarone, which can be used for children weighing more than 11kg. The number of tablets given is calculated by weight so it is helpful to know the weight of any children under 40kg travelling with you.

The antibiotic doxycycline (100mg daily) is almost as effective as mefloquine and Malarone and is much cheaper than the latter so may be more cost-effective for longer trips. Like Malarone, it need only be started one to two days before travel but, like mefloquine, must be taken for four weeks after leaving. It may also be used by travellers with epilepsy, although anti-epileptic therapy may make it less effective. Also there is a possibility of allergic skin reactions developing in sunlight; this can occur in about 1–3% of users. The drug should be stopped if this happens, as there is a risk of more serious allergic reactions. You should then seek medical advice as soon as is practical as to what to do next. Women using the oral contraceptive should use an additional method of protection.

Chloroquine and paludrine should no longer be used for this part of Africa except as a last resort.

Some travellers like to take a treatment for malaria, as well as prophylaxis or sometimes instead if they are travelling for more than six months. Whatever you decide, you should take up-to-date advice to find out the most appropriate medication.

There is no malaria transmission above 3,000m; at intermediate altitudes (1,800–3,000m) the risk exists but is low.

In addition to taking anti-malarial medicines, it is important to avoid mosquito bites between dusk and dawn, which is when the *anopheles* (malaria-carrying) mosquito is most active. Pack a DEET-based insect repellent, such as one of the Repel range, and take either a permethrin-impregnated bednet or a permethrin spray so that you can treat bednets in hotels. Permethrin treatment makes even very tatty nets protective and mosquitoes are also unable to bite through the impregnated net when you roll against it. Putting on long clothes (including long-sleeved shirts or blouses) at dusk means you can reduce the amount of repellent needed; but be aware that malaria mosquitoes hunt at ankle level and will penetrate through socks, so apply repellent to your feet and ankles too. Travel clinics usually sell a good range of nets, treatment kits and repellents.

Important While you are away, assume that any high fever lasting more than a few hours is malaria, regardless of any other symptoms. Always seek medical

LONG-HAUL FLIGHTS
Felicity Nicholson

There is growing evidence, albeit circumstantial, that long-haul air travel increases the risk of developing deep vein thrombosis. This condition is potentially life threatening, but it should be stressed that the danger to the average traveller is slight.

Certain risk factors specific to air travel have been identified. These include immobility, compression of the veins at the back of the knee by the edge of the seat, the decreased air pressure and slightly reduced oxygen in the cabin, and dehydration. Consuming alcohol may exacerbate the situation by increasing fluid loss and encouraging immobility.

In theory everyone is at risk, but those at highest risk are shown below:

- Passengers on journeys of longer than eight hours' duration
- People over 40
- People with heart disease
- People with cancer
- People with clotting disorders
- People who have had recent surgery, especially on the legs
- Women on the pill or other oestrogen therapy
- Women who are pregnant
- People who are very tall (over 6ft/1.8m) or short (under 5ft/1.5m)

A deep vein thrombosis (DVT) is a clot of blood that forms in the leg veins. Symptoms include swelling and pain in the calf or thigh. The skin may feel hot to touch and becomes discoloured (light blue-red). A DVT

help. And remember that malaria may occur anything from seven days into your trip to up to one year after leaving Africa. If symptoms appear after you have returned home, visit your doctor immediately, and mention that you have been travelling in a malarial area.

Travel clinics and health information

A full list of current travel clinic websites worldwide is available on www.istm.org/. For other journey preparation information, consult www.tripprep.com. Information about various medications may be found on www.emedicine.com/wild/topiclist.htm.

UK

British Airways Travel Clinic and Immunisation Service There are two BA clinics in London, both on tel: 0845 600 2236; web: www.britishairways.com/travel/healthclinintro. Appointments only at 101 Cheapside; or walk-in service Mon–Sat at 213 Piccadilly. Apart from providing inoculations and malaria prevention, they sell a variety of health-related goods.

is not dangerous in itself, but if a clot breaks down then it may travel to the lungs (pulmonary embolus). Symptoms of a pulmonary embolus (PE) include chest pain, shortness of breath and coughing up small amounts of blood.

Symptoms of a DVT rarely occur during the flight, and typically occur within three days of arrival, although symptoms of a DVT or PE have been reported up to two weeks later.

Anyone who suspects that they have these symptoms should see a doctor immediately as anticoagulation (blood thinning) treatment can be given.

Prevention of DVT

General measures to reduce the risk of thrombosis are shown below. This advice also applies to long train or bus journeys.

• Whilst waiting to board the plane, try to walk around rather than sit.
• During the flight drink plenty of water (at least two small glasses every hour).
• Avoid excessive tea, coffee and alcohol.
• Perform leg-stretching exercises, such as pointing the toes up and down.
• Move around the cabin when practicable.

If you fit into the high-risk category (see above) ask your doctor if it is safe to travel. Additional protective measures such as graded compression stockings, aspirin or low molecular weight heparin can be given. No matter how tall you are, where possible request a seat with extra legroom.

Edinburgh Travel Clinic Regional Infectious Diseases Unit, Ward 41 OPD, Western General Hospital, Crewe Rd South, Edinburgh EH4 2UX; tel: 0131 537 2822. Travel helpline open 09.00–12.00 weekdays. Provides inoculations and anti-malarial prophylaxis and advises on travel-related health risks.

Hospital for Tropical Diseases Travel Clinic Mortimer Market Centre, 2nd Floor, Capper St (off Tottenham Ct Rd), London WC1E 6AU; tel: 020 7388 9600; web: www.thehtd.org. Offers consultations and advice, and is able to provide all necessary drugs and vaccines for travellers. Runs a healthline (09061 337733) for country-specific information and health hazards. Also stocks nets, water purification equipment and personal protection measures.

MASTA (Medical Advisory Service for Travellers Abroad) at the London School of Hygiene and Tropical Medicine, Keppel St, London WC1 7HT; tel: 09068 224100. This is a premium-line number, charged at 60p per minute. For a fee, they will provide an individually tailored health brief, with up-to-date information on how to stay healthy, inoculations and what to bring.

MASTA pre-travel clinics Tel: 01276 685040. Call for the nearest; there are currently 30 in Britain. Also sell malaria prophylaxis memory cards, treatment kits, bednets, net treatment kits.

NHS travel website www.fitfortravel.scot.nhs.uk, provides country-by-country advice on immunisation and malaria, plus details of recent developments, and a list of relevant health organisations.

Nomad Travel Store 3–4 Wellington Terrace, Turnpike Lane, London N8 0PX; tel: 020 8889 7014; fax: 020 8889 9528; email: sales@nomadtravel.co.uk; web: www.nomadtravel.co.uk. Also at 40 Bernard St, London WC1N 1LJ; tel: 020 7833 4114; fax: 020 7833 4470 and 43 Queens Rd, Bristol BS8 1QH; tel: 0117 922 6567; fax: 0117 922 7789. As well as giving health advice, Nomad stocks mosquito nets and other anti-bug devices, and an excellent range of adventure travel gear.

Thames Medical 157 Waterloo Rd, London SE1 8US; tel: 020 7902 9000. Competitively priced, one-stop travel health service. All profits go to their affiliated company, InterHealth, which provides health care for overseas workers on Christian projects.

Trailfinders Immunisation Centre 194 Kensington High St, London W8 7RG; tel: 020 7938 3999.

Travelpharm The Travelpharm website, www.travelpharm.com, offers up-to-date guidance on travel-related health and has a range of medications available through their online mini-pharmacy.

Irish Republic

Tropical Medical Bureau Grafton Street Medical Centre, Grafton Buildings, 34 Grafton St, Dublin 2; tel: 1 671 9200. Has a useful website specific to tropical destinations: www.tmb.ie.

USA

Centers for Disease Control 1600 Clifton Rd, Atlanta, GA 30333; tel: 877 FYI TRIP; 800 311 3435; web: www.cdc.gov/travel. The central source of travel information in the USA. Each summer they publish the invaluable *Health Information for International Travel*, available from the Division of Quarantine at the above address.

Connaught Laboratories PO Box 187, Swiftwater, PA 18370; tel: 800 822 2463/717-839-7187. They will send a free list of specialist tropical-medicine physicians in your state.

IAMAT (International Association for Medical Assistance to Travelers) 417 Center St, Lewiston, NY 14092; tel: 716 754 4883; email: info@iamat.org; web: www.iamat.org. A non-profit organisation that provides lists of English-speaking doctors abroad.

Canada

IAMAT Suite 1, 1287 St Clair Av W, Toronto, Ontario M6E 1B8; tel: 416 652 0137; web: www.iamat.org

TMVC (Travel Doctors Group) Sulphur Springs Rd, Ancaster, Ontario; tel: 905 648 1112; web: www.tmvc.com.au

Australia, New Zealand, Thailand

TMVC Tel: 1300 65 88 44; web: www.tmvc.com.au. Twenty-two clinics in Australia, New Zealand and Thailand, including:

Auckland Canterbury Arcade, 170 Queen St, Auckland; tel: 9 373 3531
Brisbane Dr Deborah Mills, Qantas Domestic Building, 6th floor, 247 Adelaide St,
Brisbane, QLD 4000; tel: 7 3221 9066; fax: 7 3321 7076
Melbourne Dr Sonny Lau, 393 Little Bourke St, 2nd floor, Melbourne, VIC 3000; tel: 3
9602 5788; fax: 3 9670 8394
Sydney Dr Mandy Hu, Dymocks Building, 7th Floor, 428 George St, Sydney, NSW
2000; tel: 2 221 7133; fax: 2 221 8401
IAMAT PO Box 5049, Christchurch 5, New Zealand; web: www.iamat.org

South Africa
SAA-Netcare Travel Clinics PO Box 786692, Sandton 2146; fax: 011 883 6152;
web: www.travelclinic.co.za or www.malaria.co.za. Clinics throughout South Africa.
TMVC 113 DF Malan Drive, Roosevelt Park, Johannesburg; tel: 011 888 7488; web:
www.tmvc.com.au. Consult the website for details of clinics in South Africa.

Switzerland
IAMAT 57 Voirets, 1212 Grand Lancy, Geneva; web: www.iamat.org

Travel insurance
Before you travel, make sure that you have adequate medical insurance –
choose a policy with comprehensive cover for hospitalisation as well as for
repatriation in an emergency. Nowadays the range of cover available is very
wide – choose whatever suits your method of travel. Be aware (if you plan to
use motorbike taxis in Rwanda) that not all policies cover you for this form of
transport. Remember to take all the details with you, particularly your policy
number and the telephone number that you have to contact in the event of a
claim.

Personal first-aid kit
The more I travel the less I take. My minimal kit contains:

- a good drying antiseptic, eg: iodine or potassium permanganate (don't take
  antiseptic cream)
- a few small dressings (Band-Aids)
- sunscreen
- insect repellent; malaria tablets; impregnated bednet
- aspirin or paracetamol
- antifungal cream (eg: Canesten)
- Ciprofloxacin antibiotic (take 500mg followed by a second tablet six to
  twelve hours later for diarrhoea with blood and/or slime and or a fever.
  Norfloxacin may be prescribed as an alternative in countries outside the
  UK.
- Tinidazole (2g taken in one dose then repeat seven days later) for amoebic
  dysentery or giardiasis
- another broad-spectrum antibiotic like amoxycillin (for chest, urine, skin
  infections, etc) if going to a remote area

TREATING TRAVELLERS' DIARRHOEA

It is dehydration which makes you feel awful during a bout of diarrhoea and the most important part of treatment is drinking lots of clear fluids. Sachets of oral rehydration salts give the perfect biochemical mix to replace all that is pouring out of your bottom but they do not taste nice. Any dilute mixture of sugar and salt in water will do you good, so if you like Coke or orange squash, drink that with a three-finger pinch of salt added to each glass. Otherwise make a solution of a four-finger scoop of sugar with a three-finger pinch of salt in a glass of water. Or add eight level teaspoons of sugar (18g) and one level teaspoon of salt (3g) to one litre (five cups) of safe water. A squeeze of lemon or orange juice improves the taste and adds potassium, which is also lost during a bout of diarrhoea. Drink two large glasses after every bowel action, and more if you are thirsty. If you are not eating, then you need to drink three litres a day plus the equivalent of whatever is pouring into the toilet. If you feel like eating, take a bland, high-carbohydrate diet. Heavy, greasy foods will probably give you cramps.

If the diarrhoea is bad, or you are passing blood or slime, or you have a fever, you will probably need antibiotics in addition to fluid replacement. A three-day course of Ciprofloxacin 500mg twice daily (or Norfloxacin) is appropriate treatment for dysentery and bad diarrhoea. If the diarrhoea is greasy and bulky and is accompanied by 'eggy' burps, the likely cause is giardia. This is best treated with Tinidazole (2g in one dose repeated seven days later if symptoms persist).

- pair of fine-pointed tweezers (to remove hairy-caterpillar hairs, thorns, splinters etc)
- condoms or femidoms
- possibly a malaria treatment kit
- a travel thermometer (not containing mercury; airlines ban these)

Common medical problems
Travellers' diarrhoea

At least half of those travelling to the tropics/developing world will experience a bout of travellers' diarrhoea during their trip; the newer you are to exotic travel, the more likely you will be to suffer. By taking precautions against travellers' diarrhoea you will also avoid typhoid, cholera, hepatitis, dysentery, worms, etc.

From food

Travellers' diarrhoea and the other faecal-oral diseases come from getting other peoples' faeces in your mouth. This most often happens from cooks not washing their hands after a trip to the toilet, but even if the restaurant cook does not understand basic hygiene you will be safe if your food has been properly cooked and arrives piping hot. The maxim to remind you what you can safely eat is:

PEEL IT, BOIL IT, COOK IT OR FORGET IT.

This means that fruit you have washed and peeled yourself, and hot foods, should be safe, but raw foods, cold cooked foods, salads, fruit salads prepared by others, ice cream and ice are all risky, as are foods kept lukewarm in restaurant or hotel buffets. Self-service or buffet meals are popular in Rwanda, so try to eat these when the food is hot and freshly cooked – for example a late buffet lunch eaten in mid-afternoon will have been sitting around a long while. If you do get travellers' diarrhoea, see box opposite for treatment.

From water

It is is also possible to get sick from drinking contaminated water, so try to drink from safe sources. Tap water is supposedly safe in Kigali but not elsewhere in Rwanda. To make risky water safe it should be brought to the boil (even at altitude it only needs to be brought to the boil), passed through a good bacteriological filter or purified with iodine; chlorine tablets (eg: Puritabs) are also adequate although theoretically less effective, and they taste nastier. Micropur tablets are tasteless but take at least two hours to become effective. If you buy bottled water (which is widely available in Rwanda) make sure the seal is intact. Iodine is not recommended in pregnancy so you should ask a doctor what you should do.

Dengue fever

This mosquito-borne disease resembles malaria but there is no prophylactic available to deal with it. The mosquitoes which carry this virus bite during the daytime, so it is worth applying repellent if you see them around. Symptoms include strong headaches, rashes and excruciating joint and muscle pains with high fever. Dengue fever lasts for only a week or so and is not usually fatal if you have not previously been infected. Complete rest and paracetamol are the usual treatment. Plenty of fluids also help. Some patients are given an intravenous drip to keep them from dehydrating.

Insect bites

It is crucial to avoid mosquito bites between dusk and dawn; as the sun is going down, don long clothes and apply repellent on any exposed flesh. This will protect you from malaria, elephantiasis and a range of nasty insect-borne viruses. Malaria **mosquitoes** are voracious, hunt at ankle-level, and can penetrate through socks. Sleep under a permethrin-treated bednet or in an air-conditioned room. During the day it is wise to wear long, loose (preferably 100% cotton) clothes if you are pushing through scrubby country; this will deter **ticks** as well as **tsetse flies** and day-biting *Aedes* mosquitoes which may spread dengue and yellow fever. Tsetse flies hurt when they bite and are attracted to the colour blue; locals will advise on where they are a problem and where they transmit sleeping sickness.

Minute pestilential biting **blackflies** spread river blindness in some parts of Africa between 190°N and 170°S; the disease is caught close to fast-flowing rivers since flies breed there and the larvae live in rapids. The flies bite during the day but long trousers tucked into socks will help keep them off. Citronella-based natural repellents do not work against them.

Tumbu flies or *putsi* are a problem in areas of eastern, western and southern Africa where the climate is hot and humid. The adult fly lays her eggs on the soil or on drying laundry and when the eggs come in contact with human flesh (when you put on clothes or lie on a bed) they hatch and bury themselves under the skin. Here they form a crop of 'boils' each of which hatches a grub after about eight days, when the inflammation will settle down. In *putsi* areas either dry your clothes and sheets within a screened house, or dry them in direct sunshine until they are crisp, or iron them.

Jiggers or **sandfleas** are another kind of flesh-feaster. They latch on if you walk barefoot in contaminated places, and set up home under the skin of the foot, usually at the side of a toenail where they cause a painful, boil-like swelling. These need picking out by a local expert; if the distended flea bursts during eviction the wound should be dowsed in spirit, alcohol or kerosene, otherwise more jiggers will infest you.

Bilharzia or schistosomiasis
With thanks to Dr Vaughan Southgate of the Natural History Museum, London
Bilharzia or schistosomiasis is a disease that commonly afflicts the rural poor of the tropics who repeatedly acquire more and more of these nasty little worm-lodgers. Infected travellers and expatriates generally suffer fewer problems because symptoms will encourage them to seek prompt treatment and they are also exposed to fewer parasites. However, it is still an unpleasant problem that is worth avoiding.

The parasites digest their way through your skin when you wade, bathe or even shower in infested freshwater. Unfortunately many African lakes, rivers and irrigation canals carry a risk of bilharzia. In Rwanda, the bathing areas of Lake Kivu are currently said to be safe.

The most risky shores will be close to places where infected people use water, where they wash clothes, etc. Winds disperse the cercariae, though, so they can be blown some distance, perhaps up to 200m from where they entered the water. Scuba-diving off a boat into deep offshore water, then, should be a low-risk activity, but showering in lake water or paddling along a reedy lake shore near a village carries a high risk of acquiring bilharzia.

Although absence of early symptoms does not necessarily mean there is no infection, infected people usually notice symptoms two or more weeks after penetration. Travellers and expatriates will probably experience a fever and often a wheezy cough; local residents do not usually have symptoms.

There is now a very good blood test which, if done six weeks or more after likely exposure, will determine whether or not parasites are going to cause problems, and then the infection can be treated. While treatment generally remains effective, it does fail in some cases for reasons that are not yet fully

QUICK TICK REMOVAL

African ticks are not the prolific disease transmitters they are in the Americas, but they may occasionally spread disease. Lyme disease, which can have unpleasant after-effects, has now been recorded in Africa, and tick-bite fever also occurs. The latter is a mild, flu-like illness, but still worth avoiding. If you get the tick off whole and promptly the chances of disease transmission are reduced to a minimum.

Manoeuvre your finger and thumb so that you can pinch the tick's mouthparts, as close to your skin as possible, and slowly and steadily pull away at right angles to your skin. This often hurts. Jerking or twisting will increase the chances of damaging the tick which in turn increases the chances of disease transmission, as well as leaving the mouthparts behind.

Once the tick is off, dowse the little wound with alcohol (local spirit, whisky or similar is excellent) or iodine. An area of spreading redness around the bite site, or a rash or fever coming on a few days or more after the bite, should stimulate a trip to a doctor.

understood; retreatment seems to work fine and it is not known if some drug resistance is developing. Since bilharzia can be a nasty illness, avoidance is better than waiting to be cured and it is wise to avoid bathing in high-risk areas. Take local advice about this.

Avoiding bilharzia

If you are bathing, swimming, paddling or wading in freshwater which you think may carry a bilharzia risk, try to stay in no longer than ten minutes. Afterwards dry off thoroughly with a towel; rub vigorously. Avoid bathing or paddling on shores within 200m of villages or places where people use the water a great deal, especially reedy shores or where there is lots of water weed. Covering yourself with DEET insect repellent before swimming will help to protect you. If your bathing water comes from a risky source try to ensure that the water is taken from the lake in the early morning and stored snail-free, otherwise it should be filtered or Dettol or Cresol should be added. Bathing early in the morning is safer than bathing in the last half of the day. If you think that you have been exposed to bilharzia parasites, arrange a screening blood test (your GP can do this) *more* than six weeks after your last possible contact with suspect water.

Skin infections

Any mosquito bite or small nick in the skin provides an opportunity for bacteria to foil the body's usually excellent defences; it will surprise many travellers how quickly skin infections start in warm humid climates and it is essential to clean and cover even the slightest wound. Creams are not as effective as a good drying antiseptic such as dilute iodine, potassium permanganate (a few crystals in half a cup of water), or crystal (or gentian) violet. One of these should be available in most towns. If the wound starts to throb, or becomes red and the redness starts to spread, or the wound oozes, and especially if you develop a fever, antibiotics will probably be needed; flucloxacillin (250mg four times a day) or cloxacillin (500mg four times a day). For those allergic to penicillin, erythromycin (500mg twice a day) for five days should help. See a doctor if the symptoms do not start to improve in 48 hours.

Fungal infections also get a hold easily in hot moist climates so wear 100% cotton socks and underwear and shower frequently. An itchy rash in the groin or flaking between the toes is likely to be a fungal infection. This needs treatment with an antifungal cream such as Canesten (clotrimazole); if this is not available try Whitfield's ointment (compound enzoic acid ointment) or crystal violet (although this will turn you purple!).

Prickly heat
A fine pimply rash on the torso is likely to be heat rash; cool showers, dabbing (not rubbing) dry, and talc will help; if it's bad you may need to check into an air-conditioned hotel room for a while. Slowing down to a relaxed schedule, wearing only loose, baggy 100% cotton clothes and sleeping naked under a fan reduce the problem.

Sun damage
The incidence of skin cancer is rocketing as Caucasians are travelling more and spending more time in the sun. Keep out of the sun during the middle of the day and, if you must expose yourself, build up gradually from 20 minutes per day. Be especially careful of sun reflected off water and wear a T-shirt and lots of waterproof SPF 15 suncream when swimming and Bermuda shorts to protect the back of your thighs when snorkelling. Sun exposure ages the skin and causes premature wrinkles; cover up with long loose clothes and wear a hat when you can.

Meningitis
This is a particularly nasty disease as it can kill within hours of the first symptoms appearing. The telltale symptoms are a combination of a blinding headache (light sensitivity), a blotchy rash and a high fever. Immunisation with the newer tetravalent vaccine ACWY protects against the most serious bacterial form of meningitis and is usually recommended for longer-stay trips to Rwanda or if you are working closely with the local population – in particular with children. A single injection gives good protection for three years. Other forms of meningitis exist (usually viral) but there are no vaccines for these. Local papers normally report outbreaks. If you show symptoms go immediately to a doctor.

Sexual risks
Travel is a time when we may enjoy sexual adventures, especially when alcohol reduces inhibitions. Remember the risks of sexually transmitted infection are high, whether you sleep with fellow travellers or with locals.

About 40% of HIV infections in British heterosexuals are acquired abroad and AIDS is a serious problem in Rwanda. Use condoms or femidoms, preferably bearing the British kite mark and ideally bought before travel. If you notice any genital ulcers or discharge get treatment promptly.

Ebola

So far this has never occurred in Rwanda, but it has claimed some lives in Uganda. It is a rare, but deadly, highly contagious, virally induced disease which causes haemorrhagic fever. In the unlikely event of an outbreak, protective measures will be taken and you should follow whatever local advice is given.

Useful contacts in Kigali

Central Hospital of Kigali Tel: 575555
King Faycal Hospital (Kigali) Tel: 82421
Sun City Pharmacy Bd de la Révolution. Open 24 hours.
Pharmacie Conseil Av des Mille Collines (opposite Belgian School). Open 08.00–21.00 Mon–Sat; 10.00–15.00 Sun.

Animals

Rabies

Rabies can be carried by all mammals and is passed on to man through a bite or a lick of an open wound. You must always assume any animal is rabid (unless personally known to you). The closer the bite is to the face the shorter the incubation time of the disease, but it is always wise to get medical help as soon as possible. In the interim, scrub the wound with soap and bottled/boiled water, then pour on a strong iodine or alcohol solution. This helps stop the rabies virus entering the body and will guard against wound infections including tetanus. If you intend to have contact with animals and/or are likely to be more than 24 hours away from medical help, then pre-exposure vaccination is advised. Ideally three doses should be taken over four weeks. Contrary to popular belief these vaccinations are relatively painless! If you are exposed as described, then treatment should be given as soon as possible, but it is never too late to seek help as the incubation period for rabies can be very long.

Those who have not been immunised will need a full course of injections together with rabies immunoglobulin (RIG), but this product is expensive (around US$800) and may be hard to come by – which is a reason why pre-exposure vaccination should be encouraged in travellers who are planning to visit more remote areas. Tell the doctor if you have had pre-exposure vaccine as this will change the treatment you receive. Remember that if you do contract rabies, mortality is 100% and death from rabies is probably one of the worst ways to go!

Snakebite

Snakes rarely attack unless provoked and bites to travellers are unusual. You are less likely to get bitten if you wear stout shoes and long trousers when in the bush. Most snakes are harmless and even venomous species will only dispense venom in about half of their bites. If bitten, then, you are unlikely to have received venom; keeping this fact in mind may help you to stay calm. Many so-called first-aid techniques do more harm than good: cutting into the wound is harmful; tourniquets are dangerous; suction and electrical inactivation devices do not work. The only treatment is antivenom. In case of a bite which you fear may have been from a venomous snake:

• Try to keep calm – it is likely that no venom has been dispensed.
• Prevent movement of the bitten limb by applying a splint.
• Keep the bitten limb BELOW heart height to slow the spread of any venom.
• If you have a crepe bandage, bind up as much of the bitten limb as you can, but release the bandage every half hour.
• Evacuate to a hospital which has antivenom.

And remember:

• NEVER give aspirin; you may offer paracetamol, which is safe.
• NEVER cut or suck the wound.
• DO NOT apply ice packs.
• DO NOT apply potassium permanganate.

If the offending snake can be captured without risk of someone else being bitten, take it to show to the doctor – but beware, since even a decapitated head is able to dispense venom in a reflex bite.

Further reading
Self-prescribing has its hazards so, if you are going anywhere remoter than Rwanda, or if you like to have facts at your fingertips, then consider taking a health guide. For adults there is *Bugs, Bites & Bowels: The Cadogan Guide to Healthy Travel* by Jane Wilson-Howarth (1999); if travelling with children look at *Your Child's Health Abroad: A Manual for Travelling Parents* by Jane Wilson-Howarth and Matthew Ellis, published by Bradt Publications in 1998.

SAFETY
Big game
If you are venturing into the bush remember that it is inhabited by some threatening wildlife. The most dangerous species are the big primates and wild buffalo; hippos are dangerous if you happen to frighten them and you are between them and the safety of their waterhole.

Theft
The following security hints are applicable anywhere in Africa:

• Most casual thieves operate in busy markets and bus stations. Keep a close watch on your possessions in such places, and avoid having valuables or large amounts of money loose in your daypack or pocket.

- Keep all your valuables and the bulk of your money in a hidden money belt. Never show this money belt in public. Keep any spare cash you need elsewhere on your person – a button-up pocket on the front of the shirt is a good place as money cannot be snatched from it without the thief coming into your view. It is also advisable to keep a small amount of hard currency (ideally cash) hidden in your luggage in case you lose your money belt.
- Where the choice exists between carrying valuables on your person or leaving them in a locked room I would tend to favour the latter option (thefts from locked hotel rooms are relatively rare in Africa). Obviously you should use your judgement on this and be sure the room is absolutely secure. Bear in mind that some travellers' cheque companies will not refund cheques which were stolen from a room.
- Leave any jewellery of financial or sentimental value at home.

Useful contact
Police Tel: 08311117

Other hazards

People new to exotic travel often worry about tropical diseases, but it is accidents which are most likely to carry you off. Road travel isn't as dangerous in Rwanda as in some other African countries but still accidents aren't uncommon, and the number of vehicles is increasing; so be aware and do what you can to reduce risks. For example, try to travel during daylight hours and refuse to be driven by anyone who is drunk. Always heed local advice about where you should (or should not) travel, or about areas where you should take particular care. At the time of writing, Rwanda is a relatively safe country – but, sadly, it has been seen elsewhere that an increase in tourism can lead to an increase in opportunistic crime. Be as sensible in Rwanda as (I hope!) you would be in any other strange country about carrying your cash discreetly and not flaunting jewellery, and (particularly in towns) about where you walk after dark. Also be sensible in hotels and guesthouses: don't leave tempting items too readily accessible.

Travelling in Rwanda

TOURIST INFORMATION AND SERVICES

The **Office Rwandais du Tourisme et des Parcs Nationaux**, more commonly referred to as ORTPN (*Or-ti-pen*), doubles as both tourist office and national parks authority. The ORTPN offices in the airport arrivals hall and in central Kigali stock a fair range of booklets and maps, and are the best places to seek out current information relating to the national parks and other reserves. The office in central Kigali (No 1, Boulevard de la Révolution at its junction with Avenue de l'Armée) handles advance bookings and issues permits for gorilla-tracking in the Volcanoes National Park. It's open 07.00–17.00, Monday–Friday; 07.00–12.00 weekends and holidays. Permits can sometimes – depending on availability – also be bought at the ORTPN office in Ruhengeri, but check this in Kigali first.

ORTPN can also provide details of hotels around the country, as well as lists of car-hire agencies in Kigali, tour operators, public transport and local events. It's best to call in personally, otherwise contact details are: ORTPN, BP 905 Kigali; tel: 573396, 576514; fax: 576515; email: ortpn@rwanda1.com and info@rwandatourism.com; web: www.rwandatourism.com.

Two bookshops in central Kigali with a reasonable stock of guidebooks and maps, as well as a wide selection of background reading, are the **Librairie Caritas** near the GPO, and the **Librairie Ikirezi** in Avenue de la Paix. See advertisement on page 69. (Remember that in French *librairie* means bookshop; lending library is *bibliothèque*.)

Tour operators and travel agents (see pages 120–1) are also sources of local information.

PUBLIC HOLIDAYS

In addition to the following fixed public holidays, Rwanda recognises Good Friday and Easter Monday.

January 1	New Year's Day	August 15	Assumption Day
January 28	Democracy Day	September 8	Culture Day
April 7	Genocide Memorial Day	September 25	Republic Day
May 1	Labour Day	October 1	Heroes' Day
July 1	Independence Day	November 1	All Saints' Day
July 4	National Liberation Day	December 25	Christmas Day
August 1	Harvest Festival	December 26	Boxing Day

MONEY

The unit of currency is the Rwanda franc (Rfr). In January 2004, the exchange rate against the dollar was around Rfr500, depending on whether the transaction involved cash or travellers' cheques, and where it took place. In Rwanda more than most African countries, US dollars are by far the most widely recognised foreign currency, and, except in Kigali, US dollars cash are the only foreign currency easily exchangeable outside of banks.

If you intend visiting the mountain gorillas – and who in their right mind would not! – then bear in mind that your permit will cost US$250 which currently must be paid in US$ *cash,* so bring at least that much with you.

Foreign exchange

See *Chapter 2,* page 35, for details of exchange transactions. All Rwandan banks have branches in Kigali and there's at least one bank in each other main town. There are also several private bureaux de change (known locally as forex bureaux) in the capital, which generally offer better rates than banks against cash but don't handle travellers' cheques. Elsewhere in the country, there are very few forex bureaux, and bank rates tend to be poorer than in the capital.

The best rates for US dollars cash anywhere in the country are offered by the private individuals who hang out around the main post office in Kigali. Their activities are technically illegal, but they operate in the open (and, conveniently, at times when banks are closed) and appear to be tolerated. The atmosphere when you're changing money here can be pretty fraught, with up to a dozen individuals breathing down your neck, so that being cheated or hustled is probably of greater concern than falling foul of the law, and you should always decide beforehand the minimum rate you're prepared to accept. Fortunately, the money-changers in Kigali do have a reasonable reputation for honesty: they might well quote a sub-standard rate, but are unlikely to get into more elaborate con tricks. This could change, however, so keep your wits about you, and – once you've decided who to deal with – try to get the mob to disperse before you start the transaction. These private money-changers generally offer a slightly better rate for cash than the forex bureaux which offer a slightly better rate than banks. The bank rate for travellers' cheques is even lower.

In other towns, particularly those close to international borders, it is also possible to change US dollars cash on the street, at rates significantly better than those offered by the bank, but lower than the street rate in Kigali. As in Kigali, there is always a risk of being duped by street operators. One way around this is to ask the manager of your hotel to exchange your US dollars – you may lose slightly on the deal, as the hotel will effectively be acting as a broker, but it will save a lot of hassle.

Banking hours are from approximately 08.00 to 12.00 and 14.00 to 17.00 Monday to Friday (some banks stay open longer), and 08.00 to 12.00 Saturday. Private forex bureaux may keep slightly longer hours than banks. Both are closed on Sundays and public holidays.

Credit cards

The situation is bad at present but due to improve. See *Chapter 2*, page 35, for details. Don't be misled by the gleaming ATMs you may see around the city – they accept only cards issued by a local bank (the BCDI).

Transfers from abroad

If your budgeting has fallen apart and you need a rescue transfer from home, there are Western Union facilities at the Banque Commerciale du Rwanda, and Moneygram facilities (accessed via any branch of Thomas Cook in the UK) at the Banque Continentale Africaine Rwanda, both in Boulevard de la Révolution in Kigali. Western Union has various other offices in Kigali (including at the Novotel) and in all main towns.

Prices in this book

Most services in Rwanda are best paid for in local currency. The exceptions are gorilla-tracking fees and some upmarket hotels, which charge in US dollars. Throughout this guide, **prices are quoted in US dollars using an approximate exchange rate of Rfr500 per US$1**. Prices were correct as of January 2004, but you'll need to adjust them if the Rwandan franc either strengthens or weakens, so check this before travelling.

GETTING AROUND
Self-drive

Most trunk roads in Rwanda are surfaced and in reasonable condition, including the main road from Kigali to Cyangugu via Butare; to Gisenyi via Ruhengeri; to Rusumo via Kibungo; to Kibuye via Gitarama; and to the Uganda border via Byumba or Umutara. A big programme of road improvement is under way; meanwhile there are still some pot-holed sections along all these routes which, together with the winding terrain and the tendency for Rwandans to drive at breakneck speeds and particularly to overtake on sharp or blind corners, necessitate a more cautious approach than one might take at home.

The unsurfaced roads most likely to be used by tourists include the long stretch running parallel to Lake Kivu between Gisenyi, Kibuye and Cyangugu; the approach roads to Akagera National Park (and roads within the park); and approach roads to the Parc des Virungas and Lakes Burera and Ruhondo from Ruhengeri. In all cases, these roads are in fair condition, and should be 'do-able' in a saloon car during the dry season, though a 4WD would certainly be preferable.

On all routes, be alert to cyclists swaying from the verge, and for livestock and pedestrians wandering blithely into the middle of the road. Putting one's foot to the floor and hooting like a maniac is the customary Rwandan approach to driving through crowded areas; driving rather more defensively than you would at home is a safer approach. Try to avoid driving at night, because of the risk posed by vehicles lacking headlights.

Several travel agencies in Kigali rent out saloons and 4WDs, with or

APPROXIMATE DISTANCES BETWEEN MAIN TOWNS
(in kilometres)

	Kigali	Butare	Byumba	Gitarama	Kibungo	Kibuye	Gisenyi	Gikongoro	Ruhengeri	Cyangugu
Kigali		135	60	53	112	144	187	164	118	293
Butare	135		210	82	247	129	237	29	190	158
Byumba	60	210		128	187	219	173	240	104	349
Gitarama	53	82	128		165	91	177	112	108	221
Kibungo	112	247	187	165		256	299	277	230	386
Kibuye	144	129	219	91	256		108	258	199	130
Gisenyi	187	237	173	177	299	108		366	69	238
Gikongoro	164	29	240	112	277	258	366		220	128
Ruhengeri	118	190	104	108	230	199	69	220		307
Cyangugu	293	158	349	221	386	130	248	128	307	

without drivers. For their contact details see *Chapter 6,* pages 120–1. Further up-to-date listings are given in the tourism section of the Rwanda website www.rwandatourism.com; also you can get details from ORTPN in Kigali. Rates vary according to whether you'll be driving outside Kigali, and whether fuel is included. A 4WD can cost from US$100 to US$150 per day including driver, depending on its type/size.

Mountain biking or cycling

The relatively short distances between tourist centres and the consistently attractive scenery should make Rwanda ideal for travelling by mountain bike. These cannot easily be bought locally, so you would have to bring one with you (some airlines are more flexible than others about carrying bicycles; you should discuss this with them in advance). More and more Rwandans are using cycles now, and if you ask around you should be able to find some for hire – but check the brakes carefully and carry a repair kit. Minibuses will allow you to take your bike on the roof, though expect to be charged extra for this. Minor roads vary in condition, but in the dry season you're unlikely to encounter any problems. Several of the more off-the-beaten-track destinations mentioned in this book would be particularly attractive to cyclists.

Hitching

This is an option on main routes, though you should expect to pay for lifts offered by Rwandans. Some minor roads carry little traffic so you could face a long wait.

Previous page Waterfall, Nyungwe Forest National Park
Above Baby mountain gorilla, Volcanoes National Park
Left Angola colobus monkey, Nyungwe Forest Reserve
Below left L'Hoest's monkey, Nyungwe Forest Reserve
Below right Mountain gorilla, Volcanoes National Park

Public transport
Boat and rail
There are no rail services in Rwanda (although a rail link with Tanzania is on the drawing board), nor is there at present a functional ferry on Lake Kivu, although transport links are being renewed now as the situation with the DRC improves. You may be able to get a place on a cargo boat serving the main lake ports, and it's possible to rent local dugouts for short excursions on the lake. Motor boats are also available for hire on Lake Kivu – see *Cyangugu* in *Chapter 7* and *Gisenyi* in *Chapter 8*. Small boats can be used to get around the smaller lakes, such as Burera and Ruhondo, by making an informal arrangement with the boat owner.

Road
The main mode of road transport is shared **minibuses** or *matatus*, generally known as *taxis* or *taxi-minibuses*, which connect all major centres (and most minor ones) and leave from the town's minibus station (*gare taxi/minibus*) when they are full. No smoking inside is the rule, as it is on all public transport. Departures continue throughout the day but it's best not to wait until too late, in case the last one proves to be full. Fares generally work out at around US$1 per 50km. Travel times along main surfaced roads typically average about 50km per hour, with frequent pauses to drop off passengers balanced against driving that verges on the manic between the stops. Overloading is not the problem it is in many African countries, nor are tourists routinely overcharged, though the latter does happen from time to time so check the fare with other passengers if it feels too high. You pay just before you alight rather than when you board, so there's the opportunity to see what other people are paying. On some routes **buses** are also available, which leave at fixed times. In and around Kigali there's a network of **urban minibuses**, running on set routes through the capital and its suburbs.

In some larger towns you'll also find normal **taxis** – identifiable by a yellow or orange stripe round the side – known as *taxi-voitures* to distinguish them from taxi-minibuses. The same rules apply as in most African countries – agree a price in advance and haggle if it seems extortionate. Fares in Kigali are fixed according to distance.

Private minibuses
Between Kigali and all main towns, private companies operate minibuses to fixed timetables and with bookable seats. These start and finish at the company's offices rather than at the public minibus stations. The price is generally much the same as for public minibuses. Details appear under the relevant towns in *Part Two*.

There are also privately owned minibuses which operate flexibly throughout the country, in much the same way as taxis, with passengers sharing the fare. If you're hitching, you may well come across these.

Two-wheeled taxis
In and around minibus-taxi stations you may find 'taxis' in the form of motorbikes (*motos*) or bicycles. They're handy for short distances – but be

aware that your travel insurance may not cover you for accidents when on either of them, and you certainly won't be offered a safety helmet. Agree a price beforehand, and check with a passer-by if it seems excessive. If you've got a heavy bag, a comfortable alternative is to stick it on the saddle of the bicycle and walk alongside.

LOCAL TOUR OPERATORS
See the *Kigali* chapter (pages 120–1) for details of local tour operators who can fix up trips within the country for you.

ACCOMMODATION
There are hotels of international standard in Kigali, Kinigi, Akagera and Gisenyi. Elsewhere, accommodation consists of mid-range hotels, geared to local businesspeople as much as to tourists, and cheaper local guesthouses. With a few exceptions, accommodation in Rwanda is good value for money when compared with that of other countries in the region. Where mid-range hotels are available – in Ruhengeri, Butare and the Lake Kivu resorts – rates generally work out at comfortably under US$30 for a clean double with en-suite hot bath or shower. Budget accommodation mostly falls into the US$7–15 price range, and in many cases this will get you a very clean room with en-suite hot shower. In hotels of all standards, if you're staying for more than a few days you may be able to negotiate a lower rate.

Most accommodation establishments are recognisably signposted as a hotel, *logement,* guesthouse or similar, but some local places are signposted as *Amacumbi* (pronounced amachoombi) – which literally means 'Place with Rooms' in Kinyarwanda. Note, too, that in the Swahili language – not indigenous to Rwanda but more widely spoken by locals than any other exotic tongue – a *hoteli* is a restaurant, which can create confusion when asking a non-French speaker for a hotel.

Few formal campsites exist in Rwanda. Some hotels will permit camping in the gardens, but at little saving over the price of a budget room. There are campsites at the Volcanoes and Akagera national parks and in Nyungwe Forest. At Nyungwe, the campsite is far more attractively located than the resthouse for travellers without a vehicle. A tent may also come in handy for travellers backpacking or cycling through relatively untouristed rural areas, where you are strongly advised to ask permission of the local village official before setting up camp.

EATING AND DRINKING
Eating out
Kigali boasts a good range of restaurants representing international cuisines such as Indian, Italian, Chinese and French. In most other towns, a couple of hotels or restaurants serve uncomplicated Western meals – chicken, fish or steak with chips or rice. Possibly as a result of the Belgian influence, restaurant standards seem to be far higher than in most East African countries, and Rwandan chips are probably the best on the continent. Servings tend to be

dauntingly large, and prices very reasonable – around US$5 for a main course.

Wherever you travel, local restaurants serve Rwandan favourites such as goat kebabs, grilled or fried tilapia (a type of lake fish), bean or meat stews. These are normally eaten with one of a few staples: *ugali* (a stiff porridge made with maize meal), *matoke* (cooking banana/plantain), *chapatti* (flat bread), and boiled potatoes (as in Uganda, these are somewhat mysteriously referred to as Irish potatoes) – not to mention rice and the ubiquitous chips. At local restaurants, you should be able to fill yourself adequately for US$2 or less.

My favourite 'food discovery' anywhere in Rwanda when I (Janice) was researching this new edition of the guide was a cheery little restaurant, La Tranquilleté, opposite the minibus-taxi stand in Gitarama, not normally a place one would visit in search of culinary delights. An unprepossessing alley with clothing pinned up for sale on one wall opens out into a simple courtyard with clean tables, a blackboard announcing the dishes of the day and a handful of young waitresses bustling to and fro. Out of a choice of chicken, beef and

CHEDDAR IN RWANDA

Many's the long night I've dreamed of cheese – toasted, mostly.

Treasure Island, Robert Louis Stevenson.

I don't know about toasted, but certainly there's more locally made cheese available in Rwanda now, although shortage of refrigerated transport limits its distribution. On supermarket shelves in Kigali you'll see Rwandan 'gouda', Rwandan 'feta' and less ambitiously named 'local goats' cheese'.

For Rwandan 'cheddar' you must head off to Nyabisindu. Take the Nyanza turning from the Gitarama–Butare road and, after 1–2km, take a right turn signed 'Oakdale Demonstration Farm'. Follow a twisty dirt road down into the valley (bearing left at a confusing fork with coffee trees); turn right just before crossing the valley floor. The Lac du Roi Rudahigwa is ahead on your left and you'll come to the 'cheese factory' on your right – a small, new building on the edge of the road. In the spotless interior, four women (widows) prepare the cheeses.

Much is made from the milk of the farm's own cows, but farmers can also bring in their own milk – it is checked for quality and then, if suitable, made into cheese. The cheeses are waxed for storage, so can be transported. Bought at the farm, a 1kg Oakdale cheese costs US$7; bought in Kigali, many times more. (To make four 1kg cheeses takes 38.5 litres of milk.)

To make an appointment beforehand (the manager will show visitors round by request) phone 83139 or 08540565. The farm has pigs and turkeys as well as cows and will soon be digging fishponds; already some fish is farmed in the lake. Even if you don't want to buy cheese, the beautiful and peaceful valley is worth a visit.

liver with chips and/or salad I had liver – tender, in a very tasty sauce – followed by a well-presented plate of fresh fruit. Service was friendly and exceptionally quick; including a fruit juice I spent less than US$3. Tables were full, so I shared with (and chatted to) a Rwandan electrical engineer. I shall now plan all my Rwandan routes so that lunchtime coincides with Gitarama!

Buffet or self-service meals are often offered in restaurants – and are said to originate from a period in the 1980s when the government decreed that civil servants should have shorter lunch breaks. As a result, enterprising restaurants dreamed up this way of enabling them to eat faster. Smarter restaurants, especially in Kigali, may be closed or take a while to rustle up food outside of normal mealtimes.

Unless you have an insatiable appetite for greasy omelettes or stale *mandazi* (deep-fried dough balls not dissimilar to doughnuts), breakfast outside of Kigali (where good French bread and croissants are available) or the larger hotels can be a problematic meal. One area in which Rwanda is definitely influenced more by its anglophone neighbours than by its former coloniser is baking: in common with the rest of East Africa, the bread is almost always sweetish and goes quickly stale. In such cases a bunch of bananas, supplemented by other fresh fruit, is about the best breakfast option: cheap, nutritious and filling.

Cooking for yourself

The alternative to eating at restaurants is to put together your own meals at markets and supermarkets. The variety of foodstuffs you can buy varies from season to season and from town to town, but in most major centres you can rely on finding a supermarket that stocks frozen meat, a few tinned goods, biscuits, pasta, rice and chocolate bars. If you're that way inclined, and will be staying in hotels rather than camping, bring a small electric immersion heater for use in your bedroom (sockets take standard continental two-pin plugs), plus some teabags or instant coffee, so you can supplement your picnic with a hot drink.

Fruit and vegetables are best bought at markets, where they are very cheap. Potatoes, sweet potatoes, onions, tomatoes, bananas, sugar cane, avocados, paw-paws, mangoes, coconuts, oranges and pineapples are seasonally available in most towns.

For hikers, about the only dehydrated meals available are packet soups. If you have specialised requirements, you're best doing your shopping in Kigali, where a wider selection of goods (cheese, local yoghurt...) is available in the supermarkets; there are also a handful of excellent bakeries, with mouthwatering goodies hot from the oven.

Drinks

Brand-name soft drinks such as Pepsi, Coca-Cola and Fanta are widely available, and cheap by international standards. Tap water is debatably safe to drink in Kigali, although the smell of chlorine may put you off; bottled mineral water is widely available if you sensibly prefer not to take the risk. Locally bottled fruit juice (passion fruit, orange, pineapple...) isn't bad and comes in concentrated versions too.

The most widely drunk hot beverage is tea (*chai* or *icyayi* in Swahili/Kinyarwanda). In rural areas, the ingredients are often boiled together in a pot: a sticky, sweet, milky concoction that definitely falls into the category of acquired tastes. Most Westernised restaurants serve tea as we know it, but if you want to be certain, specify that you want black tea. The milk served separately with it is almost always powdered, but of a type that dissolves well and doesn't taste too bad. Coffee is one of Rwanda's main cash crops, but you'd hardly know it judging by the insipid slop that passes for coffee in most restaurants and hotels – unless they are serving Maraba coffee (see box below). You're on safe if unexciting ground with instant coffee (ask for *Nescafé*); after a few days in the country we made a policy of checking whether coffee was of the brewed or instant variety before we ordered – if the former, we settled for tea.

MARABA BOURBON GOURMET COFFEE

Rwanda's Maraba Bourbon coffee is one of the country's most recent success stories. Beans being grown at Maraba, near Butare, have excelled in international taste tests – in a US study they were classed as second best worldwide – and are being marketed actively in the UK and US. Maraba is a very special type of Arabica coffee from Bourbon coffee trees, characterised by a smooth, full-bodied, almost fruity flavour with no astringency or after-taste.

The coffee plantation is run by the Abahuzamugambi Co-operative, many of whose 1,500 members are women widowed in the genocide who were struggling to support their families. The sale of the Maraba coffee has enabled them to pay school fees, rebuild damaged homes and acquire livestock. Of the 31 tonnes of speciality coffee produced by the co-operative in 2002, Britain's Union Coffee Roasters bought 13 tonnes and Community Coffee of Baton Rouge, US, bought 18 tonnes. In the UK, Sainsbury's sold Maraba coffee in 353 of its stores during the 2003 Comic Relief campaign. In the US, it is finding its way into speciality stores whose customers care more about quality than price.

Traditionally, Arabica coffee has been Rwanda's principal export, but quality and quantity declined seriously after the genocide. According to OCIR-Café, the state coffee board, the 19,600 tonnes produced in 2001 were about half the pre-1994 output. With Maraba Bourbon, this is changing.

Many organisations have contributed to the success story: USAID, ACDI/VOCA, PEARL, Comic Relief, Union Coffee Roasters... enabling new washing stations to be built and adequate equipment to be installed. The overseas markets are still enthusiastic, and Maraba Bourbon is also being promoted in Rwanda by restaurants and hotels. Its growth is self-perpetuating. Watch out for it – whether in the UK, the US or Rwanda – and enjoy!

The most popular alcoholic drink is beer, brewed locally near Gisenyi. The cheaper of the two local brands (and I thought the tastier) is Primus, which comes in 700ml bottles which cost anything from US$0.75 in local bars to US$2 in Kigali's swankiest hotels. The alternative is Mutzig, which tastes little different, costs about 30% more, and comes in 700ml or 350ml bottles. There's also the local banana beer, *urwagwa*.

South African and French wines are sold at outrageously inflated prices in a few upmarket bars and restaurants. Far more sensibly priced are the boxes of Spanish or Italian wine sold in some supermarkets. If you want to check out your capacity for locally brewed banana wine (also called *urwagwa*) before ordering it with a meal (at least one of the authors finds it delicious…!) most supermarkets and some small grocers/snackbars have bottles on sale. It comes in many varieties – some have honey added, and I've heard of a kind made in the northeast that contains hibiscus flowers. There's also a banana liqueur.

As for the harder stuff – *waragi,* a millet-based clear alcohol from Uganda, is available everywhere; either knock it back neat or mix it as you would gin. (In its undistilled form it could strip away a few layers of skin!) The illegal Rwandan firewater, *kanyanga,* is also available widely: treat with care.

LANGUAGE

The local language is Kinyarwanda, but almost all Rwandans speak at least a little of at least one international language. In rural areas, this is most likely to be KiSwahili, a coastal Bantu language with strong Arabic influences which, thanks largely to the 19th-century slave caravans, has come to serve as the lingua franca of East Africa. Most educated Rwandans who were brought up within the country also speak passable to fluent French, but may not speak English. By contrast, many returned long-term exiles were educated in Uganda, Kenya or Tanzania or another anglophone territory, and don't know any French, but do speak fluent English.

The upshot of this is that French speakers will have no difficulty getting by in the towns, and should always be able to find somebody who can speak French in rural areas. English speakers will struggle more, though particularly in Kigali and Ruhengeri they'll find that a fair number of people speak English. Travellers who know some Swahili will also find this very useful, particularly in rural areas. The potential for chaos is, of course, immense: in Ruhengeri, I (Philip) regularly tried my faltering Swahili in a bar or hotel to no avail, followed up on this in my even more limited French, only to have the person I was addressing ask me whether perhaps I spoke English!

Both French and English are now taught from primary school onwards, with the aim of making Rwanda a trilingual country; however, *the* national language, spoken by everyone, remains Kinyarwanda, and for the sake of friendliness and courtesy you should try to take on board a few words. At the very least aim for *yégo* (yes), *oya* (no), *murakozé* (thank you), *muraho* (hello, good morning/afternoon), *bitesé*? (how are you?) and *byiza* (good). For me, an essential phrase in any language is 'What's your name?', to be used on children;

their faces light up and they start to take you seriously! Then point to yourself and say your own name, and the introduction is complete. In Kinyarwanda it's easy – *Witwandé*? The above words are written phonetically – the value of consonants may change a bit in different parts of the country; for example 'b' may sometimes sound more like 'v' or 'w'. If you're linguistically ambitious, turn to the more comprehensive vocabulary in *Appendix 1*.

Place names

In Kinyarwanda, as in most African languages, place names are more or less phonetic, so that the town of Base, for instance, is pronounced *Bah-say*. But the transcription of place names in Rwanda displays some other quirks that I've not encountered anywhere, namely the occasional pronunciation of 'g' as 'j' (Kinigi, for instance, is pronounced Kiniji), and of an initial 'k' as 'ch' and 'cy' as 'sh' (Kigali = Chigali, Cyangugu = Shangugu). Further complication is created by the African tendency to treat 'r' and 'l' as interchangeable, and the local custom of distinguishing certain towns from the synonymous region by adding the French word *ville* to the end of the town's name. Hence, when you hear a bus conductor yelling *Chigari-ville* at the top of his voice, he is in fact referring to the city of Kigali!

Particularly when travelling in off-the-beaten-track areas, it can pay to recognise that the names of communes – the smallest administrative unit in the country – are often used interchangeably with town or village names. This can create confusion where a commune and its principal settlement have the same name, something that happened to us on the east side of Lake Burera, where it took me quite some time to understand why we were in Butaro and not in Butaro at the same time – Butaro is the name of both the commune and its administrative centre. The opposite thing happened to us when we crossed into the next commune: later I grasped that the town people referred to as Cewyu is actually called Kirambo, but is referred to by the name of the commune for which it serves as an administrative centre. There are no hard and fast rules; just be alert to the fact that the names given on maps and in other secondary sources of information – this travel guide included – may not entirely coincide with local conventions.

WHAT THE 'ELL...?

The transposition of r and l can be tongue-twisting as well as confusing. I have friends named Hilary and Florence – in Rwanda aka Hiraly and Frolence. The multiple mwamis or kings of Rwanda – *les rois* – can be called *les lois* (the laws); while the queen (*la reine*) can sound like *la laine* (the wool!). In a recent letter, a young girl asked me to 'play' for her – which, unmusical as I am, would be difficult. She meant 'pray'. And New Year greetings wished me the 'fun and floric of the festive season'. Fortunately I've never heard the transposition applied to gorilla.

HASSLES
Overcharging and bargaining
Tourists may sometimes need to bargain over prices, but this need is often exaggerated by guidebooks and other travellers. Hotels, restaurants and supermarkets generally charge fixed prices, and deliberate overcharging is so rare that it's not worth challenging a price unless it is blatantly ridiculous. In other situations – mostly markets or in the street – you're bound to be asked a higher price than the vendor will expect, and a certain degree of bargaining is considered normal. It is, however, important to keep this in perspective. Some travellers, after a couple of bad experiences, start to haggle with everyone from hotel owners to old women selling fruit by the side of the road, often accompanying their negotiations with aggressive accusations of dishonesty. This may be the easiest way to find out whether you are being overcharged, but it is unfair on the majority of Rwandans who are forthright and honest in their dealings with tourists.

Minibus conductors may occasionally ask tourists for higher fares than normal. The way to counter this is to watch what other people are paying, or to ask a fellow passenger what the fare should be. The main instance where bargaining is essential is when buying handicrafts or curios. However, the fact that a curio seller is open to negotiation does not mean that he or she was initially trying to rip you off. Vendors will generally quote a starting-price knowing full well that you are going to bargain it down – they'd probably be startled if you didn't – and it is not necessary to respond aggressively. It is impossible to say what size of reduction you should expect (some people say that you should offer half the asking price and be prepared to settle at around two-thirds, but my experience is that curio sellers are far more whimsical than such advice allows for). The sensible approach is to ask the price of similar items at a few different stalls before you actually contemplate buying anything.

In fruit and vegetable markets and stalls, bargaining is often the norm, even between Africans, and the most healthy approach to this sort of haggling is to view it as an enjoyable part of the travel experience. There will normally be an accepted price-band for any particular commodity. To find out what it is, listen to what other people pay (it helps if you know some Kinyarwanda) and try a few stalls – a ludicrously inflated price will drop the moment you walk away. When buying fruit and vegetables, a good way to feel out the situation is to ask for a bulk discount or a few extra items thrown in. And bear in mind that the reason why somebody is reluctant to bargain may be that they asked a fair price in the first place.

Above all, don't lose your sense of proportion. No matter how poor you may feel, it is your choice to travel on a tight budget. Most Rwandans are much poorer than you will ever be, and they do not have the luxury of choosing to travel. If you find yourself quibbling with an old lady selling a few piles of fruit by the roadside, stand back and look at the bigger picture. There is nothing wrong with occasionally erring on the side of generosity.

Theft

Rwanda, of all the African countries I've visited, is perhaps the most free of crime against tourists. Kigali is a very safe city, even at night, though it would probably be courting trouble to stumble around dark alleys with all your valuables on your person. Be aware, too, that this sort of thing can change very quickly: as recently as 1995, muggings and petty theft were practically unheard of in Malawi, but today you won't spend long in that country without meeting somebody who has been mugged or pick-pocketed. As tourism increases, so does opportunistic and petty crime. See the *Safety* section of *Chapter 3* (pages 50–1) for a list of tips applicable to anywhere in Africa.

Begging

To anyone who knows Africa it should come as no surprise to see beggars on the streets; the surprise, in view of Rwanda's recent past, is that they aren't more numerous. Nor are they often aggressive. For a charity helping Kigali's streetkids, see page 89. The maimed, handicapped and very old tell an obvious story. I can't advise you what to do about them. It's true that if you give to one you risk being surrounded by a dozen – but sometimes it's hard to walk on by. Rwandans themselves often recommend that you give something; they and the country's budget have little enough to spare. I set aside a 'ration' of small notes each day – when they're used up, that's it. If you don't believe in giving cash, *Chapter 5* lists some charities where your money will be well used.

Women travellers

I (Janice) experienced far less hassle and anxiety in Rwanda during my visits in 2000 than I have (as a lone female traveller) in many other countries. I travelled all over the country by public transport feeling completely safe. There was a refreshing absence of 'smart Alecs' trying to engage me in dubious conversation.

In one town, a young man (Congolese, as it turned out) overheard me asking directions to the guesthouse and spontaneously walked with me, chatting occasionally, to make sure I found it safely. Then he shook my hand and went off. Another time I left my unlockable duffel bag with a smiling girl in a small wooden drinks kiosk near a minibus stop while I explored a village; when I returned to collect it, it had been stowed safely in a corner and the girl's baby was gurgling happily on top. I felt a kind of 'sisterhood', particularly with village women – if I smiled it was always reciprocated, although often shyly, and I always asked a woman first if I needed help or directions.

In Kigali I spent a lot of time walking both in and outside the city centre and never felt threatened, although there are some poorer areas which (and a Rwandan woman friend agrees with me) become scarier after dark. This applies to men too, of course, but women are generally seen – rightly or wrongly! – as a target less likely to put up resistance. The rule here is to take the same sensible precautions you'd take in any capital city, and then relax.

As a matter of courtesy, watch what the local women wear and don't expose parts of yourself that they leave covered, particularly in village areas. In business areas people are smartly dressed; I was glad I'd brought a skirt and some crumple-free tops. Be sensitive to the fact that people here have suffered a great deal; if someone is reluctant to talk or to answer questions, don't push it.

You may not be as fortunate as I was. Nor do I suggest that you drop your guard and behave over-confidently. There can be bad apples in any barrel. Would-be Lotharios exist in any country and they tend to home in on female travellers. In fact, one night in Kigali a strange man did knock on my bedroom door at 11pm, but it turned out that he needed money to take a sick street kid to hospital (yes, honestly!).

I place Rwanda very high on the list of relatively hassle-free countries where good manners, honesty and trust are the order of the day – and of course this should be a two-way process.

Bribery and bureaucracy

For all you read about the subject, bribery is not the problem to travellers in Africa that it is often made out to be. Those who are most often asked for bribes are the ones with private transport; and even they only have a major problem at some borders and from traffic police in some countries (notably Mozambique and Kenya). If you are travelling in Rwanda on public transport or as part of a tour, or even if you are driving yourself, I doubt whether you need to give the question of bribery serious thought, although if you make a day trip into the DRC you may encounter someone inventively explaining why you should part with a few thousand francs.

There is a tendency to portray African bureaucrats as difficult and inefficient in their dealings with tourists. As a rule, this reputation says more about Western prejudices than it does about Africa. Sure, you come across the odd unhelpful official, but then such is the nature of the beast everywhere. The vast majority of officials in the African countries I've visited – Rwanda included – have been courteous and helpful in their dealings with tourists, often to a degree that is almost embarrassing.

A factor in determining the response you receive from African officials – and those in Rwanda are unlikely to be an exception – will be your own attitude. If you walk into every official encounter with an aggressive, paranoid approach, you are quite likely to kindle the feeling held by many Africans that Europeans are arrogant and offhand in their dealings with other races. Instead, try to be friendly and patient, and remember that the person to whom you are talking does not speak English (or French) as a first language and may thus have difficulty understanding you. Treat people with respect rather than disdain, in Rwanda as elsewhere, and they'll tend to treat you in the same way.

FOREIGN REPRESENTATION IN RWANDA

Foreign embassies and consulates in Kigali (or in other East African countries, if there is none in Rwanda) are given below. International dialling codes are Rwanda 250; Kenya 254; Uganda 256.

Austria (Kenya) City House, Wabera St, PO Box 30560 Nairobi; tel: (2) 228281/2; fax: 331792

Belgium Rue de Nyarugenge, BP 81 Kigali; tel: 575551; fax: 573995

Burundi 4 Rue Ntaruka, BP 714 Kigali; tel: 575512, 575718, 73465; fax: 576418
Canada 1534 Rue Akagera, BP 1177 Kigali; tel: 573210; fax: 572719
China 44 Bd de la Révolution, BP 1545 Kigali; tel: 575415; fax: 510489
Denmark (Uganda) 3 Lumumba Av, PO Box 11234 Kampala; tel: (41) 256687, 256783, 250938; fax: 254970; email: denmark@emul.com
Egypt Av de l'Umuganda, BP 6073 Kigali; tel: 87560; fax: 87510
France Av Paul VI, BP 53 Kigali; tel: 575206, 575225; fax: 576957; email: ambafrance@rwanda1.com
Germany 8 Rue de Bugarama, BP 355 Kigali; tel: 575141, 575222; fax: 577267; email: amball@rwanda1.com
India (Uganda) 11 Kyadondo Rd, PO Box 7040 Kampala; tel: (41) 257368, 342994; fax: 254943
Ireland (Uganda) Plot 12, Acacia Av, Kololo, Kampala; tel: (41) 344348, 344344; fax: 344353
Japan (Kenya) ICEA Building, Kenyatta Av, PO Box 60202 Nairobi; tel: (2) 332955/6/7/8/9; fax: 216530
Libya Libyan People's Bureau, 8 Rue Cyahafi, BP 1152 Kigali; tel: 572294; fax: 572347
Netherlands (Kenya) Uchumi House, Nkrumah Av, PO Box 42537 Nairobi; tel: (2) 227111/2/3/4; fax: 339155
Norway (Uganda) Acacia Av Quarter, Kololo, PO Box 22770 Kampala; tel: (41) 343621, 346733, 346757, 340848; fax: 343936
Russian Federation 19 Av de l'Armée, BP 40 Kigali; tel: 575286; fax: 574818
South Africa 1370 Bd de l'Umuganda, BP6563, Kigali; tel: 583185; fax: 511758
Switzerland 38 Bd de la Révolution, BP 1257 Kigali; tel: 575534, 575072; fax: 572461
Tanzania Plot 1253, Kimihurura III, BP 3973 Kigali; tel: 505400; fax: 505402
Uganda Plot 9, Av de l'Akagera, BP 656 Kigali; tel: 576854
United Kingdom Parcelle 1131, Bd de l'Umuganda, BP 576 Kigali; tel: 86072, 84098, 85771; fax: 82044
USA 55 Bd de la Révolution, BP 28, Kigali; tel: 505601–3; fax: 570319

For updates and/or additions, either ask ORTPN or check website www.rwanda1.com or www.rwandatourism.com.

MEDIA AND COMMUNICATIONS
Newspapers and magazines
Rwanda has two English-language newspapers: *The New Times* (twice weekly; web: www.newtimes.co.rw) which supports the government, and *Rwanda Newsline* (weekly) which works hard at being independent. Imported dailies and weeklies from Uganda are also widely available on the streets of Kigali and Butare. A very limited range of international papers can be bought at the kiosks of upmarket hotels such as the Mille Collines in Kigali. News magazines such as *Time* and *Newsweek* are available from street vendors and some bookshops. The Ikirezi bookshop in Kigali has a good stock – see advertisement, page 69.

Internet, email and fax
The electronic communications age has fast gained a foothold in Rwanda, with increasing use of email. The local servers tend to be slow, however, and

subject to breakdowns. Judging by developments in neighbouring countries, it is simply a matter of time before internet facilities become more reliable. Most hotels of mid-range and upwards have email and fax facilities, and in Kigali there's an efficient fax office at the main post office in Avenue de la Paix. Sending faxes here costs under US$2 to Europe and US$2.50 to the US; receiving a fax costs under US$1. If you want someone at home to fax you there, the number is (250) 576574.

Telephone

Rwanda's telephone system is reasonably efficient. From overseas, it is definitely one of the easier African countries to get through to first time. The international code is 250. Because of the small size of the country, and limited number of phones, no area codes are in use.

In Kigali, international phone calls can be made from the central post office in Avenue de la Paix and from various other shops and kiosks in the city. For calls within Rwanda the street kiosks and shops with public phones work well – calls are metered and you pay when you've finished, so there's no fussing with coins or tokens. Some of these can handle international calls too.

Cell phones (mobiles) have caught on in a big way in Rwanda. Cell-phone numbers can be recognised by an '08' prefix. Most cannot be accessed internationally. It's possible to buy a package to convert your own mobile (if compatible) for use in Rwanda: see *Chapter 6*, page 110.

Post

Post from Rwanda is cheap and reasonably reliable, but can be slow. The best place to arrange to collect poste restante is the main post office in Kigali. Address letters as follows:

> Philip Briggs
> Poste Restante
> Kigali (centre ville)
> Rwanda

(The 'centre ville' bit is because there's another main post office in Kigali, out in Kacyiru which is the government and business area, but it's less conveniently positioned for collecting mail.)

Yellow post-buses with *Iposita* on the side shuttle mail around Rwanda. Letterboxes outside post offices have a variety of appellations – sometimes *Boite aux Lettres*, sometimes (eg: in Butare) *Box of Letters* and sometimes (a Belgian/Flemish relic in Kibuye) *Brievenbus*.

Radio and television

The BBC World Service comes across loud and clear, on different frequencies according to the time of day. Local radio stations broadcast in Kinyarwanda, French, English and Swahili. TV is largely piped in from elsewhere, giving CNN, Sky, BBC News, etc at different times of day: generally more informative for visitors than the local channel, although that does have occasional news bulletins in English.

SHOPPING

All basic requirements (toiletries, stationery, batteries and so forth) are available in Kigali, and, away from the capital, most towns of any size have a pharmacy as well as a reasonable supermarket or general store. In Kigali, the pharmacy in Boulevard de la Révolution is open 24 hours. Photographic equipment (film etc) is available in Kigali – try the photographic shop in Avenue de la Paix or the well-established Fotolab in Rue Kalisimbi, opposite the Isimbi Hotel – but may be scarcer (or out of date) in smaller places, so it's best to bring whatever you'll need.

For handicrafts you've a very wide range – wood-carvings, weaving, pottery, baskets, clay statues, beadwork, jewellery, masks, musical instruments, banana-leaf products, batik – see *Handicrafts* in the Kigali chapter (pages 116–18) and the Butare section (page 212) for more details. CDs or cassettes of Rwandan music make good gifts, as does local honey: buy it in a market and decant it into a screwtop soft-drinks bottle for travelling. In Kigali market you can buy candles of local beeswax. Locally made wines, spirits and liqueurs are heavier to carry but generally appreciated! For traditional musical instruments, you need a well-informed local advisor to help you to pick the best and most authentic.

Women can buy lengths of brightly dyed fabric in the market and have street dressmakers make up a garment on the spot; men can similarly kit themselves out with hand-tailored shirts. And just browsing in any large street market will give you dozens more ideas…

ARTS AND ENTERTAINMENT

Concerts (whether pop or classical) and displays of traditional dance are held from time to time in the various stadiums – check for details with the ORTPN (see page 53). The Centre for Franco-Rwandan Cultural Exchanges (see page 114) organises presentations of theatre, music, dance and cinema in its theatre in Kigali – either contact the centre for its current programme or ask at the ORTPN. The cinema in the Kigali Business Centre (see pages 113–14) has daily screenings of international movies.

The National Museum of Rwanda in Butare (see pages 137–8) is excellent, and there are plans to open more museums around the country as part of a project to record '500 years of Great Lakes History'. It may or may not happen during the lifetime of this guide.

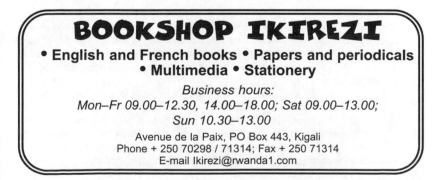

PHOTOGRAPHIC TIPS
Ariadne Van Zandbergen
Equipment
With some thought and an eye for composition you can take reasonable photos with a 'point and shoot' camera, but you need an SLR camera with one or more lenses if you are at all serious about photography. If you carry only one lens in Rwanda, a 28–70mm or similar zoom should be ideal for anything but wildlife photography, whereas a 80–200mm or 70–300mm or similar will be better for candid shots and wildlife. Carrying both will allow you to play more with composition. If you're serious about wildlife photography a higher magnification than 300 is useful but expensive and bulky. For a small loss of quality, tele-converters are a cheap and compact way to increase magnification: a 300 lens with a 1.4x converter becomes 420mm, and with a 2x it becomes 600mm. Note that tele-converters reduce the speed of your lens by 1.4 and 2 stops respectively. For wildlife photography from a safari vehicle, a solid beanbag, which you can make yourself very cheaply, will be necessary to avoid blurred images and is more useful and less cumbersome than a tripod.

Film
Print film is the preference of most casual photographers, slide film of professionals and some dedicated amateurs. Slide film is more expensive than print film, but this is broadly compensated for by cheaper development costs. Most photographers working outdoors in Africa favour Fujichrome slide film, in particular Sensia 100, Provia 100 (the professional equivalent to Sensia) or Velvia 50. Slow films, ie: those with a low ASA (ISO) rating, produce less grainy and sharper images than fast films, but can be tricky without a tripod or beanbag in low light. Velvia 50 is extremely fine-grained and shows stunning colour saturation; it is the film I normally use in soft, even light or overcast weather. Sensia or Provia may be preferable in low light, since 100 ASA allows you to work at a faster shutter speed than 50 ASA. Because 100 ASA is more tolerant of contrast, it is also preferable in harsh light. For extreme situations, such as photographing gorillas or chimps in a dark forest interior, it is always good to carry some faster films. Provia 400 ASA is a relatively fine-grained fast film.

For print photography, a combination of 100 or 200 ASA film should be ideal. For the best results it is advisable to stick to recognised brands. Fujicolor produces excellent print films, with the Superia 100 and 200 recommended.

Some basics
The automatic programmes provided with many cameras are limited in the sense that they are able to calculate but not to think. A better investment than any amount of electronic wizardry would be to read a photographic manual for beginners and get to grips with such basics as the relationship between aperture and shutter speed.

Beginners should also note photographs taken at a low shutter speed are often affected by camera shake, resulting in a fuzzy image. For hand-held photographs of static subjects using a low magnification lens such as 28–70mm, select a shutter speed of at least 1/60th of a second. When hand-holding lenses of higher magnification, the rule of thumb is that the shutter speed should be at least the inverse of the highest magnification of the lens (for instance, a speed of 1/300 or faster on a 70–300mm lens). You can use far lower shutter speeds with a tripod or beanbag.

Most modern cameras include a built-in light meter, and allow a choice of three different types of metering, ie: matrix, centre-weighted, or spot metering. You will need to understand how these different systems work to make proper use of them. Built-in light meters are reliable in most circumstances, but in uneven light, or where there is a lot of sky, you may want to take your metering selectively, for instance by taking a spot reading on the main subject. The meter will tend to under- or overexpose when pointed at an almost white or black subject. This can be countered by taking a reading against an 18% grey card, or a substitute such as grass or light grey rocks – basically anything that isn't almost black, almost white or highly reflective.

Dust and heat

Dust and heat are often a problem in Africa. Keep your equipment in a sealed bag, stow films in an airtight container (such as a small cooler bag), leave used films in your hotel room, and avoid changing film in dusty conditions. On rough roads, I always carry my camera equipment on my lap to protect against vibration and bumps. Never stow camera equipment or film in a car boot (it will bake), or let it stand in direct sunlight.

Light

The light in Africa is much harsher than in Europe or North America, for which reason the most striking outdoor photographs are often taken during the hour or two of 'golden light' after dawn and before sunset. Shooting in low light may enforce the use of very low shutter speeds, in which case a beanbag (from a vehicle) or tripod (on foot) or monopod (lighter but less steady than a tripod) will be required to avoid camera shake. Be alert to the long shadows cast by a low sun; these show up more on photographs than to the naked eye.

With careful handling, side lighting and back lighting can produce stunning effects, especially in soft light and at sunrise or sunset. Generally, however, it is best to shoot with the sun behind you. Because of this, most buildings and landscapes are essentially a 'morning shot' or 'afternoon shot', depending on the direction in which they face. When you spend a couple of nights in one place, you'll improve your results by planning the best time to take pictures of static subjects (a compass can come in handy).

When photographing people or animals in the harsh midday sun, images taken in light but even shade are likely to look nicer than those taken in direct sunlight or patchy shade, since the latter conditions create too much contrast. Fill-in flash is almost essential if you want to capture facial detail of dark-skinned people in harsh or 'contrasty' light. Note that flash photography is not allowed with gorillas and chimps.

Protocol

Except in general street or market scenes, it is unacceptable to photograph people without permission. Expect some people to refuse or to ask for a donation. Don't try to sneak photographs as you might get yourself into trouble. Even the most willing subject will often pose stiffly when a camera is pointed at them; relax them by making a joke, and take a few shots in quick succession to improve the odds of capturing a natural pose.

Culture and People

RELIGION

The Christian religions are a powerful force in Rwanda today, as witnessed by the great number of active churches throughout the country. Roman Catholicism leads the field with 65% adherence, followed by 9% for Protestantism. Pope John Paul II visited Rwanda in 1990. Some evangelical sects are now gaining ground. There is a small (1%) Muslim population, leaving a 25% following for minority and traditional beliefs, some of which may have absorbed traces of Christianity.

Traditional religion and beliefs

Rwandans traditionally believe in a supreme being called *Imana*. While *Imana*'s actions influence the whole world, Rwanda is his home where he comes to spend the night. Individuals hold informal ceremonies imploring *Imana*'s blessing. There is a tradition that, before retiring, a woman may leave a pitcher of water for *Imana* in the hope he will make her fertile.

Since words can have a magical impact, the name of *Imana* is often used when naming children, also in words of comfort, warnings against complacency, blessings, salutations, and during rites associated with marriage and death. Oaths take the form of 'May *Imana* give me a stroke', or 'May I be killed by *Imana*'. In instances when a long-desired child is born, people say to the new mother, '*Imana* has removed your shame.' Tales of *Imana* granting magical gifts to humans, who then lose these gifts through greed and disloyalty, are common.

There is a special creative act of *Imana* at the beginning of each person's life. Impregnation in itself would not be sufficient to produce a new human being. This is why the young wife, at evening, leaves a few drops of water in a jar. *Imana*, as a potter, needs some water to shape the clay into a child in her womb. Then after birth, *Imana* decides what life is to be for that individual: happy or unhappy. If, later on, a man is miserable, poverty-stricken or in bad health, it is said that he was created by *Ruremakwaci*, a name given to *Imana* when he does not create very successfully, when 'he is tired', or, for some inscrutable reason, decides that a certain destiny will be unhappy.

Rwandans traditionally believe that a life force exists in all men and animals. In animals this invisible soul disappears when the creature dies, but in humans it is transformed into *bazimu*, spirits of the dead who live in *Ikuzimu*, the underworld or the world below the soil. While the deceased kings of Rwanda constitute a kind of governing body in the underworld, there are no social distinctions. Life is neither pleasant nor unhappy. The *bazimu* continue the individuality of living persons and have the same names. Though non-material, they are localised by their activity. They do not drink, eat, or mate but their existence in other respects is similar to that in the world of the living. *Bazimu* return to the world, often to places where they used to live. Some may stay permanently in the hut where their descendants live or in the small huts made for them in the enclosure around the dwelling. *Bazimu* are generally bad. They bring misfortune, sickness, crop failure and cattle epidemics because they envy the living the cherished things they had to leave behind. Their power, actuated by the male spirits, or grandfathers, extends only over their own clan. The living members of a family must consult a diviner to discover the reason for the ancestor's anger. Respect to *bazimu* is shown principally by joining a secret cult group.

The cult of Ryangombe

Ryangombe is said to be the chief of the *imandwa*, Rwandans who are initiated into the cult of *Ryangombe*. According to Rwandan legend, *Ryangombe* was a great warrior who was accidentally killed by a buffalo during a hunting party. In order not to leave *Ryangombe*, his friends threw themselves on the bull's horns. *Imana* gave *Ryangombe* and his followers a special place, the Karisimbi volcano in the Virunga volcano chain, where they have a notably more agreeable afterlife than the other *bazimu*. The cult of *Ryangombe* became an important force of social cohesion, with Tutsi, Hutu and Twa being initiated into the cult. *Ryangombe* has said himself that he should be called upon by everybody. He is propitiated by the *babandwa*, a politico-religious fraternity, who perform rituals, chants and dances in his honour. They are not a permanent group and meet only once a year during July, at which time initiation takes place. During their festival the members of the fraternity paint themselves and decorate the spirit huts. A member of the group appears as the personification of the spirit of *Ryangombe,* carrying his sacred spear. After a ritual is performed, all members purify themselves at the stream. While the cult of *Ryangombe* is not common today, Rwandans can recall when their grandfathers or fathers participated in the *Ryangombe* festival and a popular Rwandan song recounts *Ryangombe*'s exploits as a warrior and lover.

THE ARTS
Literature

A written language was not introduced until the Europeans arrived in Rwanda at the end of the 19th century, so there is no great tradition of written literature. However, there is a wealth of oral literature in the form of myths, folk stories, legends, poetry and proverbs. These have passed on not only stories but also moral values and historical traditions from generation to generation. Before (and to some extent after) the arrival of the Europeans, the Mwami's court was a centre for training young nobles in various art forms, particularly the composition and performance of songs and poems dedicated to valour in warfare and the magnificence of their cattle.

The historian Alexis Kagame wrote extensively about oral poetry and recorded many poems in both Kinyarwanda and French. A display in Butare's National Museum (see pages 137–8) gives an idea of the intricacy of some poetic structures.

Music

Music is of great importance to all Rwandans, with variations of style and subject among the three groups. Traditionally, Tutsi songs praised excellence and valour; Hutu songs were lighter, sometimes humorous and linked to social occasions; Twa songs related more directly to aspects of their original occupation, hunting. During the time of the monarchy, the court was dominated musically by the royal drummers, and drumming is still of great artistic importance.

A full drum ensemble typically consists of either seven or nine drums. The smallest of these, sometimes called the soprano, which is often (but not invariably) played by the director of the orchestra, sets the rhythm for each tune and is backed up by some or all of the following drums: a tenor, a harmonist alto, two baritones, two bass and two double bass. The other widely used musical instrument is the *lulunga*, an eight-stringed instrument somewhat resembling a harp. It is most often played solo, perhaps as the background to singing or dancing, but may also be used to provide a melodic interlude and/or as a counterpoint to drums.

Dance

Dance is as instinctive as music in Rwanda and its roots stretch back through the centuries. As with music, there are variations of style and subject among the three groups. Best known today are the **Intore dancers**, based in Nyanza and Butare, who perform both nationally and internationally. At the time of the monarchy and for centuries before the arrival of the Europeans, the Intore dancers at the royal court were selected young men who had received a privileged education and choreographic training in order to entertain their masters and to perform at special functions. The name *intore* means 'best', signifying that only the best of them were chosen for this honour.

Traditionally their performances consisted mainly of warlike dances, such as the *ikuma* (lance), *umeheto* (bow) and *ingabo* (shield), in which they carried authentic weapons. In the 20th century dummy weapons were substituted, the dances were given more peaceful names and rhythm and movement (rather than warfare) became their main feature. The Intore dancers were divided into two groups. The first group, the *indashyikirwa* or 'unsurpassables', were all Tutsi. The second, the *ishyaka* or 'those who challenge by effort', were Twa led by a Tutsi. A description nearly three-quarters of a century old leads us through a performance:

> In the opening movement, the group of Twa advances with measured
> step. The musicians also are Twa. The dancers form a square or line
> up in double file. They perform the opening sequence and then a

dance representing 'safety'. Next they stand at ease, chanting the exploits of real or imaginary Rwandan heroes. Then come movements representing 'tattooing', 'stability', 'the incomparable' and 'the most difficult case'. At this point the Tutsi dancers leap into the arena, armed, to mingle with the Twa and demonstrate that they deserve the name of 'unsurpassables'. The names of some of their dances translate into English as 'that which puts an end to all discussion', 'the crested crane', 'the exit dance' and 'thanks'.

The costume worn by the Tutsi dancers consists of either a short floral skirt or a leopard skin wound around their legs. Crossed straps decorated with coloured beads are generally worn across the chest. On their heads they wear a fringe of white colobus monkey fur. Depending on the theme of the dance and the region they may carry a bow, a spear or a stick decorated with a long tail of raffia. Around their ankles they wear bells, the sound of which adds to the rhythm of the dance.

The Intore dancers perform regularly today and it's a dramatic spectacle. You may come across them in Kigali, Nyanza, Butare – or abroad, on one of their tours. Ask ORTPN in Kigali for details of any scheduled performances.

Another striking performance of dance – equally traditional – is given by a group of Twa in Kigali – see pages 77–8.

Handicrafts

As in other countries, most genuinely traditional handicrafts have a practical use or are decorated forms of everyday objects. An object which gives purely visual pleasure and is unrelated to any function has probably evolved for the tourist market – although it is none the worse for that. In Rwanda the weaving (of bowls, mats, baskets, storage containers, etc) from various natural fibres is particularly fine. The quality of wood-carving is variable, but at best it's excellent. Pottery made by the Twa community is plain but strong and its uncluttered style is attractive. See *Chapter 6* (pages 116–18) for details of where in Kigali to find handicrafts on sale.

PEOPLE

To quote from the website of the Rwandan Embassy in Washington, DC (www.rwandemb.org):

> Inhabitants of Rwanda are called 'Banyarwanda'. They speak the same language, have the same culture, live on the same hills and, for centuries, have intermarried. The three 'ethnic' groups are the Bahutu, the Batutsi and the Batwa, referred to in the West as Hutus, Tutsis and Twas.

In fact, matters may not be quite so clear-cut and the insistence on 'same-ness' should not be carried to the extent of concealing historical individuality. But there's no doubt that the people of Rwanda in general are committed to overcoming any awkward or damaging differences. There's a story, well known now, about a group of schoolgirls who, during the genocide, were told by the killers to divide up into Hutus and Tutsis (with the implication that the Hutus would be spared). The girls refused, saying that they were all Rwandans. So all of them died. In a different context, a genocide survivor wrote: 'Before the genocide, Hutus and Tutsis lived together. I remember we used to play with Hutu children and share everything. There were even intermarriages. The only time when we felt discriminated against was when a place at school, or a job, was given to a Hutu, even if there was a Tutsi more qualified for it. But this was no reason for hatred between the two groups.' However, of course individual attitudes cannot accurately be extrapolated to the whole country.

The following section generally describes what people – just *people*, without any other label – are doing in and about Rwanda today. The exception is the Twa, who do have a problem specific to their origins and are therefore named.

The Twa of Rwanda and CAURWA
Elaine Gardner

> Sheer delight – and what is particularly appreciable, the authenticity...
> and to discover a whole aspect of Rwandan culture that I didn't know
> existed!

So commented a recent visitor at a display of traditional dance organised at a Twa pottery in Kigali – Batwa are, both currently and historically, Rwanda's favourite exponents of this particularly distinctive and highly reputed dance. In olden times, they were dancers and potters at the Royal court.

The Batwa (or Twa) are a pygmy people, comprising Rwanda's third 'ethnic' group – today numbering around 22–25,000. That they are indigenous Rwandans is surprisingly little known; even the recent film *A Hundred Days* mentioned only two groups as making up Rwanda's cultural diversity.

They lived originally as hunter-gatherers in the high mountain forests around Central Africa's Great Lakes. As the forests were felled and national parks established, the Batwa evolved another lifestyle, as potters, using the clay found in the marshes that lie between Rwanda's many hills. They left the forests with virtually no material possessions – and they process the clay with none. They use their feet to trample it into malleability and then their hands to shape cooking pots, stoves, decorative vases, traditional lamps, candle-holders and charming little replicas of local animals, from cattle to gorillas. The pots are fired without kilns, largely in a hollow in the ground, by burning grasses and natural debris, and sealed with earth.

Because of their pygmy origins the Batwa have suffered extreme prejudice over the years; they are socially and economically marginalised and extremely poor. Only 28% of Batwa children attend primary school (and far fewer start secondary school) compared with 88% in the population as a whole. Only 1.6% Batwa have enough land to feed their families. Most survive by begging, working on the land of others in return for food, or carrying loads. An estimated 30% of the Batwa population, as against 14% of the population overall, was lost during the 1994 genocide. So, income-generating schemes are vital – which is where the pottery and dance come into their own.

The UK-based charity, Forest Peoples' Project (FPP, see page 85), works in Rwanda in partnership with CAURWA (*Communauté des Autochtones Rwandais* or Community of Indigenous Rwandans) which FPP has been supporting since 1995. In December 2001, the UK Community Fund awarded FPP a three-year grant to start a Pottery Commercialisation Project with the Batwa potters.

In these days of advanced techniques, new materials, mass production and modern marketing, the Batwa's simple, traditional methods were being left behind and becoming stale for want of access to up-to-date resources and information. And for a poor and marginalised people, living from hand to mouth, immediate reality often takes precedence over any possibility of long-term planning. How can you hold out for a higher price when the low one offered will at least provide a bite to eat? So what if the lower price doesn't even cover your costs and labour? Those were yesterday; today your child is crying, and the customer passes by...

The FPP's **Twa Pottery Project** (*Projet Poterie*) takes account of the many difficulties faced by the Batwa potters. It has started to train potters in improved production methods and the introduction of new designs, business skills and marketing, as well as developing a retail outlet to increase sales of pottery in Kigali. The project, which is based on Fair Trade principles, started by training six potters' groups in the principles and modalities of Fair Trade and the steps to building successful businesses. As a result, these potters have decided to set up the first Rwandan Potters' Association. The project has also raised funds from several local donors to help resolve the potters' dire lack of workshop-buildings and kilns. It is also developing links to 'sustainable fair tourism', by arranging for tourists to visit the Batwa pottery workshop to see the pottery being produced, and to enjoy performances of the distinctive and joyful Batwa dancing.

To buy Batwa pottery, visit their container among the artisans' stands on Avenue de Armée (at the back of Hotel des Mille Collines) – open 09.00–12.00 and 14.00–16.30 Monday to Saturday. To arrange to visit the pottery workshop or a dance display, phone 08689551 or email projetbus@yahoo.fr. For further information about CAURWA email caurwa@rwanda1.com.

Women's access to education
Marie Chantal Uwimana
After the genocide, with up to a million of its people slaughtered, the political, social and economic structures of Rwanda were at rock bottom. To rehabilitate, reintegrate and reconcile the country was a colossal task for the Government of National Unity. In every sector, they were starting from scratch. Among the priorities, education initially took second place to the more urgent needs of food, clothing and health.

Historically, education – and particularly that of girls – had not been greatly developed in Rwanda before and even after independence. Missionaries did build schools, but they were mainly for the children of chiefs and those in power. The intake of girls was very low.

Before 1994, the low enrolment rate for girls at primary school (and the still lower rate at secondary school and college) was explained by the ignorance of the parents (a belief that girls should not study scientific subjects), by custom (that after primary school girls should stay in the family and work at home or on the land) and by enforced early marriage.

After 1994, their parents now dead, many of these girls had also become single 'parents', head of their household and caring for their younger siblings. Recognising the problem, the government began setting in place mechanisms to support Rwandan women, and particularly to motivate girls to go to school. The statistics began to change rapidly, and by 2003 the number of girls at primary school equalled that of boys. At secondary school, however, girls continued to be oriented towards the more 'feminine' subjects and the drop-out rate for girls was 10.8% versus 9.5% for boys.

Although primary schooling had theoretically been compulsory, the fees were beyond the reach of some parents. Under the new constitution, state primary schools are now free and thus available to all – as long as the law is enforced that defines 'free education' as 'students receiving without payment education provided by the teacher together with learning aids and basic textbooks needed by both the teacher and the students'.

Problems remain, and steps still needing to be taken include:

- Possible sanctions against parents who fail to send their children to school
- Elimination of discriminatory practices against schoolgirls who fall pregnant
- Non-discriminatory guidance for career selection
- Improved access for girls to non-traditional education subjects
- Provision of literacy programmes and literacy trainers
- Grants and scholarships awarded with no bias towards gender
- Information and training in sexually transmissible diseases and HIV/AIDS
- Social integration measures for disadvantaged girls/women

Then, little by little, Rwanda's women can play their full part in rebuilding and running their country.

College of Gisenyi Karate Club for Girls
Lindsay Hodgson

'They won't come' was the overwhelming consensus from my colleagues. Either that or simply 'Why?' I had spent my lunchtime putting '*Coming soon – karate club for girls*' posters at various vantage points around the school. I don't usually condone discrimination, 'positive' or otherwise, so why did I decide on a girls-only club? I guess it was a question of balance.

During one of my first lessons here as a maths teacher in Rwanda, I showed the pupils photographs from home. A few of them were of me in my karate gear and I explained how I wanted to start a club at the school. At the end of the lesson, one of the girls hung around for a while and when everyone else had left she asked if the club would only be for boys. I was genuinely surprised – I am, after all, female myself - so I asked why she had thought this. She told me that the boys already had a karate club - one of the older pupils was the sensei - but girls weren't allowed. 'Right then', I thought, 'why not have a club just for girls too?' So I set to designing posters.

Initially, admittedly, I was concerned. Virtually every colleague was so sure of a poor turn-out. In addition I was finding it difficult to get the girls to add their names to my list. 'But karate's for boys, teacher, very aggressive' to quote but one girl's opinion. With only three names in as many days I worried that the line 'Limited to 20 places' would come to haunt me. Would I have to invite the boys after all? I set myself a minimum of ten girls to make it worthwhile.

I'm glad I persevered. A week after the posters went up (and several pep talks later) I had 15 names in total. I found that once one girl plucked up the courage to join, her friends usually followed. We had a meeting to discuss logistics and the College of Gisenyi Karate Club for Girls was born!

The first few sessions were rather 'interesting'. It seemed as if every student and his or her goat was trying to sneak a peek! The girls found this, and the karate, difficult at first. Their level of confidence was low and I spent a lot of my time chasing away the spectators!

However, very quickly the girls' style and fitness both improved. Instead of a shy whimper I started getting a veritable roar for each 'KIAI' (the motivational shout used in karate). Soon I had girls coming to see me after classes to ask if there were any places left and, if so, could they join. And so it continued, every Tuesday and Thursday.

Seven months on and our dojo is 25 strong. I had to start turning girls away as the room is too small to accommodate any more. Now, rather than chasing the spectators away, the girls train regardless, with a real sense of pride and achievement – they know they look and feel great.

The girls have demonstrated for delegates at a gender workshop in Kigali, the general public in Gisenyi and, all importantly, for the boys' club at school. It was during this last demonstration that the girls were invited to train with the boys each weekend. The boys were delighted at seeing the girls participate in karate just as enthusiastically and with as much focus as they did.

As for my colleagues, I think the girls' progress and determination has shocked them more than anyone. But they are delighted nonetheless. As for me, if the girls and boys ultimately join into one club, I would be done out of a job. I can honestly say that this would delight me too!

Lindsay has been teaching in Rwanda for Voluntary Service Overseas – see below.

Voluntary Service Overseas (VSO) in Rwanda
Information provided by VSO
The genocide and related unrest of the 1990s in Rwanda destroyed what was already a weak economy, and the education system was devastated, as teachers were a particular target for the extremists. For countries such as Rwanda that are at the bottom end of the Human Development Index education is one of the keys to development and poverty alleviation. Even though enrolment at

secondary level is pathetically low and in this sense secondary school students could be described as relatively 'advantaged', the grim reality for Rwandans is that almost no-one is affluent and the vast majority of secondary school students are deeply affected by poverty.

Education is one of VSO's six Development Goals globally, and the aim to 'increase the accessibility, gender equity, relevance and quality of education for disadvantaged people in poorer countries' (Focus For Change) is the central plank of VSO Rwanda's Strategic Plan.

The education policy currently being developed in Rwanda also emphasises a trilingual approach (Kinyarwanda, French and English), which makes languages a central part of efforts towards national reconciliation. VSO's provision of teachers of English, and of maths and science who can teach through French, is a vital part of making this vision a reality in the short-to-medium term, while efforts to train local teachers have yet to bear fruit.

The use of VSO teachers is playing a role in the national effort to improve the poor access rates to secondary education. Without enough teachers, schools are unable to enrol more students. VSO is a significant partner in making the provision of this basic right open to more young Rwandans.

VSO Rwanda (VSOR) is also working to improve the quality of educational provisions. By linking classroom teaching posts with posts that combine teaching with teacher training, we are one of the few agencies actively promoting an ethos of integrated professional development for teaching staff. We aim to help teachers to communicate with each other through our own networks, and actively promote Skills Development Workshops where VSO teachers and local colleagues can learn from each other.

Our education programme is also developing a management support element for both central and provincial level offices, whose lack of capacity is a critical issue in the development of quality educational services.

We also believe that a rights-based approach to our education programme is important, as improving access alone will not guarantee progress. VSO volunteers are well placed (as expatriate workers within Rwandan schools) to be points of information and advice, as well as role models, for issues of gender equity and HIV/AIDS. Without considering these fundamental issues across the sector as a whole, sustainable progress will be impossible. The VSOR programme seeks ways to support volunteers so that they can approach these issues with confidence and cultural sensitivity.

Voluntary Service Overseas, 317 Putney Bridge Road, London SW15 2PN; tel: 020 8780 7200; web: www.vso.org.uk.

Solar ovens in Rwanda

Katot Meyer

Ever since I can remember I have had a heart for renewable energy, especially solar energy. After my studies I joined an overland company in order to see more of Africa without spending too much money. After my first trip I bought a South-African-produced solar oven. I took this oven on all my trips and tested it in many African countries. It performed very well. I mainly used it for baking bread and cakes. The highlight of my oven was baking a chocolate birthday cake in the middle of Botswana's Okavango Delta.

After my overland chapter I started my first real job here in Rwanda. I work as an electrical engineer at a small tin smelter. When I saw how little of Rwanda's forests were left I immediately decided to start a small solar oven project. My oven is based on one produced by a South African company, which shares all its drawings and research with anyone who is interested.

The oven measures about 650mm long, 500mm wide and 500mm high. It is in the shape of a monitor (the speaker you get on a music stage used by the singer/musicians to hear themselves). I constructed it out of a simple wooden frame. The inside and outside are then covered by thin aluminium plates. I get these at the price of scrap aluminium from printing companies (litho plates). The inside layer of plates act as reflectors, reflecting sunlight on a black pot placed inside the oven. The outside layer forms an air insulation between the two sets of plates. I am still experimenting with better insulation material like sawdust. The box has a glass lid to keep the heat inside.

I constructed my first oven for about US$8 (glass US$2, wood US$3, aluminium plates US$2, nails and some silicone US$1). I introduced it to the workers at our factory by heating some water. They did not believe me and said I changed the water with hot water. The next day I arrived with a cup of rice. I let them all inspect the rice and then placed it in the oven with some water. This was at about 9am. I placed the oven in a sunny spot near where they were working and only returned at 12 midday. They were all there when I opened the oven and pot. To their amazement – a pot of cooked rice!

The second oven was constructed only recently by one of my workers. I make the aluminium plates available to them at cost price since this is the only unknown item to them. Considering the number of copies of the oven plans I have been asked to make, I believe that many more ovens will be built soon! *Katot is contactable on email kattermaai@yahoo.co.uk.*

Kigali Public Library

In 1999, the Rotary Club of Kigali-Virunga decided to build a public library, its first major project as a chartered Rotary Club, to counter the striking scarcity of books in Rwanda and the resulting lack of a culture of reading. Also, a key aspect of ending violence and preventing another genocide is to make books filled with knowledge and ideas freely available to all Rwandans, regardless of social and economic status. In Rwanda, a public library can safeguard freedom and help develop a healthy democracy. Libraries make democracy work by providing access to information so that citizens can make the decisions necessary to govern themselves. A library also offers users the knowledge that will help them to gain employment or start a business.

Rwanda's first public library will play a major role in opening children's minds. Bringing children into a library can transport them from the commonplace to the extraordinary. Finally, it will help to build a sense of community, and will preserve the past with special collections on subjects such as Rwandan history and literature.

This is no daydream! The library has received generous financial support both from overseas and from local Rwandan companies. It is supported by the American Friends of the Kigali Public Library (AFKPL) – via whom the international literary association, PEN, pledged US$45,000 in April 2002. The Government of Rwanda has pledged US$500,000 of which US$100,000 was released in July 2003. Construction work started on the foundations in 2002 and by now the frontage is clearly visible. Funds are still urgently needed and fundraising has taken place at all levels, from large companies to small schools and individuals. Secondhand book sales (another 'first' for Kigali) are held regularly and major fundraising is planned for 2004. Collection boxes will be placed in Kigali hotels and at the airport – look out for these!

In 2002, a young Rwandan boy named Sam called into the office of the Chairman of the Kigali Public Library Project – who initially thought he had come to ask for school fees, a common practice among Rwanda's youth who struggle every year to find the necessary amount. However, what Sam wanted was to donate 200 Rwandan francs (less than 50 US cents, but for him a large sum). He knew about the project from one of the secondhand book sales, and wanted to contribute in order to make sure the library was built.

Check out the progress of the library on its website, www.kigalilibrary.com.

BECOMING INVOLVED

You may leave Rwanda without a backward glance, or you may find that it has affected you more than you realised. It's an amazing country. If you do want to become further involved with its people and its culture, a few suggestions are given below, to add to those already mentioned. For gorilla conservation charities, see pages 188–9.

Rwanda United Kingdom Goodwill Organisation (RUGO)
Mike Hughes

The genocide in 1994 made Rwanda known to everybody in the international community through the horror shown on TV screens and in the newspapers.

RUGO was formally launched on July 4 1997, coinciding with the third anniversary of the end of genocide in Rwanda. The aim of the organisation is to provide a channel whereby the people of UK can support the people of Rwanda as they rebuild. It received charity status in February 1999 with Baroness Chalker of Wallasey as the patron; it is a registered UK charity, number 1074088. RUGO's stated mission is:

> The advancement of education and training of the people of Rwanda, and the relief of poverty, sickness and distress, through the provision and support of community based projects designed to improve the conditions of life for those in necessitous circumstances.

Since its launch RUGO has:

- Issued newsletters to inform people about the situation in Rwanda
- Received donations of computers and books for the National University of Rwanda, and other educational establishments in Rwanda

- Held social events to fundraise and promote Rwandan culture
- Raised funds to help equip a vocational school in Nyamata
- Supported other centres in Rwanda such as: Kigali Junior Academy; Kigali Parents' School; Village of Hope (part of the Rwanda Women's Network); Village d'Orphelins (Orphanage in Kibuye)
- Held memorial services in remembrance of the victims of genocide
- Supported similar UK-based groups such as a Nottingham group collecting donations for orphanages in Rwanda
- Facilitated and raised funds for the construction of a Parish Community Centre in Kayonza in partnership with St Andrew's parish in Harrow

RUGO is managed by a committee, elected at the annual general meeting, which considers applications for help and the running of RUGO projects and events. Its income derives from members' subscriptions, donations from well-wishers and fundraising activities. The organisation employs no-one, is administered by volunteers, and thus almost every penny contributed goes towards RUGO's objectives. By joining RUGO, members support genuinely good causes, are kept in touch with events in Rwanda, and are invited to open meetings and social events which refresh old friendships and create new ones. The annual subscription (September 2003) stands at £20 for an individual, £30 for a family and £100 for corporate bodies.

For further information, contact either Mike Hughes (Chairman) on 01252 861059, email: mike.hughes@ntlworld.com or Ernest Sagaga (Secretary) on 020 8427 3186. Or write to Ernest Sagaga, 26 Thurlby Close, Harrow, Middlesex, HA1 2LZ, UK. Web: www.rugo.org.

Nyamata Vocational School Project

The progress made by Rwanda in rebuilding after the genocide is demonstrated by the many different projects which are run across the whole of Rwanda either by the Rwandan government or by NGOs. One of the consequences of the genocide is that most of Rwanda's artisans were lost, and the Nyamata Vocational School is one of the projects instigated by the government to help rebuild this skill base. Nyamata is about 30km south of the capital Kigali and some of the worst massacres of the genocide took place there. Construction of the initial stage of the school is now complete with the initial six classroom blocks, administration block and workshop block. This has been funded by the Rwandan Government.

As vocational training is high among the objectives of RUGO, the government asked for its help to support the school. RUGO's initial contribution was to equip the vocational departments, which included masonry & construction, carpentry, plumbing & appropriate technology, information technology, and tailoring.

The cost of this was in the order of £120,000. RUGO secured these funds partly through its fundraising activities and also through a grant of £25,000 from the Tudor Trust. In addition donations were received from many companies and individuals including RMC and Barclays Bank. Energis provided sponsorship through their Chairman's Award scheme and National Grid Company, George Wimpey and the Institution of Electrical Engineers donated computing equipment for use in the school and other educational establishments. Alfred McAlpine carried out a nationwide appeal to all of their sites on behalf of RUGO and secured a significant quantity of second-hand tools and equipment. A container of tools and equipment was sent by RUGO to the Ministry of Education in 2002 and the school opened in October 2003 with just a small number of classes. These will be increased year by year as additional facilities are constructed.

Future courses to be included within the curriculum include motor vehicle repair, welding & fabrication, electrical installation, fitting & turning, home economics, refrigeration & air conditioning, and electronics for TV and radio repair.

Support of all kinds is welcomed from individuals and companies:

- Donation of equipment – not necessarily new – for any of the courses
- Short-term secondment of suitable personnel to help with the project
- Cash donations
- Storage and transport facilities

If you are able to help please contact Mike Hughes of RUGO (see above)

The Forest Peoples' Project
This is the UK-based support partner of CAURWA (see pages 77–8), and is the charitable wing of the Forest Peoples' Programme which was established in 1990 to promote a people-centred approach to resolving the crisis facing the world's forests.

The Forest Peoples' Project works to:

- Promote the environmental and human rights of forest peoples
- Educate policy makers, practitioners and civil society about forest peoples' aspirations
- Support forest peoples in the conservation of their lands, sustainable management of their resources and sustainable development

It achieves these aims by means of support activities and capacity building with grassroots organisations; networking with NGOs, indigenous support organisations and agencies; research and analysis; and outreach. Donations to CAURWA (above) can also be made to the Forest Peoples' Project.

For further information contact Forest Peoples' Project, 1c Fosseway Centre, Stratford Road, Moreton-in-Marsh, GL56 9NQ, UK; tel: 01608 652893; email: info@fppwrm.gn.apc.org; web: www.forestpeoples.org.

Send a Cow
Livestock for life
Antoinette remembers vividly the day in April 1994 when ten armed men appeared outside her house. The Rwandan genocide was just getting under

way, so Antoinette and her family fled. Her mother and all her other adult relatives were caught and killed. Her father had died the previous year, so at the age of 12 Antoinette became 'mother' to four younger siblings. Life became an unremitting struggle to keep the little ones fed, clothed and in school – Antoinette herself, a bright girl who had been doing well in her lessons, had to drop out to cope with her new responsibilities.

Antoinette is typical of the child-orphan household-heads being helped to make a new future for themselves by the British charity Send a Cow. Send a Cow provides livestock, plus training in livestock care and sustainable organic farming, to poor farmers in Africa. Again and again, we see gifts of livestock – cows, goats, pigs or poultry – enabling families to transform their lives.

They can add milk, eggs and meat to their own diets, and sell the surplus for desperately needed extra income. They can use that money for such household 'extras' as salt, soap and cooking oil. As their herd or flock grows, they may bring in enough to invest in further livestock, more land or other ways of generating income, such as a small shop. For most, first call on this new income is seeing their children through school – even countries with free primary education expect families to pay for pencils, paper, books and secondary schooling.

When Send a Cow started its programme in Rwanda in 2000, our first challenge was finding partners to work with – normally we work through local community groups, but the genocide had smashed the old social networks. Our Rwanda Team Manager, Richard Munyerango, had to encourage old groups around Kabuga, the town where we were first based, to come back together. It was a less difficult task than he had feared, with people eagerly embracing this opportunity to work together again.

But young people like Antoinette had fallen right out of sight. Orphaned families, both Hutus and Tutsis, were isolated and demoralised. The first Send a Cow preparatory training course for orphans started to change all that. Meeting each other for the first time, they grabbed the chance to exchange experiences with other young people in the same circumstances. Long before Send a Cow distributed the first livestock to them, the orphan families had decided to set up their own Orphans' Association, and start working together.

Many families in Rwanda lack enough land to rear cows, and in any case a cow can be difficult for children to manage. So Send a Cow's first livestock distribution – to both young orphan families and families who had taken in orphaned relatives - was of goats, a pair at a time. These are already producing young, for their new owners either to sell or keep, in order to build up a herd.

And recently we were delighted when Antoinette was among those receiving the first cows we gave out. We have helped her to start back at school, and we watch with joy as she and her family move forward into new hope and security.

By Pat Simmons of Send a Cow

How it began

Send a Cow is a UK-based charity that started in Uganda over 15 years ago. Back in the 1980s Uganda was devastated by a long civil war. Many of the quality dairy cows died, making milk a luxury that few could afford. In 1988 a Ugandan bishop, having seen milk surpluses in the UK, appealed to British farmers for help. A group of Christian farmers responded: by sending not milk, but cows. The first plane-load of cows left Gatwick in June 1988, arriving at Entebbe quarantine farm 12 hours later. Over 300 cows were flown from the UK between 1988 and 1996; but the policy of Send a Cow is now to purchase all the animals in Africa. Currently the scheme is active in Uganda, Kenya, Ethiopia, Sudan – and Rwanda.

Send a Cow UK, Unit 4, Priston Mill, Priston, Bath BA2 9EQ; tel: 01225 447041; web: www.sendacow.org.uk

Engalynx

This is a small UK charity operating from Manningtree in Essex and set up after the genocide to help Rwanda rebuild. Its name, Engalynx, meaning 'England links with...', was chosen by the children of a local school which also became involved. Since then, with the help of local friends and businesses and even a football club, Engalynx has sent not only funds but also packages and a container with computers, tools, clothes, shoes. Stationery, sewing machines, hairdressing equipment, photocopiers, cycles, seeds, etc. It is working with CARE International to support a school in a particularly poor area of Gitarama, and helping to provide equipment (donated by retired medical staff or local hospitals) for Rwanda's hospitals. Recently it launched a 'kid for a kid' appeal, which provided around 200 goats to child-headed households. It is also helping craftspeople to market their handicrafts in the UK. Wherever Engalynx sees a need and a possibility, it steps in!

Engalynx, 35 Birch Drive, Brantham, Suffolk, CO11 1TG; tel: 01206 395089; email: lantern@cpwpost.com. Founder and director: Maralyn Bambridge.

PASSEVU

The 1994 genocide left so many of Rwanda's children vulnerable and facing an uncertain future. André Jackson Nsabiyera, a teacher before the genocide, tackled their needs by setting up this small charity. 'Passevu' stands for *Projet d'Appui à la Scolarisation et la Sauvegarde des Enfants exposés à la Vulnérabilité*. The programme promotes the rights of the child and covers a whole range of activities aimed at education and training, self-help and income-generating schemes, as well as medical care. Children are provided with basic schooling, older students can learn subjects such as dressmaking, weaving, cookery (to make them employable in hotels and restaurants), agriculture, embroidery, hairdressing, plumbing, masonry, garage repairs, general electronics, painting, wood-carving, printing, information technology... and are helped with the marketing of their products. In Gisenyi (where much of the work is based), PASSEVU runs the only computer-training classes in the area as well as a children's library. Sport (football, basketball, volleyball, running, swimming, cycling, tennis...) is also a vital component, allowing children and youngsters to take a pride in their skills and work as a team. There is a small home for the homeless.

Funds are raised locally by recycling plastics, aluminium, etc, and by selling the products of the various courses. The project is run on a shoestring and new sources of finance are welcome, as are gifts of equipment for the courses and books for the library. Tourists can visit the Gisenyi activities and help by donating unwanted items at the end of a visit: leftover medical supplies or toiletries, notebooks, T-shirts and other clothing, sewing kits, batteries, pencils and pens, etc. Ring André and he'll arrange to collect them – and answer any questions about PASSEVU.

PASSEVU, BP 4261 Kigali; tel: 08534152; fax: 517222; email: passevu@yahoo.fr. Founder and director: André Jackson Nsabiyera.

CICODEB

CICODEB (*Centre d'Initiatives Communautaires de Base pour le Développement*) is a Rwandan non-profit organisation that started work in 1995. Its aim was and is the improvement of food security, based on the strategy of supporting small-scale farmers by means of technical education, financial assistance and the provision of inputs. CICODEB is legally authorised by the Rwandan Administration Ministry.

From 1995 to 2000, CICODEB assisted 129 farmers' groups in the area of Bugesera (three communes of Kigali province) with distribution of laying hens, goats, pigs and agricultural inputs. In 2001 it shifted to Gikongoro province (the country's poorest), where it identified 92 small-scale groups to benefit from its intervention within a five-year plan (starting in 2001). That province, with its high mountains, is naturally infertile, and had suffered greatly from the devastation of its people and livestock in 1994. In 2002/3 CICODEB continued to support local groups, spread information, and hold training courses on such diverse subjects as credit management, AIDS, gender and development, poultry farming and micro-projects. Also it provided small livestock (pigs, goats), seeds and agricultural material to 24 farmers' groups and 26 farming families, as well as loans for the launching of micro-projects. Around 500 people are benefiting directly, many of them women widowed in the genocide or its aftermath.

CICODEB is recognised nationally and internationally – for example the UK government's Department for International Development (DFID) and the Cellule Micro Realisations of Rwanda's MINALOC have provided (respectively) US$5,200 and US$7,291. Its long-term aim is to continue to improve the food situation in Karaba district of Gikongoro province. It appeals to international groups and NGOs for any support they can provide such as funds, foreign breeds of cattle and goats to increase milk production, improved varieties of poultry, seed for various crops, agricultural inputs, training equipment, volunteers and expert trainers. Contact its enthusiastic director when you're in Rwanda and he'll quickly persuade you to help!

CICODEB, BP 1579 Kigali; tel: 519043, 08530185; email: cicodeb@yahoo.fr. Director: Alfred Kayisharaza.

Centre Presbytérien d'Amour de Jeunes

This very practical organisation is doing a terrific job for Rwanda's streetkids. They can come here to sort themselves out and learn a trade in its many workshops. Although run by the Presbyterian Church it's completely open-handed – it 'sees the person, not the religion', someone commented to me – and the youngsters have a free choice of what trade they learn. Before deciding, they can check out the workshops and discuss with the trainees in them. In many cases former students have now become the teachers, taking a pride in passing on their skills.

The centre is in the southeast of Kigali, in Kicukiro district. Workshops include metalwork (buckets, watering cans, household pots and implements), dressmaking, hairdressing (the kids on this course have the shortest hair I've ever seen, as they all practise on each other!), designing and printing T-shirt patterns, embroidery and other handicrafts, traditional cow-dung art, bakery and cooking – and the making of sturdy, colourful furniture (tables, chairs, cupboards, chests of drawers...) from recycled cardboard. 'If it can be made from wood, it can be made from cardboard,' the teacher, a former streetkid, told me firmly.

At the end of their course, students are helped either to go into business as a group or to work independently. Items made on the courses are sold to raise funds for the centre (and the makers earn their share). Visitors can tour the workshops and make purchases on the spot; phone the number below to arrange this. The amazing thing about the centre is the difference it has made to youngsters, previously destitute and living miserably on the streets, who now take pride in their ability and face the future confidently. If you've been troubled by the plight of streetkids as you travel round Rwanda, a donation to this centre (or buying handicrafts here) is a practical way of helping.

Centre Presbytérien d'Amour de Jeunes, BP 56 Kigali; tel: 576929.

Parrainages Mondiaux (World Sponsorships)

This Belgian organisation was providing sponsorships for Rwandan children and students when they were exiled in Uganda in the 1970s – and has continued its help in various forms through all Rwanda's troubles. Many students in today's Rwanda still benefit from PM sponsorships.

Now, in partnership with CLADHO (the Collectif des Ligues et Associations des Droits de l'Homme au Rwanda), it aims to strengthen the capacity and efficiency of existing education-oriented organisations and to identify students most urgently needing sponsorship. In partnership with Benimpuhwe (which means 'those who have compassion'), it is helping to provide training (dressmaking/tailoring) for vulnerable young women. In partnership with ASOFERWA (see pages 182–3), it provides practical training (plumbing, car maintenance, electrical repairs...) for boys, genocide orphans who have been taken in by very poor families. One-off donations and regular support are always needed; contact the office below in either English or French.

Action Développement – Parrainages Mondiaux, 33 rue du Marché, 4500 Huy, Belgium; tel: 085 613520; fax: 085 230147; email: asbl.adpm.huy@belgacom.net.

INVESTING IN RWANDA

The ultimate involvement in Rwanda is to invest in one of the many opportunities that the country's rapid development has created! The **Rwanda Investment Promotion Agency** (PO Box 6239 Kigali; tel: (250) 510248, 585221/3, 585179; fax: 510249; email: investrw@rwanda1.com; web: www.rwandainvest.gov.rw) can provide full information, including the generous incentives and concessions available. The mechanisms are straightforward and investor-friendly, with a minimum of red tape.

Openings exist in many sectors; for example the agro-industrial field offers tea estates, coffee processing plants, commercial production and processing/marketing of food crops (cereals, potatoes, tomatoes, green vegetables, beans, passion fruit, mangoes, avocados, pineapples, strawberries and many more) as well as the production and export of cut flowers. Fish farming in the river valleys is still in its infancy. There is also potential for modern commercial livestock breeding, the processing of hides and skins, and the production/processing and storage of dairy and meat products. Manufacturing opportunities exist in the production of electronic and electrical goods, glass and glass products, garments, building materials, textiles and chemical and paper products, as well as in the expansion of existing industries. There is a need for the provision of solar energy, electricity from biomass and biogas, electricity in rural areas, and the extraction of methane gas from Lake Kivu, while the telecommunications and IT sectors offer a whole range of possibilities.

In the medical sector there is a great need for investors in specialised medical services such as urology, cardiology, neurology, orthopaedics, plastic surgery and dentistry; while the financial field offers openings in banking, insurance, etc.

Finally, tourism – a glittering field with possibilities ranging from small rural guesthouses to amphibious aircraft on Lake Kivu! Hotels, lodges, safari camps, transport, watersports, boats, cultural displays, hospitality services, the training of personnel, marketing handicrafts... it's an Aladdin's cave of opportunity.

If any of the above raises even a tiny flicker of interest, do check it out. If you don't, you may miss a life-changing opportunity. And Rwanda needs you!

Part Two

The Guide

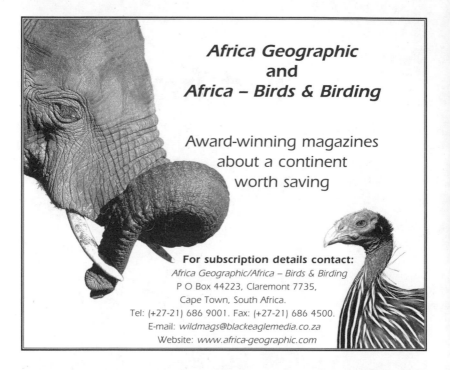

Kigali

6

Rwanda's attractive capital, Kigali, straggles over several hills, with the city centre on one and the government/administrative quarter on another. When Ruanda-Urundi (the capital of which was Usumbura, now Bujumbura) split into Rwanda and Burundi at the time of independence in 1962, the strongest contender to become Rwanda's new capital seemed to be Butare, which had been used by the Belgians as Rwanda's administrative capital during colonisation.

However, Kigali's central position and good road links to the rest of the country won out. As a result, while Butare has avoided capital-city brashness and remains relatively calm, Kigali has grown dramatically, its population rising from 25,000 to almost 600,000 in three and a half decades. Empty spaces on the hillsides are filling with new housing, and pollution in the valleys (from the increasing volume of traffic) could soon be a problem.

The centre of Kigali is bustling, colourful and noisy, but (for an African city) surprisingly clean and safe. Its occupants, from smart-suited business-persons to scruffy kids hawking newspapers or pirated cassettes, go purposefully about their activities, only lessening tempo briefly in the middle of the day. Occasional traffic lights, roundabouts and a cacophony of car horns manage (more or less) to regulate the traffic, although it's heavy and congested at peak times. Peaceful, tree-lined residential streets stretch outwards and generally downwards from the city's heart, and give visitors scope for strolling.

The government and administrative area, in Kacyiru quarter on a neighbouring hill, is newer and quieter, with wide streets and some striking modern architecture. Kigali was the centre of much fighting during the genocide and offices were ransacked; when workers returned after the end of the war they had virtually no usable typewriters, phones, stationery or furniture and had to start again from scratch. Also files, archives and other documentation had been destroyed.

There aren't many tourist attractions in Kigali itself and you're unlikely to want to spend many full days there, but there are some good hotels, the services (shops, banks, etc) are plentiful and the ambience is pleasant, making it an excellent base for exploring the rest of Rwanda, all parts of which are easily accessible by road in less than a day. Car-hire is easily arranged via one of the many tour operators and travel agencies – see pages 120–1.

GETTING THERE AND AWAY
By air

See pages 25–6 for details of flights to and from Rwanda – which means to and from Kigali, since that's where the international airport is situated, about 10km from the centre of town. There are plans to relocate it to Nyamata, about 30km south of Kigali, which would free the land for further development and bring jobs and opportunities to an under-used area, but it's unlikely to happen within the lifetime of this edition.

In the arrivals hall of the airport you'll find exchange and telephone facilities, various shops and a branch of ORTPN (*Office Rwandais du Tourisme et des Parcs Nationaux*) which is Rwanda's tourist office, where you can get a preliminary stock of maps, guides and so forth. (The main ORTPN office is in Kigali town centre.) At present there is no pestering from porters – there aren't any – just grab a trolley from the stack in the baggage reclaim area and deal with your own bags.

To get into Kigali town you've three options. (Or four, if you're prepared to beg a lift from some fellow traveller who has a vehicle.) If your hotel does airport pick-ups, you'll have arranged this at the time of booking; give them a ring if no-one has turned up to collect you. (At the telephone counter, calls are metered, so you talk first and pay afterwards, removing the need to have coins or phonecards.) If you've very little luggage and some small change in Rwandan francs, you can pick up a minibus-taxi in the road outside the airport and it'll take you to Kigali's central bus station. Otherwise take a *taxi-voiture* (a normal taxi, as opposed to a minibus-taxi). Agree a price with the driver in advance. At the time of writing the going rate is about US$12, but rates do legitimately rise over time. (If, for any reason, the exchange bureau in the airport is closed, taxi-drivers generally accept US dollars, but check the exchange-rate on the list in the window of the bureau.)

Whatever airline you've used, you MUST confirm your return flight at least three days in advance of departure – airline offices or travel agents in Kigali will deal with this for you. If you don't, you risk being 'bumped' or having your reservation cancelled.

By road

Kigali is a well-connected little city – literally. Good roads and bus services link it to all the main border crossings with neighbouring countries: Uganda, Tanzania, Burundi and the Democratic Republic of Congo.

GETTING AROUND

The centre of Kigali – for shopping, banks, airline offices, tour operators, etc – is tiny, so once you're there, you'll never be far from what you're looking for. It's based around two streets, Boulevard de la Révolution and Avenue de la Paix, and the various roads branching off them. However, if you ask directions you'll soon become aware that people don't go much on street names, rather on well-known landmarks. Remember that a lot of people working in Kigali don't actually *know* Kigali all that well – they'd never been there until they returned from some other country after the genocide.

Maps covering the whole of Kigali (as opposed to just the centre) are available from ORTPN (see page 53), also from some tour operators and hotels. There's a network of urban **minibuses** (minibus-taxis, commonly called taxis) serving all areas of the city, and plenty of **taxis** (saloons, commonly called *taxi-voitures* and recognisable by the yellow/orange stripe along the side) – they park, among other places, in Boulevard de la Révolution and at the top of Place de la Constitution, and also cruise the streets waiting to be flagged down. The **central minibus-taxi station** in Kigali is at the junction of Avenue de Commerce and Rue Mont Kabuye – you'll recognise it by the gaggle of beat-up white minibuses (with no indication of their destinations) and general air of chaos, but in fact there's an underlying level of sanity and, if you ask someone, you'll be pointed to the bus that you need. This is where you pick up minibus-taxis to take you down to the **Nyabugogo minibus-taxi station** (see page 121), from which transport to other parts of Rwanda leaves.

WHERE TO STAY
Virtually all of the Kigali hotels in the 'Luxury' to 'Middle' categories can arrange airport pick-ups – just ask (and check the cost, if any) at the time of booking. Unless otherwise specified, bedrooms in all of the Kigali hotels listed here have en-suite facilities with either bath or shower. Hotels in Remera suburb are closer to the airport than are those in the centre.

Luxury (above US$100 double)
Three hotels fall into this bracket: the Hotel des Mille Collines in the centre of Kigali, the Novotel in the administrative quarter (midway between the centre and the airport), and the brand-new five-star **Hotel InterContinental Kigali** that opened at the end of 2003 (on the site of the old Diplomates in the tree-lined Boulevard de la Révolution, a flat, ten-minute stroll from the centre), so too late for its details or prices to be included here. But it promises the full works – 104 bedrooms, pool, 500-seat conference centre, full guest facilities … everything appropriate to its five-star status. You can check it out on the InterContinental website: www.intercontinental.com. It's part of the South African Southern Sun group – www.southernsun.com.

Both the Novotel and the Mille Collines have swimming pools; both are extremely comfortable, have the facilities you'd expect for the price and offer a relaxing stay. Both have good restaurants/bars, tennis courts, conference and business facilities including internet access, and various boutiques (it's hard to resist the patisserie stall in the foyer of the Novotel...). The **Hotel des Mille Collines** (BP 1322 Kigali; tel: 576530/3; fax: 576541; email: millecollines@millecollines.net; web: www.millecollines.net) has 112 rooms and suites from US$140 to US$250; a standard double room on the city side (there's sometimes traffic noise at night) costs around US$160 including tax,

Novotel Kigali Umubano.
Welcome to the heart of a tropical garden.
Bienvenue au coeur d'un jardin tropical.

Discover the Novotel Kigali Umubano, with its luxuriant surroundings and spectacular two-hectare tropical garden set on a lush hillside. 98 rooms, including 14 suites, as well as 5 meeting rooms, for relaxing or working in total comfort. Novotel Kigali Umubano also features a restaurant with terrace, pool, tennis and volleyball courts, mini golf ... In other words a paradise where everything is designed for your enjoyment.

En plein coeur d'une nature exubérante de beauté, découvrez le Novotel Kigali Umubano. Un magnifique jardin tropical de deux hectares vous contemple de sa verte colline. 98 chambres dont 14 suites ainsi que 5 salles de réunion vous permettent de vous reposer ou de travailler dans un parfait confort. Le Novotel Umubano Kigali c'est aussi : restaurant avec terrasse, piscine, tennis, terrains de volley, mini golf ... En un mot un paradis où tout est pensé pour votre détente.

Novotel Kigali Umubano, Bd de i'Umugnada, BP 874, Kigali-Rwanda
Informations, reservations tel: (250) 821 76 or 77 or 78 - fax: (250) 829 57 - www.novotel.com

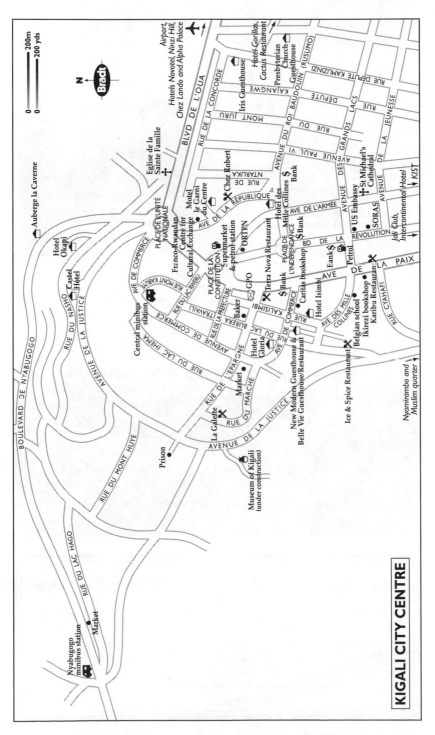

KIGALI CITY CENTRE

on the pool side US$176. Deduct 10% for single occupancy and add US$12 for breakfast. Rates are negotiable for groups or long stays. Credit cards are accepted. The hotel has a pleasant garden where you can engage in a spot of urban birdwatching. (The massive tree, home to many species, which looks as if it has been there since time began, is only 30–40 years old.) Some tour operators and travel agents, including Volcanoes Safaris, have offices here. It's an easy walk (ten minutes) to the centre, via a street (Avenue de l'Armée) filled with handicrafts stands: bargain hard here! (See advertisement opposite.)

The **Novotel** (BP 874 Kigali; tel: 82176/7/8; fax: 82957; email: h3410@accorhotels.com), sometimes still known locally by its old name of Umubano, is more quietly situated (in the administrative quarter, between Kigali and the airport) and there's plenty of transport, whether minibus-taxis or *taxi-voitures,* to and from the centre. A *taxi-voiture* can be up to US$1 cheaper if you pick it up in the street outside ($3.50) rather than in the hotel driveway; a minibus costs less than US$1. The hotel is very popular with local people for functions and the staff are friendly; an efficient but relaxed place. It has 98 rooms including 14 suites: standard doubles are around US$125–135 excluding breakfast. Credit cards are accepted. There's a post office near by and banking facilities (with Western Union) in the hotel. Maxim's nightclub, which used to be noisy at night, closed in 2003. (See advertisement on page 96.)

Upper/middle range (US$60–100 double)
The new **Hotel Gorillas** (rue des Parcs; BP 1782 Kigali; tel: 501717/8; fax: 501716; email: gorillashotel@rwanda1.com) has one of Kigali's best (and priciest...) restaurants and 31 very comfortable rooms: US$70 single, US$95 double, excluding breakfast. Less than two years old, it's a smart, calm, efficient place. Ambling downhill to it from the centre of town is manageable but the upward walk is tough; however there are plenty of *taxi-voitures* and minibus-taxis run nearby. See advertisement opposite.

The little **Motel le Garni du Centre** (BP 548 Kigali; tel/fax 572654, 571274; email:garni@rwanda1.com) is tucked away down a side street close to the centre of town, near the Centre Culturel d'Echanges Franco-Rwandaises. It has 11 quiet, comfortable rooms (TV, phone, fridge) overlooking the garden and small swimming pool. Prices start at US$67 single and US$77 double, including a good buffet breakfast; but drop for longer stays. Lunch and dinner can be provided by prior request, or guests can eat at the nearby Restaurant Chez Robert, Hotel des Mille Collines or (slightly further away) in the town centre. There's a log fire in the lounge for chilly evenings. (See advertisement opposite.)

Middle range (US$30–60 double)
The **Ninzi Hill Hotel** (tel: 87711–5; fax: 87716; email: ninzihill@yahoo.fr and ninzi@rwanda1.com), in the administrative quarter not far from the Novotel, is a quiet, comfortable place well away from city bustle. Rooms at the back look out over gardens and greenery and it has a pleasantly laid-back feel to it. There are 15 rooms with phone and TV at US$40 single/$60 double

including 'tropical' breakfast – ie: continental plus fruit! Reductions are possible for groups or long stays. Each time I've checked it out, the receptionist has spontaneously offered to show me a bedroom – elsewhere I normally have to ask, although the response is then willing. The hotel has a good (not cheap) restaurant; also there's the Shangai Chinese Restaurant nearby, with swings for the children and a family shopping centre – and it's a ten-minute flat and downhill walk to the Kigali Business Centre, with its cinema, bar-restaurant and shops.

The modern **Hotel Okapi** (BP 1775 Kigali; tel: 571667; fax: 574413; email: okapi@hotmail.com) in central Kigali has 39 rooms/suites with balconies and TV, and a back terrace with a panoramic view across the Kigali landscape. Unfortunately it's in a side street (Rue Musima), between Boulevard de Nyabugogo and Avenue de la Justice, which is unsurfaced and a bit tatty – guests might not feel safe walking back there at night. But the area is being reconstructed, so this may improve. Rooms US$35–58 single, US$36–70 double; suites US$70–93 single, US$81–104 double. (Prices, which include breakfast, depend on standard and view. There are some cheaper rooms in an annexe.) The restaurant offers an acceptable range of international meals and snacks.

Out in Remera suburb, but an easy taxi or minibus-taxi ride from town, **Hotel Chez Lando** (BP 1519 Kigali; tel: 82050, 584328, 84394; fax: 84380; email: lando@rwandatel1.rwanda1.com; web: www.hotelchezlando.com) is a well-established place with a quiet garden, popular with locals and visitors alike. It has 22 rooms in its main building and (nicer) 10 in bungalows in the garden; all have TV and phone: US$50 double and US$40 single, with reductions possible for groups or long stays. Internet facilities are available. The Zoom nightclub/disco is popular at weekends. The indoor, upstairs restaurant does a good buffet breakfast but can be slow and cheerless for other meals; for these the outdoor, downstairs restaurant is brisker and livelier. Also in Remera, the **Alpha Palace Hotel** (Boulevard de l'OUA, BP 2632 Kigali; tel: 82981; fax: 84134; email: alphapalace@rwanda1.com; web: www.alphapalace.com) is a comfortable, modern hotel, with a swimming pool, about 1km from the airport and 4km from the centre of town. There's a 24-hour restaurant with French, African and oriental cuisine, also a snack-bar for grills etc, and a nightclub on Friday/Saturday. Its 38 double rooms and suites have colour TV and phone: US$38 single, US$48 double, US$57 twin and US$67 suite, all including continental breakfast. A few minutes from the Alpha Palace, on the opposite side of the same road, the much smaller, three-year-old **Agasaro Motel** (tel: 83293) offers simpler but good-value accommodation: 13 rooms with TV and hot water, US$20 single/$30 double including breakfast. If you're arriving late by air and just want a straightforward night's sleep near the airport before moving on the next day, give it a try – reception is open 24 hours and it seems a well-cared-for place. (A few doors away is the Pleiade Motel – I couldn't check it as no-one was around but it looked less inviting than the Agasaro.)

The **Hotel Isimbi** (BP 1163 Kigali; tel: 572578/81; fax: 575109; email: isimbi@hotmail.com), the most central hotel in this range, is right in the centre of town (Rue Kalisimbi) just a few minutes' walk from the market, post office and shops – which does mean that guests may be a target for street vendors. It's an efficient, clean, business-type hotel, with 26 plain rooms (the back ones are quiet), hot water, helpful staff, a non-smoking snack-bar, a restaurant for main meals (main dishes up to around US$6), and room service. Single US$35, double US$40. See advertisement below.

The **Sky Hotel** (BP 206 Kigali; tel: 516693, tel/fax: 516690; email: skyhotel1@yahoo.fr) in Avenue de la Justice has 28 comfortable rooms (some with small sitting rooms), hot water, and a lovely view over the valley from the back: standard doubles US$30 per room upwards excluding breakfast (about US$3). The restaurant is reasonable. There's an internet café next door and a night-club (not exorbitant) at weekends. It's a bit of a walk into the centre (go straight up Rue Cyahafi, which is almost opposite, turn left at the top and you'll reach the Ikirezi bookshop) but *taxi-voitures* cruise along the main road and there's a minibus-taxi stop opposite. Also in Avenue de la Justice, but at the other end as it approaches the Place de l'Unité Nationale, the new **Castel Hotel** (tel: 576377, 578491; fax: 87456; email: castelhotel@rwanda1.com; web: www.castelhotel.com) has 23 rooms/suites with TV, phone and small fridge: rooms US$26 single, US$30 double, suites US$40. The hotel is built on a steep hillside so the restaurant at the back has dramatic views across the valley. It's spotlessly clean, and the rooms seem good value – but be warned (if it bothers you) that this is a no-alcohol place. .

The **Hotel Baobab** (BP 1406 Kigali; tel: 575633, 516616; fax; 571048; email: baobab@inbox.rw) is a great place, full of character but some distance from the city centre, down in the southwest of outer Kigali near Mount Kigali and the Islamic cultural centre. If you have your own transport (or don't mind taking taxis), do consider it. The area is peaceful, with widespread views across the valley and to Mount Kigali, and the possibility of quite rural walks. The Baobab has nine rooms with hot water, phone and TV; US$25 single, US$30 double. Breakfast is US$3. The restaurant (mostly outdoor) has a good reputation locally.

Much nearer the centre, a ten-minute walk downhill from the Hotel des Mille Collines, is the **Presbyterian Church Guesthouse** (Rue Député Kayuku; tel: 578915; fax: 578919; email: epr@rwandatel1.rwanda1.com) – a clean, relaxing place with cheerful rooms and a good-value dining room. It can get busy with church guests so book in advance. US$25 single, US$30 double – sometimes reduced rates for charities, aid workers, etc. Another church guesthouse is that of the **Episcopal Church** (Avenue Paul VI; tel: 573219) in Biryogo (aka Bilyogo) district, a considerable distance southwest of the centre – it's clean and friendly, and you can park there safely. US$20 en-suite single, US$30 double, cheaper dormitory accommodation.

A few minutes' walk from the Presbyterian Guesthouse is the **Iris Guesthouse** (BP 228 Kigali; tel: 501172, 501181; fax: 576929) in Rue Député Kajangwe, opened in January 2001: 17 clean, quiet rooms ($30 single, US$38 double excluding breakfast) and two apartments ($60 per night or US$1,500 per month). In a shady street away from traffic, it's really more hotel than guesthouse and has a good restaurant.

Finally in this category (although almost in the Budget category below) the **One Love Guesthouse** (rue de Kinamba; BP 3032 Kigali; tel/fax: 575412, 513154; email: onelove@rwanda1.com) is a very new and welcoming place run by an NGO (the Mulindi Japan One Love Project) that supports the disabled and works practically to help them – all profits from the guesthouse are ploughed back into the NGO. There are ten simple but spacious twin rooms with balconies and some cooking facilities at US$30 per day or US$500 per month, and by the time you read this it may also be possible to pitch a tent in the garden. Young people and backpackers would feel comfortable here. There's also a restaurant with a range of snacks/meals. It's a secure place, with good parking, in the valley between Kiyovu and Kaciru – Rue de Kinamba is also known as Rue Poids Lourd. All but the most energetic will need transport up to the centre of town – but there are minibus-taxis and *taxi-voitures* nearby. (Cat-lovers or cat-haters take note – when I checked it out, there were numerous – and very appealing – cats and kittens sunning themselves in the garden. This is quite rare in Rwanda.)

Budget (below US$25 double)

High on my budget list for central Kigali is still the **Auberge la Caverne** (tel: 574549), a pleasant, clean, new place (it opened in May 2000) with 12 simple but spacious en-suite rooms (hot water) set away from the traffic around a central courtyard in Boulevard de Nyabugogo. Back windows have a good view out over the valley. US$10 single, US$20. The restaurant does a standard range of meals. It's a steepish walk up into town, but as usual there are taxis.

Very central is the **Gloria Hotel** (tel: 571957), in the commercial area near to the market, at the traffic-light junction in Rue du Lac Burera (aka Bulera, aka Rue du Travail) just downhill from the Caritas bookshop. It's basic, safe, clean, functional and friendly. There's no restaurant, not even for breakfast (although they may start providing continental breakfast for residents one of these days), but there are plenty of eateries in the area. They'll take phone calls for you at reception but you can't phone out – however there's a phone kiosk next door. En-suite rooms (cold water in the taps, but they'll bring you a bucket of hot on request) cost US$12 single (some are quite small) and US$16 double. Being near the market, this is a less glamorous part of Kigali – probably safe, but be sensible if you come and go after dark.

Two cheaper places opposite each other near the Gloria (in a small, unnamed road on the right as you go uphill from the Gloria towards the Caritas bookshop) are the **Belle Vie Restaurant/Logement** (BP 3993 Kigali; tel: 570158) and the **New Modern Guest House** (BP 1459 Kigali; tel: 574708). The Belle Vie is friendly and quite good value: four plain rooms with washbasins sharing a separate (clean) shower/WC; hot water. The restaurant serves meals by request. Rooms US$8 single, US$10 double – and they've a slightly more expensive en-suite room ($13) in another building. The New Modern is fractionally cheaper – ten rooms, shared facilities, US$7/$9 – but has no washbasins, no restaurant and is much seedier. Also in central Kigali, behind/below the Eglise de la Sainte Famille (the big church on Boulevard de l'OUA by the Place de l'Unité Nationale), the **Procure d'Accueil Kigali** (tel: 576334, 575146) has 25 simple rooms at US$7 single, US$10 double excluding breakfast. There is a restaurant for guests. It can be full with church visitors at times, so book (and check the facilities) in advance.

Out in Remera suburb near the Hotel Chez Lando (thus close to the airport) there are two good budget places: the Chez Rose Guest House and the Auberge Beau Séjour. The Remera area is lively in the evenings, with small restaurants and a buzz of people – there's also a useful supermarket nearby. A *taxi-voiture* into central Kigali costs US$4–5, a minibus-taxi less than US$1. The **Auberge Beau Séjour** (BP 3655 Kigali; tel: 582527, tel/fax: 582601; email: beausejourhotel@yahoo.com) has a good reputation locally: 19 pleasant rooms at US$20 including breakfast, other meals by request. The owner supervises personally and takes a pride in the place – there are thoughtful touches like drinking-water in the bedrooms, and a well-cared-for garden. The **Chez Rose Guest House** (tel: 84086, 08574800; email: ncuro@yahoo.com) has 20 equally cheerful rooms set round a courtyard, again with thoughtful touches; US$20 including a good breakfast with fruit, other meals by request. I can't decide which of these two I like best – both are attractive – maybe a reader can offer comments for the next edition of the guidebook! Also in the Remera area – set a little bit up from the road, near the Alpha Palace Hotel – the **Travellers' Inn** (tel: 86735) has 15 rooms, only some of them en-suite, for US$6–12. It's pretty basic, as the price suggests, but friendly. There's also a small restaurant/snack-bar.

The old **Hotel Panafrique** in central Kigali has closed now, although its sign may not yet have been removed. And you may spot a sign saying 'rooms' outside the **Karibu Restaurant** in Avenue de la Paix but there are only two, they are always full and I was advised by the staff not to bother mentioning them!

Nyamirambo suburb

Finally, a handful of little places down in Nyamirambo are worth mentioning, because the area is so appealing. This is a lively, characterful quarter, near the mosque and Islamic Centre, which was one of the first parts of Kigali to be settled. To reach it on foot (if you're energetic), continue walking southwards and downhill from the Sky Hotel. *Taxi-voitures* to the centre cost around US$3–4 depending on where you're going; minibus-taxis less than US$1.

In the 'Budget' category, a friendly place there is the **Kigali Hotel** (BP 697 Kigali; tel/fax: 571384) on Avenue de la Justice, with 18 small en-suite rooms with hot water, phone and TV; US$10 single and US$14 double, including breakfast with omelette. No restaurant. Minibus-taxis from central Kigali stop nearby – ask for 'Chez Mayaka' or the mosque. (It's in a one-way section of the road so they pass it only on the way out from Kigali; to go into the centre you need a stop in the neighbouring street.) Nearby down a turning off Avenue de la Justice is the **Hotel La Vedette** (BP 850 Kigali; tel: 573575), really no more than a guesthouse; three singles at US$6 and three doubles at US$10 with shared (clean) facilities. Guests 'live as family' there, the welcoming owner told me. Further on there's the **Auberge de Nyamirambo** (tel: 572879), near the Baha'i Centre – ten doubles with showers, US$12 single and US$18 double.

Moving into the 'Middle' category there's the **Hotel la Mise** (tel: 578369), which is clean and pleasant with a reasonable restaurant, but the en-suite rooms seem a touch expensive for the area at US$35 double, despite having phone and TV.

Apartments

The **Résidence Prima 2000** (BP 924 Kigali; tel: 583173–5, email: sorasinfo@rwanda1.com) is on Boulevard de l'Umuganda opposite Telecom House, near the Novotel. It has 36 modern, self-contained apartments, with one to four bedrooms, ranging from around US$1,000 to US$3,000 per month according to size. The minimum let is normally one month. The **Iris Guesthouse** (above) also has two apartments: US$60 per night or US$1,500 per month. The Kigali travel agency **Nord-Sud International** can arrange a 'self-contained house' but I haven't checked it personally; information from tel: 502098 or 575310, or email: nordsudinternational@yahoo.fr. The **Agence de Voyage, de Tourisme et de Logistique** near the Galette supermarket (BP 3475 Kigali, tel: 515688; fax: 574857; email: cdelucco@yahoo.com) can arrange housing and apartments for people relocating to Kigali or working there, and describes itself as a 'Multi-Service Agency'.

WHERE TO EAT AND DRINK

For this section I'm greatly indebted to the author of the 2000 guide to *50 Restaurants à Kigali*, André Verbruggen. André has lived and worked in Kigali for eight years and eats out virtually every evening – so knows every knife, fork, spoon and wineglass of the place! If you're a serious foodie, do contact him on email avak2000@hotmail.com for the latest edition of his guide, due in early 2004. Meanwhile, because no tourist is likely to spend as many as 50 days in Kigali (and André's latest list actually reaches a total of 59), here is just a brief selection to get you started, with some input also from other friends living in Kigali. The hotel restaurants listed below are included because they're particularly good, but all of Kigali's hotels offer acceptable food so, if you prefer to eat wherever you're staying, you won't necessarily miss out.

Above Mural in Kigali

Below *Intore* dance group heating the drums before playing at The National Museum of Rwanda, Butare

Above Boy in dugout canoe
Right Young boy, Cyangugu
Below Children carrying water, Ruhengeri

Expensive (main dishes above US$15)

On the top floor of the Hotel des Mille Collines (tel: 576530) is the **Panorama Restaurant**, with an appropriately panoramic view over the city. This is an exclusive place: André comments that a meal at the Panorama is 'a gastronomic pleasure that rarely disappoints'. The wine list is comprehensive. Official dinners and banquets are held here and there are regular 'themed evenings'. The 'suggestion of the day' plus dessert is around US$15 but it's easy to spend more. At the Hotel Gorillas (tel: 501717), the smaller **Restaurant Le Dos Argenté** (silver-back...), new in 2002, is a member of the *Chaine des Rotisseurs* and lives up to it – 'best decoration and best food overall', comments André. Main dishes (French cuisine) go up to around US$20, desserts to US$7. Service is relaxed. Slightly less expensive than the two above, the **Restaurant Hellenique** (tel: 583731) in Kimihurura is tucked away in a residential area not far from the Cadillac Club, in the valley between Kiyovu and Kacyiru – taxi-drivers will know it and it's signposted. The food is Greek/International with a good wine-list, the ambience is relaxed and there's a pleasant terrace. Service is attentive but may be slow. Government VIPs and ambassadors come here. It's likely that the restaurant at the new **InterContinental Hotel** (see page 95) will also fall into this category.

Medium (main dishes US$5–15)

The **Restaurant Chez Robert** (you can see the two elephants marking its entrance from the gateway of Hotel des Mille Collines) falls into the 'medium' category at present but may move up to 'expensive' once it becomes established. It used to be the Caprices du Palais, approached from Rue de Ntaruka. A new Portuguese chef has just moved in and is building up his clientele with traditional dishes before expanding his menu – it should be worth a try.

The **Cactus Restaurant** (tel: 575572) in Rue Député Kayuku (near the Hotel Gorillas) is a super place, particularly for pizza-lovers – it's very welcoming, with a pleasant outdoor terrace giving a beautiful view over Kigali, and good food (French cuisine as well as pizzas). Steak and fish main dishes up to US$8, desserts US$5. André comments: 'My best place in town – THE place to be.' There's also a take-away pizza service – phone beforehand and it'll be ready for you to collect. Open 12.00–14.00 and 18.00–22.30. Closed Tuesdays.

Ask locally about the very good **Flamingo Chinese Restaurant** – it was moving to new premises at the time of writing and is probably now installed on the top floor of Telecom House, near the Novotel.

The poolside restaurant at the **Novotel** (tel: 83361) has a good and varied midday and evening buffet ($12, sizzling main dishes, calorific desserts ...) as well as the type of general menu you'd expect from a hotel of this standard. Staff are attentive and the atmosphere is relaxed. It's one of Kigali's most popular meeting places.

Slightly cheaper than the four above, out at the edge of Remera, the Italian **O Sole Luna** has a good range of pizzas and pasta, well presented – and a beautiful view over the city from its terraces. Service is friendly and reasonably brisk.

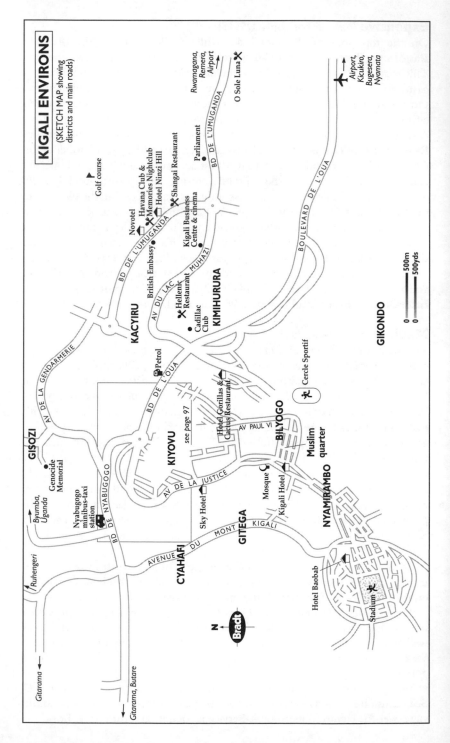

KIGALI ENVIRONS
(SKETCH MAP showing
districts and main roads)

Budget and snack (main dishes below US$5)

Popular with Rwandans, ex-pats and tourists alike is the little Indian restaurant **Ice & Spice**, in Rue du Lac Bulera/Burera (go downhill from the Belgian School, turn left and the restaurant is a little way along on your left). It has an extensive menu, with all dishes available mild, medium and hot. The 'ice' part means just that – a colourful range of ices. Staff (English-speaking) are attentive and service is relatively quick. Main dish around US$3 excluding extras. Uphill past the Belgian School, turn right into Avenue de la Paix and you're opposite the **Karibu Restaurant** with its convenient and varied lunchtime buffet (US$3) – it fills up with business people at 13.00 so try to eat earlier. At any time it's a shady place to stop for a cool drink if you're in central Kigali. Another good place for a self-service buffet lunch is the **Terra Nova**, opposite the main post office (US$3–4). In the 1980s, the government of the time decreed that civil servants should have shorter lunch breaks; so restaurants began offering buffet lunches since they took up less time – and the Terra Nova was among the first of them to do this. Neither it nor the Karibu is open in the evening.

The **Shangai Chinese Restaurant** near the Ninzi Hill Hotel and within walking distance of the Novotel is popular, friendly and good value; if you've children you can let them loose on the swings and other play equipment. Here you're not far from the Kigali Business Centre or KBC, with its **Planet Cinéma restaurant** (sandwiches, snacks, a good variety of salads, main meals…) which, you've guessed it, is right at the door of Kigali's cinema, so you can eat here if you're going to a movie. Also in the KBC, **Babito** is a friendly place. Near the Shangai, at the good and popular **Havana Club** (which is a pizzeria and not a club, despite its name) beside the Novotel, there's take-away pizza; tel: 510440.

Two good, cheap African restaurants ('for those who want a real local adventure', says André) are Chez John and Banjo. **Chez John** is in Kiyovu, in rue de Masaka (which is between rue de Kiyovu and rue de l'Akagera) – it's a rustic building opposite a school, with no visible sign so ask directions when you're nearby. The buffet (midday and evening) is around US$1.50 with meat, cheaper without. The **Banjo** is a new place in Remera, near Hotel Chez Lando, also with an African buffet.

For fast food in the city centre try either branch of **Amy's**; one is on the corner of Rue de la Préfecture on Place de la Constitution and the other is beside the petrol station just after the traffic lights on Boulevard de l'OUA as you approach the centre from Kimihurura. These are new, clean, brisk places based on the US model, with genuinely 'fast' food (and no alcohol). Close to this petrol station you'll see a sign to the Ethiopian **Addis Restaurant** – it's reached via a steepish but short mud track going down behind the petrol station. The menu is entirely Ethiopian but someone will explain to you what the (highly spiced) dishes consist of; you can opt for a selection which lets you try a little of everything. It's a simple place and service can be slow, but I know some tourists who've been delighted by the 'genuine African experience' it offers.

To combine sustenance with shopping, try the snack-bar in the **Galette** supermarket (sometimes still remembered by its old name of Baguette), rather

KIST

The **Kigali Institute of Science, Technology & Management** (KIST) was created in 1997. In July 2002 it held its first graduation ceremony, attended by Rwanda's President Paul Kagame. The Institute provides courses from faculties and other centres:

- The Faculty of Technology, with departments of ICT (information and communications technologies), various types of engineering (electrical, mechanical, civil...), food sciences and technology, training workshops and entrepreneurship development (including a cottage industry and production unit)
- The Faculty of Management, covering finance, accounting, marketing and human resources management
- The Faculty of Science, giving first-year students basic training in maths, physics and chemistry as a background for their further studies
- The Language School, with courses in English, French and African languages. In response to the government's bilingual policy, English and French are the languages of instruction at KIST, and students must pass a language exam when graduating so that they gain a working knowledge of one or both these languages
- The Centre for Continuing Education, offering part-time courses (computer applications, languages, management, practical technology...), in-service training (tailor-made courses and seminars on

awkwardly located towards the bottom of Rue du Marché just after it turns sharply to join Rue de l'Epargne. This is a popular meeting place for ex-pats and aid workers, and there are noticeboards listing various items (cars, dogs, homes, motorbikes, TVs, garden hoses...) wanted or for sale. The supermarket has a good (not cheap) range of groceries and household items; the snack-bar does breakfasts, sandwiches, salads, light meals, pastries (including croissants) and good coffee. Philip describes it as 'breakfast nirvana'.

NIGHTLIFE

For a capital city, Kigali isn't over-rich in nightclubs and discos. The biggest and best known is the **New Cadillac** in Kimihurura, of which there are two parts: one for VIPs and the smart set and one for more relaxed and younger people. The VIP part (entrance US$5) consists of a restaurant (African and European specialities), piano bar, live band and disco, and opens 11.00–15.00 and 18.00–midnight Tuesday to Sunday. Drinks aren't exorbitant, with beer at around US$2–3. If a group of visitors wants traditional music or dancers, this can be arranged. For young people, the New Cadillac Night Club functions Wednesday to Sunday, 21.00 to dawn.

Smaller than the New Cadillac but the same price is the **Planète Club** – a smart place – in the Kigali Business Centre complex. The most expensive in

demand) and distance education (including the African Virtual University, below)
- The African Virtual University, started in 1999 and financed by the World Bank in support of distance learning, has organised many seminars in (for example) accountancy, languages and management, and can provide course material in both English and French. It offers degree courses in electronics engineering, computer science and computer engineering
- The Centre for Innovations and Technology Transfer, where applied research leads to environmentally friendly, appropriate technological innovations, and their subsequent transfer to rural areas. These include solar-powered equipment, fuel-saving bread ovens, waste-water management installations and bio-gas production for cooking and lighting. For example, KIST constructed the bio-gas digesters at Cyangugu central prison

In October 2002, KIST was admitted as a member of the **International Association of Universities** (IAU). This is a UNESCO-affiliated organisation, which was formally established in 1950 to encourage links between institutions of higher learning worldwide.

Kigali Institute of Science, Technology & Management, Avenue de l'Armée, BP 3900 Kigali; tel: 574696; fax: 571924/5; email: info@kist.ac.rw; web: www.kist.ac.rw.

Kigali, but still very popular, is **Memories**, close to the Havana Club pizzeria in the Kubaho Plaza near the Novotel: entrance US$10 and drinks US$4 upwards. Smoking is allowed. The **Mango** in the Diamond Plaza on Place de la Constitution (near Amy's fast food) is a new place proving popular, with live music and a disco at weekends: entry US$4.

Other hotel nightclubs are at the **Hotel Chez Lando** and the **Sky Hotel**. Finally, the **Alpha Palace Hotel** also has one on Fridays/Saturdays: US$2 entry and a mixture of traditional/modern music.

As life in Rwanda becomes more settled and relaxed, more places may well open; please let us know about them for the next edition of this guide.

PRACTICAL INFORMATION
Money
The three most accessible **banks** in central Kigali are the Banque Commerciale du Rwanda (BCR) and the Banque Continentale Africaine Rwanda (BACAR) in Boulevard de la Révolution and the Banque de Kigali in Avenue de la Paix. Queues are slow but orderly and there's generally no hassle. The BACAR has a Moneygram service and the BCR a Western Union service via which funds can be transferred quickly from abroad. In fact Western Union has hit Rwanda in a big way – there are several other offices in Kigali,

and at least one in each of the other main towns. See also *Chapter 4*, page 54, for what transactions are possible.

In addition, there are various **foreign exchange (forex) bureaux** around the city; conspicuous ones are opposite the BCR in Boulevard de la Révolution and in Avenue de la Paix near its junction with Avenue des Mille Collines.

Money-changers hang out around the main post office in Avenue de la Paix and down Rue de l'Epargne, and may well crop up elsewhere too. They seem not to be illegal – or at any rate are tolerated – and in general they offer better rates than either banks or forex bureaux, but be vigilant, and decide in advance the lowest rate you're willing to accept.

Communications

The main **post office** in Avenue de la Paix has a counter for international phone calls and an efficient fax office; faxes to Europe cost US$2 per page, to the US$2.50. If you want someone to send a fax to you there, the number is (250) 576574. Receiving a fax costs under US$1. This is where you can collect post restante (see page 68). There's also a philatelic counter.

Cyber cafés are springing up fast and you'll see them (or internet facilities without the café) all over the city. One hour online typically costs under US$2. The main hotels (and some smaller ones) also offer internet access. Public business facilities generally close on Sundays.

Public telephones are to be found in shops and kiosks all over Kigali – they are metered, so you pay when you've finished and don't need handfuls of small change. Calls to mobile phones from these are more expensive than those to normal phones, although calls from mobile to mobile are cheaper. Rwanda is now said to have one of the most modern telephone systems in East Africa. You can get a 'starter pack' to convert most imported **mobiles** for use in Rwanda; these cost around US$25 and are available from MTN (Mobile Telephone Networks) shops – there's one in Avenue des Mille Collines opposite the Belgian School, another in Boulevard de la Révolution near the Sierra Restaurant, and various others around the city. Then it's a pay-as-you-go system: you buy cards to top up the balance in your account.

Shopping

Apart from the market area (see pages 119–20), the shops you're likely to use are in the 'square' formed by Boulevard de la Révolution, Avenue de Commerce, Avenue des Mille Collines and Rue de l'Epargne. Outside this area there's a good supermarket on the eastern side of Place de la Constitution, next to the petrol station that is opposite the ORTPN office; and the very good Ikirezi bookshop is on Avenue de la Paix but just westward of the 'square'.

In **Boulevard de la Révolution**, the large Banque Commerciale du Rwanda is on the eastern side, almost on Place de l'Indépendance (where the fountain is). Looking across the road from the bank you have, among other small shops/offices: the Poseidon Restaurant, a small supermarket, the Belvedere Restaurant, internet facilities, Sun City Pharmacy (open 24 hours), an MTN phone shop, an archway leading to Top Travel & Tours, the Sierra

Restaurant, the Banque Continentale Africaine Rwanda and a petrol station. Roughly opposite the petrol station and well barricaded is the US Embassy.

Turn right at the petrol station into Avenue des Mille Collines, then right again into **Avenue de la Paix**. On the opposite side of Avenue de la Paix before it reaches Avenue de Commerce you have (not necessarily in order) a florist, a bank, a forex bureau, various clothing and stationery shops, phone/internet facilities, various tour operators and travel agents, Fidodido ice creams, Café de la Fontaine and Dates Café-Resto.

Turn downwards into **Avenue de Commerce** (the Banque de Kigali is on the opposite corner); and on the left a little way down is the Caritas bookshop. Take the first left turn after it, into **Rue Kalisimbi** – on your right (opposite the Isimbi Hotel) is a good photographic shop (Fotolab; BP 155 Kigali; tel: 76508; web: www.aw7.com/fotolab), with a small dairy/milkbar and internet facilities just before it. (If you had continued downhill past the Kalisimbi turning, the next left would have taken you to the Belle Vie and New Modern guesthouses.)

Continue along Rue Kalisimbi passing the Isimbi Hotel and you come to the T-junction with **Avenue des Mille Collines**; there's a good supermarket opposite and to the right which has a useful range of groceries, fresh bread and pastries and (sometimes) good local honey. Turn left up Mille Collines; tour operators Primate Safaris and the Belgian School are on your right, with Changa Travel, Kenya Airways, other travel agencies, the Pharmacie Conseil (open seven days including 10.00–15.00 Sunday), an MTN phone shop and a florist opposite them on your left.

To complete your city-centre tour: go back to the junction of Avenue de la Paix and Avenue de Commerce. Go downhill but, instead of turning left into Rue Kalisimbi, turn right (also into Kalisimbi). On your right you'll come to the ASAR craft shop (see page 118). The next junction is with **Rue de l'Epargne**; if you turn left (downhill) you'll come to the market. Turn right (uphill) and you return to Avenue de la Paix, with the post office on your left at the top and the Terra Nova Restaurant (see page 107) on your right. Opposite the post office is a kiosk with a public phone; just beyond the kiosk is a craft shop/workshop which has some traditional musical instruments (bargain hard).

If you're ready for a snack or drink after your stroll, stay on the same side as the post office (keeping it on your left) and continue downhill to the Place de la Constitution – you'll see Amy's snack-bar ahead on your left.

Further information
If there's anything else you want to know, try ORTPN (below). They should have – or be able to get – most information you may need.

WHAT TO SEE AND DO IN KIGALI
Your first stop in Kigali should be ORTPN (Office Rwandais du Tourisme et des Parcs Nationaux), which is the Rwandan Tourist Office. It's in Boulevard de la Révolution where it joins Avenue de l'Armée: BP 905 Kigali; tel: 576514/5, 573396; fax: 576512; email: ortpn@rwanda1.com and info@rwandatourism.com. They should have information about all current

events and can advise you. Also they have street maps of Kigali and information about transport – minibus-taxis, car-hire and so forth.

The ORTPN office is where you buy permits to visit the national parks – you MUST do this before setting off for the park (or at the very least check with ORTPN whether you can do it on arrival at the park office), otherwise you risk being refused entry.

For a capital city, Kigali doesn't offer a great deal in terms of buildings, museums and historical/cultural sites – but it is a pleasant place for strolling and people-watching.

Museum of Kigali

This is under construction at the time of writing so may or may not be open by the time you visit Rwanda. It is located in the house formerly lived in by Richard Kandt, who first came to Africa in 1898 in search of the source of the Nile and later (1907–13) was the first and only *Kaiserliche Resident* (Imperial Resident) during German colonisation. In 1919 he wrote '*Caput Nili: ein empfindsame Reise zu den Quellen des Nils*'.

The house is not far from the prison; it's marked on the map of central Kigali. The Museum is a joint collaboration between the German Embassy in Kigali and *Coopération Française* (the French development agency). It's probable that the little geological museum, at present gathering dust in the premises of the Privatisation Secretariat, will be re-housed there.

Kigali Genocide Memorial

This has been constructed in the Gisozi area of Kigali and will open fully before the tenth anniversary of the genocide in April 2004 (so it's too early for complete details to be given here). You can see it across the valley – a large, white, modern building with terraces in front – on the right as you go downhill on Boulevard de Nyabugogo. To drive there is easy as it's in sight for much of the way – take a right turn halfway down Boulevard de Nyabugogo, continue downwards into the valley, when you're a little way past the memorial take a left turn across the valley, then (at a T-junction) go sharp left along a short dirt road and you'll come to the gate.

The Centre is already open but at present casual visitors are not accepted; you must obtain authorisation beforehand from the Office of Political and Good Governance, in Avenue de l'Armée, opposite St Michael's Cathedral, five to ten minutes' walk from the ORTPN office. Tel: 08567289.

A guide takes visitors around the memorial, telling the story and showing the skulls and bones of victims, as well as graves. The idea behind displaying bones in this and other genocide memorials is to prevent anyone, ever, from claiming 'there was no genocide in Rwanda'. There will be photos and information panels. The description in the box opposite is taken from an information leaflet currently available at the Memorial. The 'Aegis' mentioned in the box is the Aegis Trust, a non-sectarian, non-governmental organisation based in the Holocaust Centre, Nottingham, United Kingdom; web: www.aegistrust.org.

GISOZI GENOCIDE MEMORIAL AND EDUCATION CENTRE

There will be no humanity without forgiveness, there will be no forgiveness without justice, but justice will be impossible without humanity.

Yolande Mukagasana

Gisozi, in Kigali, is the burial site of over 250,000 people killed in a three-month period during Rwanda's 1994 genocide. Nine years later, victims are still being located in and around Kigali as new evidence emerges from trials of those accused of genocide. They are taken to Gisozi as their final resting place.

Founded by the mayor of Kigali, the memorial building at Gisozi was designed by a local architect. So far, the construction undertaken here has been financed largely from Kigali City Council Revenue. This means that the citizens of one of the world's poorest countries pay through their taxes to give dignity to their murdered families, whom the rest of the world abandoned.

The international community failed Rwanda. It could have prevented the loss of a million men, women and children, but the United Nations viewed the killings as an internal matter and pulled out. Now that a million people have been murdered, we need to learn how and why such tragedies happen, in order to prevent them in the future.

The UK Holocaust Centre has been invited by the Kigali City Council to work with its sister organisation Aegis, and survivors, to help complete the site by telling the story of the genocide in this building. It will assist Gisozi to function as an education centre, planned to open officially in April 2004.

The challenge facing Rwanda and the Great Lakes region is how to build a society free from the threat of dangerous ideology. Building stability starts by acknowledging the truth. Providing survivors with a place where their voice can be heard will strengthen efforts towards unity. Schoolchildren will come to Gisozi and learn about the consequences of hatred and division. The environment of Gisozi will not accuse, but rather challenge.

Adapted from a leaflet produced by Aegis Rwanda, PO Box 7251 Kigali; tel: 08567289.

Arts and entertainments

Kigali has a brand-new cinema, in the Kigali Business Centre in Avenue du Lac Muhazi. There are afternoon performances ($1) and evening performances ($2) of international movies (often in English with French subtitles), children's performances, special screenings, etc. With the Planet Cinéma Restaurant and club in the same block, a long and full evening of entertainment is possible!

Performances of traditional dancing and music take place from time to time in various venues around the city – these are publicised on local radio and in the local press. ORTPN should also have a list.

CAURWA (Communauté des Autochtones Rwandais, see pages 77–8) will arrange performances of traditional Batwa dances and take you to their pottery workshops by request. The dance is a lively affair lasting over two hours, full of colour and energy, in a covered marquee – a donation of US$10 per person is requested. For details and to arrange this, email projetbus@yahoo.fr or phone mobile 08689551; or contact the CAURWA office in Kigali on email: caurwa@rwandatel1.com; tel: 577640.

The Centre Culturel d'Echanges Franco-Rwandaises (tel: 576223), not far from the Hotel des Mille Collines, has a small theatre and presents a variety of cultural events – theatre, films, music, dance and so on. Call in to ask them for their current monthly programme or else check with ORTPN. The Centre Culturel can be a useful source of other information too, as they have a comprehensive library (see page 116).

CRICKET IN RWANDA
Chris Frean

Believe it or not, cricket is played in Rwanda. This may come as a surprise. The usual ingredients are lacking: years of contact with Britain and the games we play; sufficient sport-deprived British people; an unused area of flat ground for playing; equipment; funding; and so on.

Yet the Rwanda Cricket Association, led by law student Charles Haba, is alive and kicking, and students at the NUR in Butare play; the Asian community in Kigali can field three teams; and the British Community Team is always on the lookout for players and tourists are welcome to join in for a game. The venue is the Kicukiro Secondary School in Kigali, and matches happen on Saturdays and Sundays over 20 or 25 overs, usually all year, regardless of the rainy season.

Cricket has been played for several years in Rwanda. There was actually a match on a volcanic field in Gisenyi in the last century. In 2003 the RCA managed to get the ground at Kicukiro Secondary School into a good enough condition, and on June 14 2003 a match was played between a Queen's XI and the RCA. Players came from the University, the Indorwanda team and the Kigali Cricket Club's two elevens. The International Cricket Council's East Africa Development Officer, former Kenyan international Tom Tikolo, came over from Nairobi and the Rwandan Government's Director of Sports from the Ministry of Youth, Culture & Sport attended. Sponsors from FedEx, Akagera Motors, Sulfo and Faruki adorned the ground with their banners, and a crowd of 50 or so

Sport

Kigali caters for both golfers and cricketers! For **cricket**, see the box below. The 18-hole **Nyarutarama Golf Club** is in an attractively green corner of northeastern Kigali; the cost of a round is US$15 for non-members. For details phone 08524619 (or contact the club at PO Box 4762 Kigali). The **Cercle Sportif** in Lower Kiyovu has facilities for tennis, table tennis, basketball, volleyball, badminton, darts, swimming, etc. Also check out the current **football** fixtures – Rwanda's team is doing brilliantly just now (see box on pages 22–3) so you could be in for a treat!

Enthusiast Chris Frean explains:

> Going to a football match in Kigali is simple as long as you know that it's on. Fixtures are generally mentioned in advance on local radio – not much help unless you understand Kinyarwanda – so the simplest way is either to ask a fan (and there are many) or else to see whether there are matatu-loads of fans heading to Kisementi crossroads on Saturday and Sunday afternoons at around 3pm.
>
> The Amahoro Stadium, the venue for any big match, is situated a couple of minutes' walk from Kisementi, just off the airport road east

came to watch, later growing to a couple of hundred of intrigued Rwandans – and they are the target for the future.

We chose to play the game over 20 overs a side to coincide with the launch of Twenty20 cricket in England and the ball dominated as is the case generally in Rwandan cricket at the moment. The RCA were asked to bat and scored 63 all out off 18.2 overs; the Queen's XI made 64–6 with a few overs to spare. There were no injuries, with all batsmen wearing helmets. In the past few weeks one player has suffered a broken nose and others have been struck on the arm or head by fast balls. No holds are barred, the game is for real!

This game was not a one-off and we hope to arrange more. Indorwanda and KCC play each weekend anyway. Their players, with years of experience and regular playing, are certainly the best players at present, but the University boys, under Professor Singh, are anxious to improve, and have some impressive bowlers.

The ICC – to which the RCA has applied for membership – have set the RCA targets of getting an under-15 team to a regional tournament in Dar es Salaam in December 2003 and of getting cricket into schools as a game for boys and girls. And the long-term aim is catch up with Uganda. They are currently rated 20th in the ICC rankings.

Details of upcoming matches can be obtained from (where else!) the British Embassy in Kigali (tel: 85771, 585281/4), where the Fedex Cup is at present on display, at least until June 2004. And taking part is the name of the game. The author of this piece filled the No 11 spot for the house team at school (top score: 2*). I did not bowl either!

of the city centre. Most of the ground is inexpensive terracing, with the expensive sector being the comfy chairs in the main stand – the 'Tribune d'Honneur', which cost about US$4.

Don't expect other European things like a match programme, or introductions of players, or an operating scoreboard, or any serious regard for kicking-off on time, whatever the ticket details may say. But compared with some African football grounds, where one needs to negotiate a disorganised mob just to get in, the Rwandan football fan is a fairly reserved sort, and all is calm and well organised. Children sell (genuine) tickets outside the ground. There is a car park. Drinks are sold in the main stand. People respect national anthems.

Libraries and bookshops

Depending on how soon you visit, Kigali may have its own, brand-new, specially designed public library, built with funds raised both nationally and internationally. See pages 82–3 for more details. In connection with fundraising for the library, secondhand book sales are held regularly in Kigali – dates are generally on the noticeboard in the Ikirezi bookshop (below).

The Centre Culturel d'Echanges Franco-Rwandaises (see above) has three lending libraries: for adults, for children and for scientific research. Much of the material is in French at present. There's also a reading room.

Two good bookshops in Kigali, both of them stocking a wide range of books on the history and culture of Rwanda, the background to the genocide and an assortment of other relevant themes, are the Librairie Caritas (BP 1078 Kigali; tel: 576503; email: librcar@rwanda1.com) in Rue de Commerce just downhill from its junction with Avenue de la Paix, and the Librairie Ikirezi (BP 443 Kigali; tel: 570298; tel/fax: 571314; email: ikirezi@rwanda1.com) in Avenue de la Paix. The Ikirezi, which sometimes holds book-signings and other events, is open 09.00–12.30 and 14.00–18.00 (closes at 13.00 on Saturday) as well as 10.30–13.00 on Sunday; while Caritas keeps normal shop hours.

Finally, there's a row of secondhand bookstalls at the end of Avenue de Commerce as it joins the Place de l'Unité Nationale. The range (in Kinyarwanda, French and English) is huge and you can pick up bargains; I spotted an out-of-print book by historian Alexis Kagame at far below its internet price, not to mention a much reduced (and much thumbed) copy of *Rwanda: The Bradt Travel Guide*!

Handicrafts

A wide range of handicrafts are sold in Kigali and there's great scope for browsing.

If pottery interests you, you can visit a Twa pottery workshop and watch the pots being made – arrange this through CAURWA (see pages 77–8). A container selling Twa pottery is also set among the wood-carving stands on Avenue de l'Armée (below). Also a selection of their pots, some with plants inside, are laid out on the pavement near the bottom of Avenue du Roi Baudouin – keep walking downhill from the Hotel des Mille Collines. (Taxis generally cruise this area if you don't want to walk back up the steepish hill.)

For wood-carvings of all sorts, stroll along Avenue de l'Armée between ORTPN and the traffic lights at the junction with Avenue du Roi Baudouin; a treasure-trove of items is laid out on the pavement. The quality is variable – at best, very good indeed, but some is substandard – so check the

TOURISM AND LOCALLY MADE CRAFTS
Patrick S

The prospects for tourism in Rwanda lie mainly in the safe haven offered to the remaining mountain gorillas in our Volcanoes National Park, other various flora and fauna in the Akagera National Park and Nyungwe Forest, and physical features like the volcanoes on our border with the DRC, the Rusumo Falls in southern Rwanda, etc.

But the Rwandan people also have an important part to play. Among other talents, we are skilled at carving, sculpture and weaving. Most of this is done by the ordinary Rwandan. Weaving is particular to women and girls while wood-carving is done mostly by men.

Most importantly, the work is created according to various themes: mother nature, beauty, achievement and virtues such as valour etc, as well as everyday scenes. A woman carrying a baby on her back, a pot of milk on her head and a bundle of firewood under her arm is a common sight around here. An old man sitting on a traditional stool with a long straw dipped in a pot is also familiar.

However, it is sad when in some cases such talent is wasted through poor sales, bad storage and poor preservation. Many pieces are sold on roadsides where they gather so much dust, washed away by rains, that even an occasional tourist who passes by can hardly notice their beauty!

A lot can be done to keep this heritage alive through publicity abroad: Rwandan embassies setting up sales-points for such goods, modest though they may be, and interested individuals taking it upon themselves to sell Rwandan handicrafts for the good of it. But most of all, local government can help by giving assistance to these craftspeople and tourists can help by purchasing their products.

The price of such items is quite small and affordable. Avenue de l'Armée near our Tourism Board (ORTPN) in Kigali is one place to find them on display. Even at the Kigali International Airport there is a stall, and another near the Rwanda Revenue Authority offices. Also independent vendors display and sell their wares in the street.

Come and buy 'at your eye's pleasure'! And help to promote traditional craftsmanship in Rwanda as you explore the beauties of our Republic of a Thousand Hills.

workmanship carefully and be prepared to bargain. (But, if something has been beautifully made, consider the value of such artistry and expertise.) Here you'll see traditional carvings – adaptations or originals of genuine household objects – alongside items of no former or current practical value which have probably evolved for the tourist market. There are some traditional musical instruments on sale here too.

Weaving is one of the specialities of Rwanda – baskets, mats, hangings and pots appear in a variety of shapes and sizes, with carefully interwoven traditional patterns. They are sold by some street vendors, and there's a good selection (including woven hammocks) in the craft shop called ASAR (Association des Artistes Rwandais) in Rue Karisimbi; BP 939 Kigali; tel: 571139. This is an excellent little shop, combining the work of several craft-making co-ops; some items are very touristy but others are traditional and all make good gifts. As well as the weaving there are carvings, musical instruments, pottery, beadwork, palm-leaf crafts (including decorated notepaper and cards) and even stuffed toys. Prices are marked, so you needn't worry about bargaining – but a reduction for quantity would be legitimate.

You'll also find street vendors selling most kinds of small handicrafts – carvings, jewellery, woven baskets, masks, musical instruments, notepaper and postcards decorated with palm fibres – and so on. Handicrafts outlets are expanding and becoming more organised; so ask at ORTPN for details of any good new sources, or workshops that can be visited by tourists.

Markets

In all market areas, TAKE CARE – crowds are popular with pickpockets and opportunistic thieves, and there have been instances of crime. Also be tactful about taking photos; for every dozen people who don't object to being in a picture, there'll be someone who does. Respect their privacy.

The main market area, off and around the Avenue de Commerce, is a cramped, busy area of trestles, stalls and small shops. Just about everything you could want is on sale there, from shiny household gadgets to chunks of fresh honeycomb. There are stacks of mattresses in floral cotton covers; roughly made wooden furniture; ancient, dented kitchen utensils being recycled; clothing imported from far-off countries; cassettes blaring out of ghetto-blasters; eggs teetering precariously on shaky tables; rows of multicoloured vegetables with their damp, earthy smell; footwear; shiny watches; creamy candles made of local beeswax; chunky farm cheeses; tools, cushions, mirrors… And that's only a beginning.

In Avenue de Commerce near the central bus station (turn left as you leave the bus station) there's a good pavement market on Sundays: a wide assortment of goods laid out along the pavement so that shoppers have to step over and among them as they select. (If you're in this area – but not at weekends – look out for the men with elderly, battered typewriters who sit at tables on the pavement at the western side of Place de la Constitution, ready to type letters to order. They make a refreshing change from cyber cafés!)

Probably the most frenetic market is the one across the road from the

Nyabugogo minibus-taxi stand, at the bottom of Rue du Lac Hago. It's like a human kaleidoscope – a changing, shifting mass of colours and noise. A few minutes being jostled by these brisk crowds, determinedly going about their own business, may be enough for you – but it's a typical and non-touristy experience which it would be a pity to miss completely. See the *Walk to Nyabugogo* below.

Strolling round Kigali

If you don't mind the unavoidable hills, Kigali offers some good strolls. There are plenty of places where you can stop for a snack or a drink if you need to cool off. Two walks which could each fill up a morning, depending on how often you stop en route, are given below; but just look at a map of the whole city and you'll see that there are plenty more.

To the mosque and Nyamirambo district

One way of getting to the big mosque in the Muslim quarter is to walk southwards along Avenue de la Justice, with views out across the valley to your right; the mosque is at the junction where Rue de la Sécurité joins from the left. Continue for a few minutes and you're in a lively, busy district (Nyamirambo) of small streets and colourful little local shops. The atmosphere has a touch of London's Soho about it. This is said to be the part of the present-day city where people first settled, long ago. There's a lot of small-scale activity going on here, and small bar/cafés where you can stop for a drink.

To return to the centre, you can either catch a minibus-taxi (they serve Avenue de la Justice; look out for the yellow signs indicating bus stops) or flag down a taxi. (A short stretch of Avenue de la Justice is one-way and minibuses only travel outward from the centre; to get one going get back you'll need to be in the two-way part.) Or else retrace your steps towards the mosque and look out for Avenue Paul VI on your right – follow this upwards and it'll bring you on to the area covered by the map on page 97. Or – be adventurous and find your own variations!

To Nyabugogo market

This takes you through an area of many small shops and market stalls, finishing at the busy market opposite Nyabugogo minibus-taxi stand. If you can cope with seething crowds and a lot of jostling, try it (but don't take photos without the permission of the subjects).

Walk down Rue de l'Epargne or along Avenue de la Justice until you come to the prison. As you face it from the road, the first road beside it to your right, turning off at a sharpish angle, is Rue du Mont Huye, an unsurfaced road running downhill. Take this and follow it – you'll pass homes, small shops, an enclosed market area off it to your right, and then you arrive at the bottom – and the chaos of Nyabugogo market. Just look at the variety of people here – you'll see so many different bone structures, shades of colour, styles of clothing…

If you cross over into the minibus-taxi station (which is a 'market area' all of its own, with vendors offering everything from leather shoes and hi-fi equipment to – improbably – plastic hair curlers and freshly baked bread) you can get a minibus-taxi back to the central minibus station or else take a normal taxi; they park just inside the main gate. Or turn right up the main road as you leave the market; this upward hill is Boulevard de Nyabugogo and will take you back to Place de l'Unité Nationale and the centre of town.

EXCURSIONS FROM KIGALI
Via tour operators

All of the tour operators listed below can organise excursions for you and/or arrange vehicle hire. All have some English-speaking staff, and can book accommodation for you, collect you from the airport, arrange permits for gorilla-viewing, and so forth. In addition there are several more travel agents, who can deal with national and international travel but don't necessarily obtain gorilla permits (which are issued by ORTPN).

It is claimed that there are over 230 sites of historic or cultural interest in Rwanda (no-one has yet listed them all to me!) so you shouldn't be stuck for choice. If you're phoning from abroad, remember that the international code for Rwanda is 250. There are no regional codes in Rwanda.

Some tour operators in Kigali

One of the newest (opened since the last edition of this guide) is **Primate Safaris** (Avenue des Mille Collines next to the Belgian School; BP 158 Kigali;

tel: 511718; mobile: 08520106 and 08520103; email: primate_safaris@yahoo.com; web: www.primatesafaris.com). Very experienced operators with comfortable vehicles, they offer a full range of national and international services. In the shopping plaza opposite Primate Safaris is the **Changa Travel Agency** (tel: 577564; fax: 577669; email: changatravel@hotmail.com).

The well-established **Volcanoes Safaris** are also listed under international operators (page 28); they run regular gorilla trips and their new camp near the Volcanoes National Park (page 176) has one of the best views in Rwanda. Their Kigali office is at Hotel des Mille Collines; tel: 502452, 576530; email: salesrw@volcanoessafaris.com; web: www.volcanoessafaris.com.

In the SORAS building, on the left-hand side of Boulevard de la Révolution as you walk along from the town centre towards the new InterContinental Hotel, you'll find two agencies: **Concord Rwanda** (tel: 575988; email: info@magic-safaris.com; web: www.magic-safaris.com – they are knowledgeable about trekking in the Virungas and **International Tours & Travel** (BP 924 Kigali; tel: 57057, 578831/2; fax: 575582; email: itt@rwanda1.com).

In Avenue de la Paix there is **Swift Tours & Travel** (tel: 577472, 577074; fax: 577070; email: swift_tours@yahoo.co.uk); **Kiboko Tours & Travel** (see advertisement opposite; **Nord-Sud International Travel & Tours** (tel: 575310; fax: 575349; email: nordsudinternational@yahoo.fr); and (on the corner at the top of Avenue de Commerce) **Satguru Tours & Travel** (tel: 573079, 572643; fax: 572231; email: satguru@rwandatel1.rwanda1.com).

In Boulevard de la Révolution (set back from the road in a small courtyard near the 24-hour pharmacy) is **Top Travel Tours** (BP 10 Kigali; tel: 578646, 572552; fax: 573853; email: bernaku63@hotmail.com). Next door to the Gloria Hotel (by the traffic lights in Avenue de Commerce) is **Cité Travel & Tours Services** (tel: 577887, 571278; fax: 511138; email: cite@rwanda1.com).

A complete list would be far too long, so you will come across others that I haven't listed. Their non-inclusion doesn't mean there's anything wrong with them, so by all means give them a go – and send in recommendations for the next edition!

Independent visits
Public minibus-taxis
Most places in Rwanda are easily accessible by public minibus-taxi, leaving from the Nyabugogo minibus-taxi station (*gare routière Nyabugogo*) about 2km from the centre of Kigali. It's a huge place and they are lined up in ranks – some signposted with destinations and others not – but just ask someone and you'll be shown the right place to wait. The minibuses leave as soon as they've a full complement of passengers – and that does mean *full* as in can of sardines – but everyone gets a seat. There's a non-smoking policy on board. Fares are collected just before you alight rather than when you board; you'll see other passengers getting their money ready as their destinations approach. If you're not sure of the fare (it's helpful to offer the correct money) ask anyone what you should be paying. Fares are much the same as those of the Taxis de la

Poste, shown below. If you're carrying luggage, either (if it's small enough) keep it on your lap or else ask for it to be stuffed in at the back or put on the roof. If you have anything fragile, keep it with you.

If you're returning to Kigali the same day, don't leave it too late, as there's no set schedule; it's sensible to ask the driver for an estimate of the time of the last minibus, and to be there well before it's due to depart.

While you're waiting for your minibus to leave, vendors of all sorts will be trying to catch your eye and sell you something – including bottled drinks and fruit, as well as fresh bread and cakes, which are handy if you've a long journey ahead. You can even buy hard-boiled eggs, and season them from the salt and pepper pots conveniently provided!

Minibus-taxis to the Nyabugogo station leave from the central minibus station at the junction of Avenue de Commerce and Rue Mont Kabuye. Or take a *taxi-voiture*.

Private minibus-taxis

Many companies run these – Okapicar, Volcano Express, T2000, de la Poste, Rwanda Express, Stella, Atraco, etc – and they come and go, so there'll be new names by the time you read this. Some have offices near the central minibus station, others in Place de la Constitution. Ask around. The costs below (reasonably representative, and cheaper than some) relate to the Taxis de la Poste, which start from the central post office.

- Byumba, Kibuye and Kibungo: US$2
- Gisenyi and Nyagatare: US$2.50
- Cyangugu/Kamembe: US$5

Government-run buses

These rather smart vehicles – previously yellow but now being replaced by brand-new white ones – come under the government department Onatracom. They rattle about to all parts of Rwanda, including some rough roads which must tax their springs severely. You may see them parked in Nyamirambo, near the mosque, but that's not where you catch them; they leave from the Nyabugogo minibus station, which is where you can get current details of their timetable and destinations.

National parks

Akagera Park (see *Chapter 9*) can be visited from Kigali in a day but you'll need your own transport for a very early start. The mountain gorillas in the **Volcanoes Park** can also be visited as a day trip – but again you'll need your own transport (which any of the tour operators listed above can organise) in order to get to the park entrance by 07.30, otherwise you should spend the previous night in either Ruhengeri or Kinigi and arrange transport from there. ORTPN may be able to advise you on this when you buy your permit. See *Chapter 8*. The **Nyungwe Forest** is too far for a day trip, but minibus-taxis running between Butare and Cyangugu can drop you off nearby and you can either camp or stay overnight in the ORTPN Guesthouse – see *Chapter 7*.

Butare

Butare and the National Museum (see *Chapter* 7) are an easy day trip from Kigali, by either public or private minibus-taxi. A private operator with smart new vehicles is Volcano Express, whose office is near the central minibus station. If you go by public minibus-taxi, you can ask to be dropped at either the museum or the centre of town; to return to Kigali, you must start from the minibus-taxi station on the northern edge of town (see map on page 133). The private companies stop and start in the centre of Butare but should drop you off at the museum if you ask.

Kibuye

If you leave early and check the return times, you should be able to visit the attractive little lakeside town of Kibuye (see pages 159–63) and get back the same day, now that the very good road from Kigali has been completed. If you do, then be sure to visit the memorial church there – a beautiful, peaceful place very different from the two genocide memorials listed below and, for me, far more poignant.

Genocide memorials

There are two memorials to the south of Kigali, both accessible as a day trip. The church at Nyamata, about 30km from Kigali, was the scene of a horrific massacre. The interior has been cleared and left empty; there are still some bloodstains on the walls; and, in the courtyard outside, an underground chamber has been dug in which are stored – and displayed – the skulls and bones of many hundreds of victims. Visitors can see them and be reminded of the enormity of the crime. A guide will take you round and explain the background – and ask you to sign the visitors' book, in which you may spot some internationally known names.

Ntarama church, about 5km down a right-hand fork which branches off the Nyamata road roughly 20km outside Kigali (so you can visit both of them on the same drive), has been left empty and just as it was after the bodies had been removed – there are scraps of cloth and personal items still on the floor. Beside it is another building where more people, seeking safety, were slaughtered. It's a silent place, surrounded by trees: very evocative, very poignant. The guide (French-speaking) recounts the events precisely – and powerfully. A sign outside the gate records that around 5,000 victims died there.

Both memorials are grim, Nyamata more so than Ntarama because of the bones and skulls, and both convey the appalling scale of the tragedy. There's no charge for entry to the sites and the guides do their job with dignity – a tip is expected and deserved.

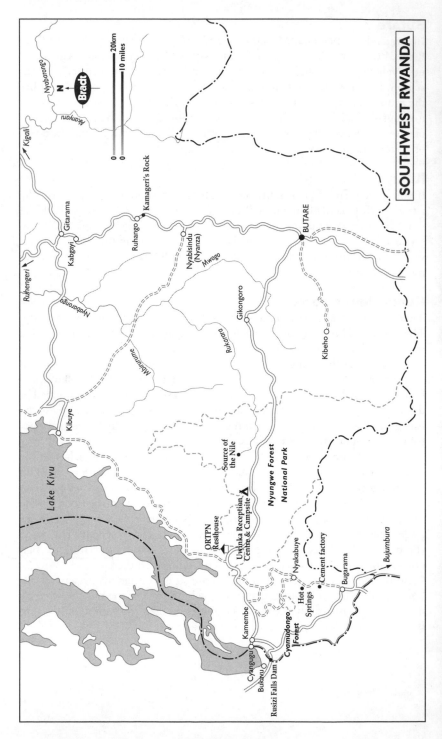

Southwest Rwanda

The mountainous southwest of Rwanda boasts a variety of different tourist attractions, among consistently memorable montane scenery.

Coming from the capital, the first regional highlight is Butare, the country's second city, and its cultural and intellectual heart. Butare is the site of the National University, as well as the fine National Museum – rated by many to house the best ethnographic collection in East Africa – and within easy day-tripping distance of the well-maintained traditional Royal Palace at Nyanza.

To the west of Butare lies the Nyungwe Forest, a 970km² expanse of Afro-montane rainforest which sprawls magnificently across the mountains that stretch towards the Burundi border. A magnet for botanists and ornithologists alike, Nyungwe is best known for the volume and variety of its primates – 13 species in all, including chimpanzee, l'Hoest's monkey and troops of 400-plus Ruwenzori colobus. Nyungwe is the most accessible of Rwanda's reserves, easily reached on public transport, while facilities include a comfortable resthouse and campsite, and an excellent network of day trails.

Other attractions in this part of Rwanda include the attractive Lake Kivu ports of Cyangugu and Kibuye, both with a good selection of hotels, and the more remote Bugarama Hot Springs and Cyamudongo Forest.

Main roads through this part of Rwanda are surfaced and covered by plenty of minibus-taxis, and in some cases buses. A good selection of mid-range and budget accommodation is available in all main centres. Altitudes range from 1,500m on the shore of Lake Kivu to a peak of 2,950m in Nyungwe; the climate is comfortably warm by day, but can be chilly at night, so take enough warm clothing.

THE ROAD FROM KIGALI TO BUTARE
Gitarama
This small and scattered town 51km from Kigali, where the road forks south to Butare and continues westward towards Lake Kivu, has often been involved in Rwanda's recent history. It is famous as the location of the historic gathering on January 28 1961 at which the people first declared Rwanda a republic (see page 14), and is also remembered as the birthplace of Grégoire Kayibanda, Rwanda's first president. Earlier, in November 1959, it was probably the

starting point for the violence that led to the imposition of martial law under Colonel Guy Logiest (see page 14).

Opposite the taxi-minibus stand in the centre of Gitarama is the helpful Banque de Kigali, a handful of small shops, and the bar/restaurants Tranquillité and Le Palmier. **Tranquilleté** is a super little place, approached via an alley with clothing hanging up for sale. It consists of a cheerful courtyard, with assorted shapes and sizes of tables; a handful of energetic waitresses serving customers really briskly (a rare thing outside of Kigali – and even inside it); and a blackboard with the dishes of the day chalked on it. The food is simple (meat, fish or chicken with chips/salad, fresh fruit for dessert) but good, and cheap. Locals have realised how good it is and it does get busy at lunchtime. The post office is about 1km away: turn right as you leave the minibus stand and keep straight on; you'll come to it on the left just after the Rwanda Revenue Authority. There are motorbike-taxis at the minibus stand – but you won't be given a helmet, so be sure that your insurance includes this form of transport. Really there's little to see here, except people, going about their daily lives, which can be a change from more intensive tourism.

Minibus-taxis pass through Gitarama en route from Kigali to either Kibuye or Butare and, if you want to break your journey, simple accommodation is available. Just outside the town and signposted on the left as you come from Kigali is the newish **Hotel Tourisme et Sports** (tel: 56269): 13 en-suite doubles with hot water, US$20 single and US$25 double. It's a pleasant, peaceful place and serves evening meals by request. In the centre of Gitarama there are two options, all small, simple and friendly: **Le Palmier** (tel: 562183), across the road from the minibus stand, has two en-suite rooms (US$13) and two with shared facilities (US$8–10). Turn right as you leave the bus station and you'll come (on your right) to the **Gloria Hotel** (tel: 562234), with some en-suite rooms (US$10) and others with shared facilities (US$8).

Heading out of Gitarama on the Butare road you pass a small and basic guesthouse – **La Planète du Centre** (tel: 562905). It has 20 rooms, only two of them en-suite and the others sharing facilities (cold water), from US$6 to US$12. On the Kibuye road the **Concord Hotel** (tel: 562720) has seven rooms, US$6 single/$10 double with shared facilities. There's no restaurant but they'll do breakfast. It's set back from the road so quieter than the Planète – except, when I was there, for an extremely vocal goat tethered nearby.

Kabgayi

The massive cathedral of Kabgayi, 3km from Gitarama along the Butare road, is the oldest in the country, dating from 1925; missionaries were already installed in Kabgayi by 1906 and it became the seat of the first Catholic bishop. The cathedral, with its huge and tranquil interior, is worth a visit, and there's a small museum nearby. Children may spot you and come to sell handicrafts. During colonisation various training schools were set up in Kabgayi – for midwives, artisans, printers, carpenters and blacksmiths, among others.

Kabgayi Church Museum

The little museum beside the cathedral opens Monday to Friday 08.00 to 17.00. Saturday and Sunday visits are also possible if booked in advance. Entry costs around U\$2.50. Within the very small interior are many historically and culturally interesting items such as:

- Ancient hand tools and weapons: knives, hoes, spears, arrows, etc
- Tools and implements connected with the iron industry
- Ancient examples of clothing: bark cloth etc
- Musical instruments
- Methods of transportation used for chiefs, high-born women and the sick
- Clay pots and pipes
- Baskets – ornamental and for domestic use
- The prestigious Milk Bar and jugs from the palace of the last queen mother (1961)

KAMAGERI'S ROCK: A traditional tale retold

It happened during the reign of Mwami Mibambwe II Sekarongoro II Gisanura, who ruled Rwanda almost four centuries ago. He was a fair and just ruler. Among other innovations, he required his chiefs to bring jars of milk from their own cows to the court – and these were then distributed to the poor and needy, three times a day: morning, noon and evening.

One day, so the story goes, a man was convicted of stealing from the Mwami, who then asked two of his chiefs to devise a suitable punishment. It seems that they saw this as an opportunity to impress the Mwami with their thoroughness.

The chief named Mikoranya suggested an instrument of torture based on a shaft of wood extending from a hut; while the chief named Kamageri proposed to the Mwami that a large, flat rock near Gitarama be heated until red-hot and the criminal be spread-eagled across it.

The Mwami asked the chiefs to demonstrate their ideas, so that he could understand what they proposed. Eagerly they set to work.

When the rock was glowing red-hot (it took a week of brushwood fires to achieve this) and the torture implement was prepared, the Mwami arrived with his retinue. 'Is everything ready?' he asked Kamageri and Mikoranya, and they nodded proudly, expecting praise and possibly some reward.

The Mwami called forward his guards, to whom he had already explained what would happen. 'Take them,' he ordered. 'And subject them to their own punishments! Let Kamageri roast on his rock and Mikoranya suffer his own torture. They were too cruel. There is no place for these men in my kingdom.'

The rock where Kamageri supposedly roasted to death can still be seen, at Ruhango on the Gitarama–Butare road. Tourists stop to photograph it and guides recount various versions of the story.

- Old indoor games such as igisoro which is still popular in Rwanda and neighbouring countries
- Ancient military officers' costumes and pips
- A national drum captured from Ijwi Island (Kivu) in 1875, thereby effectively annexing it to Rwanda
- Information about traditional medicines, and tokens (kwe) formerly used as currency
- Modern clothing and historical photographs

In the complex of associated buildings behind the cathedral in Kabgayi there's the large **Centre St André** (tel: 562450), with 82 guestrooms of various categories – single, double, triple, en suite, shared facilities and so on. The most you'll pay is about US$10 per person, but it can fill up if there's a religious convocation, so book in advance.

Ruhango

This small town is of interest primarily for *Uratare rwa Kamageri* (Kamageri's Rock), signposted by the roadside a ten-minute walk south of the town centre. See box on page 127.

Ruhango also boasts one of the largest markets in the country, which takes place on Friday mornings and contains an astonishing range of merchandise, from livestock and vegetables to hi-fi equipment and household goods. Vendors trek in from far afield, carrying their wares. You could consider spending a Thursday night here and then watching activities unfold. Ruhango has a few restaurants and supermarkets, as well as the sensibly priced **Hotel Umuco** (tel: 560017). Centrally located, and arranged around a pleasant courtyard, this nine-room hotel offers singles for US$7 and doubles with en-suite showers for US$10, as well as inexpensive meals and drinks. The newer **Pacis Hotel** (tel: 560121) has six doubles with shared facilities at US$8.

Nyanza

The turning to Nyanza is on the right as you travel southwards. *Nyanza* is the ancient name, although it's still used; on the signpost you will see the town's modern name, Nyabisindu.

Some minibus-taxis go into the town centre while others will drop you at the junction. This little town with its wide, dusty streets has almost a Wild West feeling to it. If you want to stop for a drink or a meal on your way to the King's Palace, there are several local places serving good Rwandan *mélanges* for not much more than US$1; but a smarter (and quieter) place is the new **Club Tropicana** which has a good range of (more expensive) food and drinks. It also has a public (international) phone and I guess will develop its services – it had only been open three months when I checked it out. As you head for the palace you pass right by (it's on the right) and can't miss it.

The King's Palace

This is the top touristic reason for visiting Nyanza. It's several kilometres from the centre, and signposted. The traditional ancient palace of the Mwami has

HOLLYWOOD COMES TO NYANZA
Rosamond Halsey Carr

My introduction to the Mwami and his royal court was in 1956, when the Hollywood film *King Solomon's Mines* was shown to the king and queen and the royal courtiers. The movie, which was partially filmed on location in Ruanda and starred Stewart Granger and Deborah Kerr, contains some of the most authentic African dance sequences on film, including a dazzling depiction of the dance of the Intore.

The showing had been arranged by the American consulate in Léopoldville and took place in the royal city of Nyanza. Many of the European residents of Ruanda were invited, myself included. The Mwami and his queen, their courtiers, and the Tutsi nobles who took part in the film were all present. It was a mild, clear night, charged with an air of excitement and wonder. A large screen was erected in the middle of a wide dirt road. On one side of the screen, chairs had been set up for the invited guests. On the other side (the back side), a huge crowd of Banyaruanda sat with expectant faces waiting for the movie to begin.

The king and his entourage made a ceremonial entrance. One would be hard-pressed to find a more majestic figure than this giant of a monarch who could trace his family dynasty back more than four hundred years. Rudahigwa and his courtiers were dressed in traditional white robes with flowing togas knotted at their shoulders, and his queen, Rosalie Gicanda, was wrapped in billowing layers of pale pink...

...The soundtrack for the film was in English and, as a result, the Africans were unable to understand the dialogue. Restlessness and murmurs of disappointment rippled through the crowd until the action sequences progressed to the familiar landscape of Ruanda. From that point on, the spectators provided their own soundtrack with cheers and improvised dialogue, as they followed the safari adventure across the desert to the royal city of Nyanza, shouting with glee each time they recognised friends – and in some instances themselves – on the big movie screen.

The city of Nyanza was almost entirely devoid of Western influence, as the Belgian administration had refrained from intruding upon the royal seat of the Tutsi monarchy. There were no hotels, and outside visitors were discouraged. When the movie ended, the Mwami and his entourage and most of the invited guests assembled at the one small restaurant in town for sandwiches and drinks.

From: Land of a Thousand Hills: My Life in Rwanda *by Rosamond Halsey Carr with Ann Howard Halsey. Viking, 1999. See Appendix 3, page 241.*

been reconstructed, together with some other buildings, 3–4km away from its original site, beside the newer *mwami's* palace (built for the Mwami Rudahigwa Mutara III in 1932) which is now the part-time home of Rwanda's National Ballet (the Intore dancers, see pages 75–6). In olden times, Nyanza was the heart of Rwanda and seat of its monarchy, background to the oral tradition of battles and conquests, power struggles and royal intrigues. It is where the German colonisers came, at the end of the 19th century, to visit the *mwami* – and contemporary reports tell of the great pomp and ceremony these visits occasioned, as well as the impressive size of the *mwami's* court.

> The capital of the kingdom was composed of a group of huts, an ephemeral town of some 2,000 inhabitants, well organised as far as the administration of the country and the comfort of the nobility were concerned… At his court the Mwami maintained the following retinue: the 'Ntore', adolescent sons of chiefs and notables, who formed the corps de ballet; the 'Bakoma', soothsayers, magicians and historians; the 'Abashashi', keepers of the arsenal, the wardrobe and the furniture; the 'Abasisi' and 'Abacurabgenge', mimes, musicians and cooks; the 'Abanyabyumba', palanquin bearers and night watchmen; the 'Nitalindwa', huntsmen and runners; the 'Intumwa', artisans working for the Mwami; and finally the hangmen, attentive servants of jurists, ever ready to respond to the brief order to fetch and kill.

Traveller's Guide to the Belgian Congo and Ruanda-Urundi,
Tourist Bureau for the Belgian Congo and Ruanda-Urundi, Brussels, 1951

The traditional palace has been carefully reconstructed and maintained, and contains the king's massive bed as well as various utensils. The guide relates the history and traditions of the royal court – there is even significance to some of the poles supporting the roof; for example, the one at the entrance to the king's bed is named 'do not speak of what happens here' and another conferred sanctuary on anyone touching it. Often the guides here don't speak French or English – they may be from the Intore dance troupe or have some other connection with the palace – so you'll need a Kinyarwanda speaker with you.

The newer palace is – at last – being restored to its former beauty. A 1951 report states: 'In certain circumstances, and with the permission of the local authorities, he [the Mwami] may be visited at his palace which is built on modern lines, furnished in good taste and richly decorated with trophies in an oriental manner.' For its history and for its peaceful, attractive location, it is worth seeing, especially if you go with a knowledgeable guide. Entry to the palaces costs US$1, plus a further US$2 if you want to take photos.

En route to the palaces you'll pass the **Ikivuguto National Dairy**, started during Belgian colonisation and still going strong. In theory you can just turn up and ask for a free tour, but in practice it would be courteous to ask about this on your way out to the palaces and then have your tour (if convenient) on the way back.

As you return towards the main Butare road from Nyanza, there's a left-hand turn about 2km from the junction with a sign to the Oakdale Demonstration Farm. If you fancy following this mud road to the source of some Cheddar cheese, see the box on page 59!

Back at the junction with the main road is the new **Nyanza Guest House** (tel: 533002, 533121): ten en-suite rooms (cold water for the moment but hot is planned) at US$10 double. They also have a 'villa' – four rooms containing six double beds in total with a shared shower and long-drop outside at US$6. It has only just opened so I don't know how it'll turn out.

Continuing to Butare there's a sign on the right to the Gatagara Pottery. Turn off on to the mud road and after about 3km you reach a home for the handicapped; the pottery is on the left at the entrance. You can watch potters (they are Batwa, see pages 77–8 in *Chapter 5*) at work and the clay in all its stages – also there's a small shop with a good range of finished pots, plates, animals, etc.

BUTARE

This pleasant, businesslike town is the site of Rwanda's national university and is often called the country's 'intellectual centre'. Named Astrida by the Belgians (after Queen Astrid), it reverted to its original, name of Butare in 1962. At the time of independence it seemed that it might become Rwanda's capital; during colonisation, although the capital of the joint territory of Ruanda-Urundi had been Bujumbura, Butare was the administrative capital of Ruanda. However, in the end Kigali was chosen, largely because of its more central location. So Kigali has mushroomed, while Butare remains peaceful and compact.

During term-time Butare has probably the country's greatest concentration of students, in relation to its size – not only at the university but also at other technical and training schools and colleges. In fact the first secondary school in the country opened here in 1928. It's something of a religious centre, too, with its massive cathedral and other churches.

The genocide

The intellectual and cultural spirit of Butare was so strong that initially it seemed that it could remain intact and resist the madness of slaughter. For decades Hutus and Tutsis had lived and studied peacefully together there. When the killing started, people flocked to Butare from outlying areas believing that they would find safety – as indeed they did, for a while. The prefect of Butare at the time of the genocide was the only Tutsi prefect in Rwanda; he took charge, welcoming the refugees, reassuring parishioners, and demonstrating such authority that, for two weeks while the killing raged elsewhere, relative calm (although there were isolated instances of violence) prevailed in his prefecture. But it couldn't last. Because of his defiance he was sacked from his post and subsequently murdered, to be replaced by a hardline military officer, Colonel Tharcisse Muvunyi, and an equally hard-line civilian administrator. Under their orchestration, the killing started immediately – and the massacres in Butare prefecture proved to be some of the worst of the genocide. Tharcisse Muvunyi later fled to Britain, where he was tracked down and arrested in Lewisham (London) in February 2000.

Getting there and away

Butare is 136km (a two-hour drive) from Kigali, along good tarred roads. Public minibus-taxis to Butare start from Kigali's Nyabugogo bus station; the fare is under US$3. There are also direct minibuses from Cyangugu and Gitarama. In Butare, you can be dropped either at the minibus station on the northern edge of town or opposite the market in the centre. However, for returning to Kigali (or continuing to Cyangugu) you must start from the bus station as there are no central pick-ups.

Alternatively there are private minibuses, including the Taxi Ponctuel and Volcano Express Taxi, which go direct from Kigali to Butare.

Plenty of traffic uses this road, so hitching should be easy too.

Getting around

The National Museum and the University are no more than about 5km apart, so theoretically everything is manageable on foot. If you should get weary or want to go further afield, however, a few beat-up taxis wait by the turning from the main street leading to the market. The prices asked seem to be standard, but, if you feel you're being overcharged, either bargain or ask to see the official tariff. In any case, agree on a price in advance. Rates may well have increased by the time you read this, but at the time of writing it costs about US$2.50 from the town centre to the museum, US$20 to Nyanza and US$25 to Kibeho (see page 138). Waiting time costs extra, currently US$7.50 per hour.

Where to stay

Starting at rock bottom, the cheapest (but also the least appealing) accommodation is at the **Episcopal Church Guesthouse**, by the crossroads en route to the university, where the friendly welcome doesn't compensate for cell-like double rooms ($4 per room) opening off a long dark passage, and the shared facilities are far from fragrant. Far better is the **Procure de Butare Guesthouse** (BP 224 Butare; tel: 30993) opposite the cathedral, where the shared facilities are clean, and bright rooms (with wash-basins) cost US$5 single, US$8 double. All meals are available here (breakfast US$1.50, lunch and supper US$2.50) and there's secure parking.

In the market area there are several passable small hotels all in the range of US$5–10 per person – the newest is the **Eden Garden Hotel** (tel: 530446) opened in August 2000, which has 13 plain, clean rooms set around a central courtyard for US$6 per person whether single or double, with shared facilities. The **Dusabane** (11 rooms) looks unprepossessing but the en-suite rooms (cold water) are clean and the restaurant does a generous mixed plateful of rice, vegetables and meat/fish. The **Motel Ituze** has rooms with wash-basins and shared shower/WC, set around a patch of grass and with deckchairs outside, at US$6–8 – it's clean and quiet.

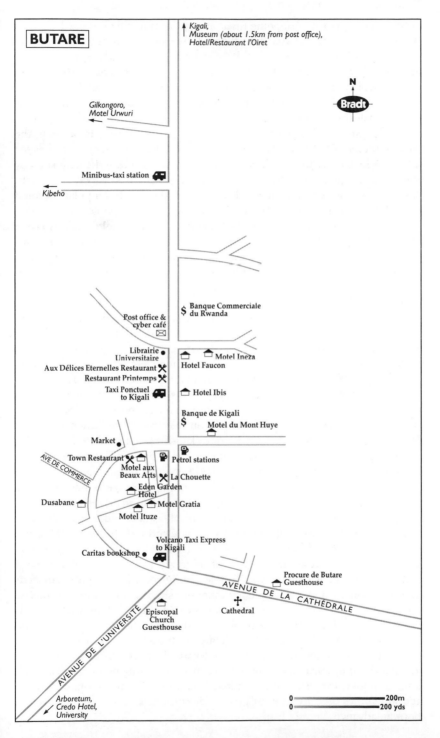

BUTARE

Kigali,
Museum (about 1.5km from post office),
Hotel/Restaurant l'Oiret

N

Bradt

Gilkongoro,
Motel Urwuri

Minibus-taxi station

Kibeho

Post office &
cyber café

Banque Commerciale
du Rwanda

Librairie
Universitaire
Aux Délices Eternelles Restaurant
Restaurant Printemps

Motel Ineza
Hotel Faucon

Taxi Ponctuel
to Kigali

Hotel Ibis

Banque de Kigali
Motel du Mont Huye

Market

AVE DE COMMERCE

Town Restaurant
Motel aux
Beaux Arts
Eden Garden
Hotel
Dusabane

Petrol stations

La Chouette

Motel Gratia
Motel Ituze

Volcano Taxi Express
to Kigali
Caritas bookshop

Procure de Butare
Guesthouse

AVENUE DE LA CATHÉDRALE

AVENUE DE L'UNIVERSITÉ

Episcopal
Church
Guesthouse

Cathedral

Arboretum,
Credo Hotel,
University

0 ———————— 200m
0 ———————— 200 yds

Still in the market area, going up a bit in price but still very good value, is the two-storeyed **Motel aux Beaux Arts** (tel: 530037). All its ten rooms have washbasin, shower and WC, and the restaurant offers a good range of meals and snacks; rooms cost US$8–12 depending on facilities. The **Motel Gratia** (tel: 531044) is also a comfortable place, with a restaurant and 11 rooms set round a small, well-watered courtyard garden: US$8 upwards. Some rooms have a small sitting room.

Down a side road opposite the post office on the north side of town, the **Motel Ineza** (BP 170 Butare; tel: 530387) has 12 tiny, en-suite rooms set around a secluded garden, where you can sit out and eat, write or just enjoy the peace and quiet. The bar/restaurant has a good range of food and snacks (the *mélanges* are tasty) and the whole place is good value. It's popular, so you'd do well to book in advance. Around US$6 single, US$8 double.

Possibly the best value of all the budget places is the **Motel du Mont Huye** (tel: 530765, 08561005), set peacefully down a side turning away from main-street traffic, with 19 clean, comfortable en-suite rooms (hot water) at US$10 and a two-room apartment at US$20. Rooms open on to a central garden, and there's a restaurant. It's used by Catholic Relief Services, NGOs, etc, so it's best to book in advance.

Two mid-range hotels in the main street which have been there for several decades are the Ibis and the Faucon. The **Ibis** (BP 103 Butare; tel: 530335; email: campionibis@hotmail.com) has 14 en-suite rooms at a variety of prices depending on facilities – suites, single, double, twin, etc. They're comfortable, with TV and phone, and the bedside lights are a welcome touch. Rooms US$30/$42 single/double upwards, apartments US$36/40; payment by Visa can be arranged on request. The main restaurant is good (quite pricey) and there's a convenient bar/snack restaurant on the street. The **Faucon** (BP 366 Butare; email: faucon@yahoo.fr) is more laid-back – an old building, thick walls, high ceilings; a few colonial echoes here! It badly needs a face-lift now but I'm told renovations are planned. The 11 en-suite rooms (some suites) are set round a courtyard, away from the street, and the back windows have a peaceful view of greenery. There's a good (not cheap) main restaurant, also a bar/snack-bar. Prices US$10–20 excluding breakfast, depending on facilities.

Finally, on the road to the university is the **Credo Hotel** (BP 310 Butare; tel: 530855/530505; fax: 530505; mobile: 08302216) which has a range of 30 comfortable en-suite rooms – some of them are suites – as well as what it calls a 'home', consisting of two simple family rooms, one with four beds and the other with two beds and a washbasin, sharing impeccably clean WC and showers, for US$8 per person. Otherwise this is an upmarket, mid-range place, with a swimming pool and restaurant. Rooms vary in size and have TV, telephone and (mostly) balcony, with a lovely view across fields at the back. It's new (opened in 1999) and very clean. Room prices run from about US$30 upwards for a double and include continental breakfast. With a bit of notice, car-hire can be arranged here for trips to Nyungwe Forest. It's sometimes used by tour groups or for conferences, so you'd do well to book in advance.

A little way from the centre of Butare are two more places: the **Hotel/Restaurant l'Oiret** (tel: 530299, 530870) out by the museum (17 rooms, some en-suite, from US$3 to US$7.50 including breakfast), and the **Motel Urwuri** (tel: 0865 2589) 2–3km from Butare on the Gikongoro road with 13 en-suite rooms (cold water, but they'll bring buckets of hot) at US$6. It's simple but welcoming and there's a reasonable restaurant.

Where to eat

Plenty of small restaurants round the market offer snacks and good-value *mélanges* of rice, vegetables and meat/fish at under US$2. For snacks or drinks in the main street, the **Ibis** and **Faucon** are both convenient and reasonably priced. Also in the main street, **Aux Délices Eternelles** opposite the Hotel Faucon has an unspectacular menu of cheapish snacks and main meals but is quiet and friendly; the next-door **Restaurant Printemps** does a reasonable lunchtime buffet for about US$3 upwards. **La Chouette** (between Motel Gratia and the petrol station) is also reasonable. **The Motel Ineza** is a pleasant and economical place for lunch or dinner (or a drink) even if you're not staying there. One traveller reports having had 'a whopping dinner there – US$9.00 for a meal and some drinks for two people'. Considerably pricier but good if you feel like a treat are the main restaurants at the **Ibis** and **Faucon**.

Nightlife

There's not a huge amount: the **Sombrero** nightclub near the Credo Hotel, the **Piscine** behind the post office and a new, unnamed one by the SORAS building near the market.

Practicalities

The **post office** is at the northern end of the main street. Of the **banks**, the Banque Commerciale du Rwanda opposite the post office and the Banque de Kigali midway down the main street offer normal services. The BCR has Western Union. There are two **bookshops**: the Librairie Universitaire at the northern end of the main street has a fair range of books and student stationery, as well as some dusty but original handicrafts. Librairie Caritas at the other end of the main street has a few more touristy books and items of stationery, as well as some international magazines and games. I felt a surge of homesickness at the sight of a set of Travel Scrabble. For **handicrafts**, there's an excellent shop opposite the Ibis Hotel, selling products made by the *Coopérative des Producteurs Artisanaux de Butare* (COPABU). The items are priced, but a little gentle bargaining will do no harm, particularly if you're buying more than one. The co-op was set up in 1997 with 47 members, working in banana-leaf products, wood-carving and reed baskets. Three years later it had 954 members (99 individuals and 35 associations) of which 66% were women. Handicrafts in the Butare area have been well organised, with the help of German aid; see www.pab-faab.org.rw. For more details, email gtzpab@rwanda1.com.

Security

For all its laid-back atmosphere, Butare is a busy town with a mixed population, so take normal precautions such as not carrying conspicuous wealth. The larger streetkids can be a bit pushy, but treat them understandingly and they're manageable. In the evenings some may gather to sniff solvents around the petrol stations. See box *After the genocide* on page 18. If you go out to eat at night it's wise to take a torch/flashlight. Yes, the streets are well lit, but if there's a power cut (rare, but it happens) they become very black indeed, and finding your way back to your hotel might not be easy.

What to see

Although not really a tourist 'sight', the **National University of Rwanda** (BP 56 Butare; tel: 530122; fax: 530121; email: nurcc@nur.ac.rw; web: www.nur.ac.rw) is by far Butare's most important institution. Created in 1963, and with only 51 students and 16 lecturers when it opened, it now has over 4,500 students and 275 lecturers. The university lost many of its students and personnel during the genocide and suffered considerable damage, but managed to reopen in 1995. It is now a vibrant and forward-looking institution, comprising faculties of agronomy, law, arts & human sciences, medicine, science & technology, economics, social sciences & management, and education, as well as schools of journalism & communication and modern languages. You may run across visiting professors in any of Butare's hotels and guesthouses.

Out by the university is the **Ruhande Arboretum**, started in 1934. Its objective at the outset was to study the behaviour of imported and indigenous species, to determine what silvicultural methods were most suitable, to evaluate the trees' productivity and timber quality, and to develop the best of them. Now, it is of interest for the range and variety of its species – and it's a peaceful, shady place. Get permission from the university if you'd like to visit.

The huge, red-brick, Roman Catholic **cathedral**, built in memory of Belgium's Princess Astrid in the 1930s, is the largest in the country and worth a visit. Its interior is fairly plain, but the atmosphere is tranquil and the size impressive. A service there can be a moving experience.

There is some attractive **architecture** and the tranquil, tree-lined residential streets away from the centre are good territory for strolling. It's possible to take a turning to the right a short distance east of the Motel Ineza and then to cross twisty tracks through the green and cultivated valley until you reach the cathedral, but ask for directions and advice. A clear heritage of Belgian colonisation (in Belgium even the motorways are lit) is the generous amount of street lighting in Butare.

The **market**, although not extensive, is crowded and atmospheric.

Spectacular displays of **traditional dance** (*Intore*) take place in Butare and can be arranged on request (and for a fee); ask at the museum (below) about this.

The National Museum of Rwanda

If you're in Butare – indeed even if you're in some other part of Rwanda – you should allow time to visit this beautifully presented collection of exhibits on Rwandan history and culture.

The museum is exceptional. Opened in 1988, and presented to Rwanda as a gift from Belgium's King Baudouin I, its seven spacious rooms illustrate the country and its people from earliest times until the present day.

Room 1 (the entrance hall) has space for temporary displays as well as numerous shelves of traditional handicrafts for sale. **Room 2** presents a comprehensive view of Rwanda's geological and geographical background and the development of its terrain and population. In **Room 3** the occupations of its early inhabitants (hunter-gathering, farming and stock raising) are illustrated, together with the later development of tools and methods of transport. The social importance of cattle is explained and there are even detailed instructions for the brewing of traditional banana beer. **Room 4** displays a variety of handicrafts and the making of traditional household items: pottery, mats, baskets, leatherwork and the wooden shields of the Intore dancers. **Room 5** illustrates traditional styles and methods of architecture – and a full-scale royal hut has been reconstructed. In **Room 6** traditional games and sports are displayed and more space is given to the costumes and equipment of the Intore dancers. Finally, **Room 7** contains exhibits relating to traditional customs and beliefs, history, culture, poetry, oral tradition and the supernatural.

At the reception desk, various pamphlets and books are on sale. At present no descriptions or background material are available in English, only in French and Kinyarwanda; but, at the time of writing, some translations are being prepared.

THE PREPARATION OF BANANA BEER
(Free translation)

When the bunches of fruit are ready, cut them.

Cover the bunches with banana leaves and leave them in the courtyard to ripen for two to three days.

Clean out the pit in which the fruit ripened.

Lay banana branches across the top of the pit.

Place the bananas on top of the branches.

Wrap the bananas in fresh banana leaves and then scatter a layer of earth on top.

Put leaves in the ditch under the bananas and set the leaves alight.

Leave for three days.

Peel the fruit, then crush it, then mix a little water into the pulp.

Press the pulp and filter the juice.

Grind up a small amount of sorghum.

Pour the juice into a large jar and add the sorghum to it.

Leave to ferment for three days.

The beer is ready to drink.

At present the museum is open daily, 07.00–17.00, but this may change. The entrance fee is US$2.50. Tel: 530586, 530207; fax: 530211; email: museumrwanda@yahoo.fr; web: www.nur.ac.rw/rwanda4.htm. If you want to go somewhere for a drink and snack after your visit, a short walk Butare-wards along the main road brings you to the Bar-Restaurant l'Oiret which is open 07.00–23.00. There's a lunchtime buffet. (It also has rooms to let, see page 135.)

If you don't fancy the walk from Butare (about 1.5km from the centre), then a taxi to the museum will cost about US$2.50, or more if you ask it to wait. If you're coming by minibus-taxi from Kigali you can ask to be dropped off there; and, if you want to go straight back to Kigali afterwards, you could try flagging down a minibus that has come from Butare – if it has spare seats inside, it will probably stop. Or to be sure of getting one you can walk to the minibus-taxi stand, which is less than 1km away.

Excursions from Butare
Viaki Crafts Village
Start this trip at the handicrafts shop (COPABU, see page 135) opposite the Ibis Hotel – they will give you a leaflet about this project. Three associations of woodcarvers have set up a workshop, a shop (selling their products) and a small snack-bar. Finance came from the Rhineland Palatinate and the German Embassy in Kigali. You can watch them at work and see carvings progress from a chunk of rough wood to the finished article. Prices at the Viaki shop are slightly lower than those in Butare.

There's a map in the leaflet – but follow the main Burundi road south for 13km and you'll see the sign. It's a lovely area and there are walks. Linked to the same project, but closed at present because it's up for sale, is the Kigembe Fish Farm in the Rwabisemanyi valley. Continue for a further 8km along the Burundi road and then follow the sign (on the left) to 'Etangs Piscicoles'. When functioning, this place should have a small restaurant serving fish fresh from the farm – and it's a beautiful valley, so do check with either COPABU or Viaki to see whether it has reopened. Also see www.pab-faab.org.rw.

The same leaflet gives details of the drive up Mount Makwaza, 40km from Butare – there's a tremendous view from the summit. A 4WD is advisable. All of these areas will see more tourist development within the next few years.

Kibeho
You pick up the Kibeho road by driving through the minibus park just north of Butare. Minibuses also make the trip, but not very frequently. It's a beautiful drive through a mixture of wooded valleys and farmland, on an unmade road. There's not a great deal to see at Kibeho just now, but developments are planned in order to attract tourists.

You may already have heard the name. Before the genocide, Kibeho hit the headlines because of the visions of the Virgin Mary allegedly seen there by young girls from 1981 onwards, starting with that of teenager Alphonsine Mumureke in November 1981. The phenomena were reported both nationally and internationally, and the small, remote community became a centre of pilgrimage and faith, as believers travelled from all over Rwanda and further afield to witness the miracles.

During the genocide Kibeho suffered appallingly: hospital, primary school, college and church were all attacked. The church was badly burned while still sheltering survivors. At the time of writing it has not been rebuilt and a genocide memorial site is beside it.

BUTARE TO NYUNGWE FOREST
Gikongoro
There's not a lot to see around here except for a few shops and some beautiful, dramatically hilly landscapes; if the area appeals to you and you feel like some steepish strolling, there's simple, good-value accommodation available in Gikongoro at the **Gikongoro Guesthouse** (tel: 535060) near the Provincial Office: nine en-suite rooms at US$10. To find it when you're coming from Butare: at the start of Gikongoro there's a hill going down with shops (including the Restaurant Dallas) on the right. At the bottom of this hill, turn right then left – then ask. An alternative is the **Hibiscus Guesthouse**, by the petrol station.

The genocide memorial at Murambi, about 2km north of Gikongoro, is one of Rwanda's starkest: over 1,800 bodies, of the 27,000-odd exhumed from mass graves here, have been placed on display to the public in the old technical school. They people the bare rooms, mingling horror with poignancy, as a mute but chillingly cloquent reminder that such events must never, ever, be allowed to recur. During the genocide, under orders from the prefect and with the support of the church authorities, between 40,000 and 60,000 inhabitants were assembled together in and around the school on Murambi hill, supposedly for protection; there were 64 rooms crammed full with people. Then the *interahamwe* attacked, throwing grenades through the windows. Within four days, most of those on the premises had been slaughtered. Later, French soldiers were installed on the site as part of *Opération Turquoise,* and a volleyball pitch was built over one of the mass graves.

NYUNGWE FOREST NATIONAL PARK
If the mountain gorillas in the Volcanoes National Park form the single best reason to visit Rwanda, then the less-publicised Nyungwe Forest (soon to be designated a national park) is probably the best reason to prolong your stay. Extending for 970km^2 over the mountainous southwest of Rwanda, Nyungwe protects the largest single tract of montane forest remaining anywhere in East or Central Africa. As such, it is a remarkably rich centre of biodiversity, harbouring (among other things) 86 mammal species, 280 birds, 120 butterflies, and about 200 varieties of orchid.

Nyungwe is magnificent. The forest takes on a liberatingly primal presence even before you enter it. One moment the road is winding through the characteristic rural Rwandan landscape of rolling tea plantations and artificially terraced hills, the next a dense tangle of trees rises imperiously from the fringing cultivation. For a full 50km the road clings improbably to steep forested slopes, offering grandstand views over densely swathed hills which tumble like monstrous green waves towards the distant Burundi border. One normally thinks of rainforest as the most intimate and confining of environments. Nyungwe is that, but, as viewed from the main road, it is also gloriously expansive.

Vast though it may be, Nyungwe today is but a fragment of what was once an uninterrupted forest belt covering the length of the Albertine Rift (the stretch of the western Rift Valley running from the Ruwenzoris south to Burundi). The fragmentation of this forest started some 2,000 years ago, at the dawn of the Iron Age, when the first patches were cut down to make way for agriculture – it is thought, for instance, that the isolation of Uganda's Bwindi Forest from similar habitats on the Virunga Mountains occurred about 500 years ago.

It is over the past 100 years that the forests of the Albertine Rift have suffered most heavily. Nyungwe, protected as a forest reserve since 1933, has fared relatively well, decreasing in extent by roughly 20% prior to the implementation of a co-ordinated forest protection plan in 1984. But it is the only substantial tract of forest left in Rwanda: the Gishwati Forest, which in the 1930s covered an area comparable to that of Nyungwe, had by 1989 been reduced to two separate blocks covering a combined 280km^2, and now little remains. See pages 199–201.

The main attraction of Nyungwe Forest is its primates. Chimp-tracking can be arranged at short notice. Several other monkeys are readily seen, including the acrobatic Ruwenzori colobus in troops of up to 400 strong (the largest arboreal primate troops in Africa) and the beautiful and highly localised l'Hoest's monkey. Nyungwe is also highly alluring to birders, botanists and keen walkers. One of the joys of Nyungwe is its accessibility. Not only is the forest bisected by the surfaced trunk road between Butare and Cyangugu, but it is serviced by an excellent and inexpensive resthouse and campsite, and easily explored along a well-maintained network of walking trails.

Natural history

Nyungwe is a true rainforest, typically receiving in excess of 2,000mm of precipitation annually. It is also one of the oldest forests in Africa, which is one reason why it boasts such a high level of biodiversity. Scientific opinion is that Nyungwe, along with the other forests of the Albertine Rift, was largely unaffected by the drying up of lowland areas during the last ice age, and thus became a refuge for forest plants and animals which have subsequently recolonised areas such as the Congo Basin. Nyungwe's faunal and floral diversity is not a function only of its antiquity, but also of the wide variation in elevation (between 1,600m and 2,950m above sea level), since many forest plants and animals live within very specific altitudinal bands.

Flora

The forest comprises at least 200 tree species. The upper canopy in some areas reaches 50–60m in height, dominated by slow-growing hardwoods such as *Entandrophragma excelsum* (African mahogany), *Syzygium parvifolium* (waterberry), *Podocarpus milanjianus* (Mulanje cedar), *Newtonia buchananii* (forest newtonia) and *Albizia gummifera* (smooth-barked albizia). A much larger variety of trees makes up the mid-storey canopy, of which one of the most conspicuous is *Dichaetanthera corymbosa*, whose bright purple blooms break up the rich green textures of the forest.

Of the smaller trees, one of the most striking is the giant tree-fern *Cyathea mannania*, which grows to 5m tall, and is seen in large numbers along the ravines of the Waterfall Trail. Also very distinctive are the 2–3m-tall giant lobelias, more normally associated with montane moorland than forest, but common in Nyungwe, particularly along the roadside. Bamboo plants, a large type of grass, are dominant at higher altitudes in the rather inaccessible southeast of the forest, where their shoots are favoured by owl-faced monkeys. Nyungwe also harbours a huge variety of small flowering plants, including around 200 varieties of orchid and the wild begonia.

Within Nyungwe lie several swampy areas whose biology is quite distinct from that of the surrounding forest. The largest of these is the 13km² Kamiranzovu Marsh, sweeping views of which are offered along the main road between the campsite and the resthouse. Formerly a favoured haunt of elephants, this open area is also rich in epiphytic orchids and harbours localised animals such as the Congo clawless otter and Grauer's rush warbler. The higher-altitude Uwasenkoko Marsh, bisected by the main road towards Butare, is dominated by the Ethiopian hagenia and protects a community of heather-like plants sharing unexpected affinities with the Nyika Plateau in distant Malawi.

Mammals

The most prominent mammals in Nyungwe are primates, of which 13 species are present, including the common chimpanzee (see box, pages 146–7) and eight types of monkey (see pages 142–4). In total, however, an estimated 86 different mammal species have been recorded in Nyungwe, including several rare forest inhabitants.

Of the so-called 'Big Five', elephant, buffalo and leopard were all common in pre-colonial times. Buffalo are now extinct – the last one was shot in 1976 – and elephant may well have gone the same way since 1990, when it was estimated that at least six and perhaps as many as 20 elephant lived in the forest. For several years after the civil war, no elephant were seen in Nyungwe. In mid-1999, elephant spoor was observed during a forest inventory, but in November of that year an elephant corpse was found (cause of death unknown) and no spoor has been seen since then. Leopard, by contrast, are still present in small numbers, and regularly seen by local villagers, but as a tourist you'd be very lucky to encounter one.

A number of smaller predators occur in Nyungwe, including golden cat, wild cat, serval cat, side-striped jackal, three types of mongoose, Congo clawless

NYUNGWE'S MONKEYS

The 13 primate species which occur in Nyungwe represent something like 20–25% of the total number in Africa, a phenomenal figure which in East Africa is comparable only to Uganda's Kibale Forest. Furthermore, several of these primates are listed as vulnerable or endangered on the IUCN red list, and Nyungwe is almost certainly the main stronghold for at least two of them.

Disregarding the chimpanzee (see box on pages 146–7), the most celebrated of Nyungwe's primates is the **Ruwenzori colobus** (*Colobus angolensis ruwenzori*), a race of the more widespread Angola colobus which is restricted to the Albertine Rift. The Ruwenzori colobus is a highly arboreal and acrobatic leaf-eater, easily distinguished from any other primate found in Nyungwe by its contrasting black overall colour and snow-white whiskers, shoulders and tail tip. Although all colobus monkeys are very sociable, the ones in Nyungwe are unique in so far as they typically move in troops of several hundred animals. A semi-habituated troop of 400, resident in the forest around the campsite, is thought to be the largest troop of arboreal primates anywhere in Africa – elsewhere in the world, only the Chinese golden monkey moves in groups of a comparable number.

Most of the other monkeys in Nyungwe are guenons, the collective name for the taxonomically confusing *Cercopithecus* genus. Most guenons are arboreal forest-dwelling omnivores, noted for their colourful coats and the male's bright red or blue genitals. The most striking of Nyungwe's guenons is **l'Hoest's monkey** (*C. l'hoesti*), a large and unusually terrestrial monkey, whose cryptic grey and red coat is offset by a bold white 'beard' which renders it unmistakable. As with the Ruwenzori colobus, l'Hoest's monkey is more or less confined to the Albertine Rift, and is very scarce elsewhere in its restricted range. In Nyungwe, it is the most frequently encountered monkey, with troops of 5–15 animals often seen along the roadside, within the forest, and even in the campsite.

One race of blue monkey – the most widespread of African forest primates – occurs in Nyungwe. Likely to be encountered along the road and around the campsite, the **silver monkey** (*C. mitis doggetti*) is similar in build and general appearance to l'Hoest's monkey, but lacks the diagnostic white beard. The silver monkey typically lives in small family parties, though solitary males are also often encountered in Nyungwe. In the remote bamboo forests close to the Burundi border is the rare and secretive **owl-**

faced monkey (*C. hamlyni*), another Albertine Rift endemic whose modern range is restricted to a handful of montane forests. This thickset, plain grey, pug-faced monkey was first recorded in Nyungwe as recently as 1989, and it remains the least-known of the monkeys in the reserve – researchers monitoring the population close to the Burundi border reckon they encounter the monkeys at most twice a week.

Another guenon whose status within Nyungwe is uncertain is the **red-tailed monkey** (*C. ascanius*), a small and highly active arboreal monkey most easily distinguished by its bright white nose. Generally associated with low-elevation forest, the red-faced monkey now faces extinction within Nyungwe owing to much of its habitat having been cleared for cultivation over recent decades. The solitary individual that hangs out with a colobus troop on the tea estate is presumably unlikely ever to find a breeding partner, though we have been told that a small but viable population of red-tailed monkeys survives on the fringes of the forest reserve near Banda.

Dent's mona monkey (*C. mona denti*) is widespread within Nyungwe, and occurs at all elevations, but it is infrequently seen by tourists. Another typical forest guenon, Dent's mona is distinguished from other monkeys in the forest by its contrasting black back and white belly, blue-white forehead, and yellowish ear tufts. It often moves with other guenons, and is mostly likely to be seen around Uwinka and the disused campsite at Karamba, not far from the ORTPN Resthouse. Some sources incorrectly list the **crowned monkey** (*C. pogonias*) for Nyungwe, but this is a West African lowland species, regarded by some to be a race of mona monkey. Unlikely to be seen within the forest proper, the **vervet monkey** (*C. aethiops*) is a grizzled grey guenon of savannah and open woodland, with a distinctive black face mask. Probably the most numerous monkey in the world, the vervet is occasionally encountered on the forest verge and around the ORTPN Resthouse, where it is often quite tame and regularly raids crops.

Another savannah monkey occasionally seen along the road through Nyungwe is the

continued overleaf

NYUNGWE'S MONKEYS continued
olive baboon (*Papio anubis*), a predominantly terrestrial primate which lives in large troops. After the chimpanzee, this is by far the largest and most stocky of the forest's primates, with a uniform dark olive coat and the canine snout and large teeth characteristic of all baboons. The olive baboon is very

aggressive and, like the vervet monkey, it frequently raids crops.

Intermediate in size between the olive baboon and the various guenons, the **grey-cheeked mangabey** (*Cercocebus albigena*) is an arboreal monkey of the forest interior. Rather more spindly than any guenon, the grey-cheeked mangabey has a uniform dark-brown coat and grey-brown cape, and is renowned for its loud gobbling call. It lives in small troops, typically around ten animals, and is localised in Nyungwe due to its preference for lower altitudes.

In addition to chimpanzees and monkeys, Nyungwe harbours four types of prosimian, small nocturnal primates more closely related to the lemurs of Madagascar than to any other primates of the African mainland. These are three species of bushbaby or galago (a group of tiny, hyperactive wide-eyed insectivores) and the sloth-like potto. All are very unlikely to be encountered by tourists.

otter, common and servaline genet, and common and palm civet. Most of these are highly secretive nocturnal creatures which are infrequently observed.

The largest antelope found in Nyungwe is the bushbuck. Three types of duiker also occur in the forest: black-fronted, yellow-backed and an endemic race of Wein's duiker. Formerly common, all the forest's antelope have suffered from intensive poaching as bush meat. Other large mammals include giant forest hog, bushpig, several types of squirrel (including the monkey-sized giant forest squirrel), Derby's anomalure (a large squirrel-like forest animal which has large underarm flaps enabling it to glide between trees) and the tree hyrax (a rarely seen guinea-pig-like animal whose blood-curdling nocturnal screeching is one of the characteristic sounds of the African forest).

Birds

Nyungwe, in my opinion, is the single most important birdwatching destination in Rwanda, with more than 280 bird species recorded, of which the majority are forest specialists and 26 are regional endemics whose range is restricted to a few forests along the Albertine Rift. Birdwatching in Nyungwe can be rather frustrating, since the vegetation is thick and many birds tend to stick to the canopy, but almost everything you do see ranks as a good sighting.

You don't have to be an ardent birdwatcher to appreciate some of Nyungwe's birds. Most people, for instance, will do a double take when they first spot a great blue turaco, a chicken-sized bird with garish blue, green and yellow feathers, often seen gliding between the trees along the main road. Another real gem is the paradise monarch, a long-tailed blue, orange and (sometimes) white bird often seen around the resthouse. Other birds impress with their bizarre appearance – the gigantic forest hornbills, for instance, whose wailing vocalisations are almost as comical as their ungainly bills and heavy-winged flight. And, when tracking through the forest undergrowth, watch out for the red-throated alethe, a very localised bird with a distinctive blue-white eyebrow. The alethe habitually follows colobus troops to eat the insects they disturb, and based on our experience it sees humans as merely another large mammal, often perching within a few inches!

The priorities of more serious birdwatchers will depend to some extent on their experience elsewhere in Africa. It is difficult to imagine, for instance, that a first-time visitor to the continent will get as excited about a drab Chubb's cisticola as they will when they first see a paradise monarch or green pigeon. For somebody coming from southern Africa, at least half of what they see will be new to them, with a total of about 60 relatively widespread East African forest specials headed by the likes of great blue turaco, Ross's turaco, red-breasted sparrowhawk and white-headed wood-hoopoe.

From an East African perspective, however, it is the 26 Albertine Rift endemics that are most alluring. Depending on your level of expertise, you could reasonably hope to tick off half of these over a few days in the forest. The more common regional endemics are handsome francolin, Ruwenzori turaco (a stunner!), stripe-breasted tit, red-collared babbler, red-throated alethe, Archer's ground robin, Kivu ground thrush, Grauer's rush warbler (confined to high-altitude marshy areas), red-faced woodland warbler, Kungwe apalis, Grauer's warbler, yellow-eyed black flycatcher, Ruwenzori batis, blue-headed sunbird, regal sunbird and strange weaver.

The guides at Nyungwe are improving and some are excellent, but others have only limited knowledge. For this reason, you will be highly dependent on a field guide, and without a great amount of advance research you are bound to struggle to identify every bird that you glimpse. Given the above, relic forest patches and the road verge are often more productive than the forest interior, since you'll get clearer views of what you do see.

Small creatures
While monkeys and to a lesser extent birds tend to attract the most attention, Nyungwe's fauna also includes a large number of smaller animals. With only 12 species recorded, snakes are relatively poorly represented, due to the chilly climate – probably good news for most visitors – but colourful lizards are often

CHIMPANZEES

Chimpanzees are distinctive black-coated apes, more closely related to humans than to any other living creatures. Two species are recognised, the  common or robust chimpanzee *Pan troglodytes* and the bonobo or gracile chimpanzee *Pan paniscus*. As the Latin name of the genus Pan indicates, scientists have long recognised the similarities between chimpanzees and humans, but only with recent DNA research has it become clear just how close we actually are – some biologists have expressed the opinion that a less partial observer would probably place us all in the same genus!

While the bonobo is relatively scarce and confined to a small area of lowland forest in the DRC, the common chimpanzee is the most numerous of the great apes. An estimated wild population of 180,000 ranges across 20 countries, from western Uganda and Tanzania through to the Senegambia. About half of the wild population – including the estimated 500–1,000 which are resident in Nyungwe – belong to the eastern race *P. t. schweinfurthii*. This has been genetically isolated from other races for about a million years, and may yet be classified as a discrete species.

Chimps live in loosely bonded troops of between ten and 120 animals, normally based around a core of related males with an internal hierarchy topped by an alpha male. Females are generally less strongly bonded to

seen on the rocks, and at least five species of chameleon occur in the forest. Nyungwe also harbours more than 100 different types of colourful butterfly, including 40 regional endemics. Look out, too, for the outsized beetles and bugs that are characteristic of all tropical forests. Equally remarkable, but only to be admired at a distance of a metre or so, are the vast columns of army ants that move across the forest trails – step on one of these columns, and you'll know all about it, as these guys can bite!

Further information

A basic fact-sheet about the forest is available from the ORTPN tourist office in Kigali. An excellent 60-page booklet entitled *Nyungwe Forest Reserve* was sold for around US$5 at the ORTPN office next to the resthouse. It has been out of print but should be reprinted soon, particularly if enough visitors ask for it!

Keen birdwatchers should try to lay their hands on the out-of-print checklist of the forest's birds, which gives Latin, English and French names as well as a good indication of each species' habitat and relative abundance within the reserve.

their core group than are males; emigration between communities is not unusual. Mother–child bonds are strong. Daughters normally leave their mother only after they reach maturity, at which point relations between them may be severed. Mother–son relations have been known to survive for over 40 years. A troop has a well-defined core territory which is fiercely defended by regular boundary patrols.

Chimpanzees are primarily frugivorous (fruit eating), but they do eat meat on occasion: young baboons, various types of monkey, small antelopes and bushpigs. Most kills are opportunistic, but stalking of prey is not unusual. Cannibalism has also been observed. The first recorded instance of chimps using tools was at Gombe Stream in Tanzania, where they regularly use modified sticks to 'fish' in termite mounds. In West Africa, they have been observed cracking nuts open using a stone and anvil. Chimpanzees are among the most intelligent of animals: in language studies in the USA they have been taught to communicate in American Sign Language, and have demonstrated their understanding, in some instances even creating compound words for new objects (such as rock-berry to describe a nut). Chimpanzee behaviour has been extensively studied in recent decades, most famously by Jane Goodall, whose research programme at Gombe Stream in Tanzania was initiated in 1960 and is still active today. Before heading out to see chimps, it's worth reading one of Jane Goodall's books (see *Further Reading*), which give detailed explanations of chimp behaviour in a highly readable style. Those who prefer their reading in a less academic form are pointed towards William Boyd's superb novel *Brazzaville Beach*, much of which is set in a fictional chimpanzee research centre.

Getting there and away

Nyungwe Forest Reserve is transected by the main surfaced road between Butare and Cyangugu. The Uwinka Reception Centre and Campsite lies alongside the main road, and is well signposted 90km from Butare and 54km from Cyangugu. The ORTPN Resthouse is also on the main road, 18km closer to Cyangugu, on the right side of the road and about 2km after you exit the western boundary of the forest reserve coming from Butare.

Where to stay and eat

Set in the heart of the forest, yet only a couple of hundred metres from the main road, the **Uwinka Reception Centre and Campsite** is the best option provided that you have a tent and are reasonably self-sufficient. The campsite has a perfect location at an altitude of about 2,300m on a high ridge, with individual sites scattered over a wide area of forest. There's a small orchid nursery near by. A semi-habituated troop of l'Hoest's monkey passes through every morning and most afternoons, as does the occasional troop of silver monkey and a variety of forest birds. The Coloured Trails start from here; so it's the most convenient base, particularly if you have no vehicle, from which

ALBERTINE RIFT ENDEMICS

Most of Rwanda's forest inhabitants have a wide distribution in the DRC and/or West Africa, while a smaller proportion is comprised of eastern species that might as easily be observed in forested habitats in Kenya, Tanzania and in some instances Ethiopia. A significant number, however, are endemic to the Albertine Rift: in other words their range is more or less confined to montane habitats associated with the Rift Valley escarpment running between Lake Albert and the north of Lake Tanganyika. The most celebrated of these regional endemics is of course the mountain gorilla, confined to the Virunga and Bwindi Mountains near the eastern Rift Valley escarpment. Other primates endemic to the Albertine Rift include several taxa of smaller primates, for instance the golden monkey and Ruwenzori colobus, while eight endemic butterflies are regarded as flagship species for the many hundreds of invertebrate taxa that occur nowhere else.

Of the remarkable tally of 37 range-restricted bird species listed as Albertine Rift endemics, roughly half are regarded to be of global conservation concern. All 37 of these species have been recorded in the DRC, and nine are endemic to that country, since their range is confined to the western escarpment forests. More than 20 Albertine Rift endemics are resident in each of Uganda, Rwanda and Burundi, while two extend their range southward into western Tanzania.

All but one of the 29 endemics that occur on the eastern escarpment have been recorded in **Rwanda's Nyungwe Forest**. Inaccessible to tourists at the time of writing, the Itombwe Mountains, which rise from the Congolese shore of northern Lake Tanganyika, support the largest contiguous block of

to explore the forest and track the 400-strong troop of colobus. The main road adjacent to the campsite is also worth exploring, for the great views and variety of birds. Camping costs US$10. Drinks are available at reasonable prices, and firewood can be arranged, but campers must bring all food and should have sufficient warm clothing to offset the chilly night temperatures at high altitude. There's also a small two-roomed bungalow at Uwinka costing US$25 per night. It's quite basic – lanterns rather than electricity, hot water is provided in the mornings and a fire at night, but guests must bring their own food.

The alternative for those unequipped for camping is the **ORTPN Resthouse**, which lies 2km outside the forest close to the Gisakura Tea Estate. The accommodation here is clean and comfortable, and good value at US$15 per person for a single or twin, or US$20 per person for a double room in a large self-contained chalet. The communal showers and toilets are also clean, though the water supply was a problem when we visited. Huge meals can be prepared with a couple of hours' notice for the reasonable charge of US$5 per person. Make bookings via ORTPN's Kigali office – see page 53. Dorette Boshoff and David Hartley wrote: 'We ended up at the guesthouse just outside the park and found it very good value for money –

montane forest in East Africa. This range is also regarded to be the most important site for montane forest birds in the region, with a checklist of 565 species including 31 Albertine Rift endemics, three of which are known from nowhere else in the world. The most elusive of these birds is the enigmatic Congo bay owl, first collected in 1952, and yet to be seen again, though its presence is suspected in Rwanda's Nyungwe Forest.

Several Albertine Rift forest endemics share stronger affinities with extant or extinct Asian genera than they do with any other living African species, affirming the great age of these forests, which are thought to have flourished during prehistoric climatic changes that caused temporary deforestation in lower-lying areas such as the Congo Basin. The Congo bay owl, African green broadbill and Grauer's cuckoo-shrike, for instance, might all be classed as living fossils – isolated relics of a migrant Asian stock that has been superseded elsewhere on the continent by indigenous genera evolved from a common ancestor.

Among the mammals endemic to the Albertine Rift, the dwarf otter-shrew of the Ruwenzoris is one of three highly localised African mainland species belonging to a family of aquatic insectivores that flourished some 50 million years ago and is elsewhere survived only by the related tenrecs of Madagascar. A relict horseshoe bat species restricted to the Ruwenzoris and Lake Kivu is anatomically closer to extant Asian forms of horseshoe bat and to ancient migrant stock than it is to any of the 20-odd more modern and widespread African horseshoe bat species, while a shrew specimen collected only once in the Itombwe Mountains is probably the most primitive and ancient of all 150 described African species.

clean, all in working order and our dinner was an absolute feast, prepared and served with a lot of TLC!' The main drawback to the resthouse – particularly for travellers dependent on public transport – is that it is outside the forest and 18km from Uwinka, the trailhead for most of the trails. The resthouse does, however, offer good access to the Waterfall Trail and the colobus troop on the Gisakura Tea Estate. Vervet monkeys occasionally pass through the resthouse grounds, and a fair variety of birds are present in the small patch of forest in front of the resthouse. A number of nearby relic forest patches offer good birdwatching, as well as a chance of encountering forest monkeys.

Fees

Any non-primate forest visit costs US$10; so a morning and an afternoon walk will cost you US$20. Any primate walk (whether to the nearby colobus on the Gisakura tea estate or to the more distant chimps) costs US$20 – but if you do a primate walk and a non-primate walk on the same day you pay only US$25 instead of US$30. For groups of more than ten persons, the cost drops to US$15 for a primate walk. (And it is normal to tip the guides.) Double-check these fees with ORTPN because I've a suspicion they may change in 2004.

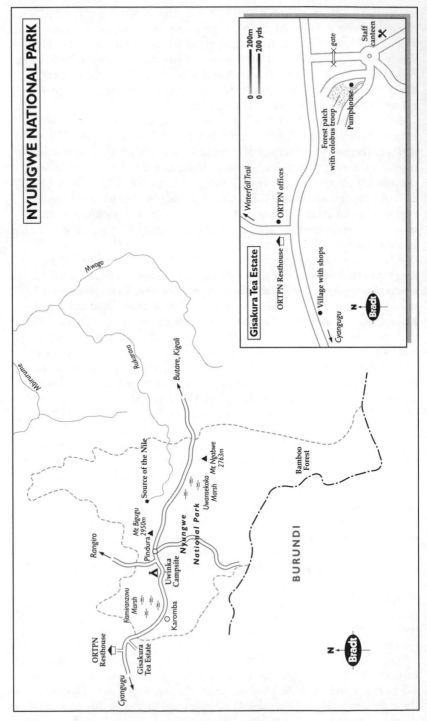

NYUNGWE NATIONAL PARK

Gisakura Tea Estate

Waterfall Trail

• ORTPN offices

ORTPN Resthouse

• Village with shops

Cyangugu

Forest patch
with colobus troop

Pumphouse•

gate

Staff
canteen

N
Bradt

0 ———— 200m
0 ———— 200 yds

Mwogo

Mbirurume

Rukarara

Butare, Kigali

Source of the Nile

Mt Ngabwe
2763m

Uwansekoko
Marsh

Mt Bigugu
2950m
Pindura

Uwinka
Campsite

Nyungwe
National Park

BAMBOO
Bamboo
Forest

Rangiro

Kamiranzovu
Marsh

ORTPN
Resthouse

Gisakura
Tea Estate

Karomba

Cyangugu

BURUNDI

N
Bradt

Walks and excursions

A large selection of walking possibilities and other excursions is available within Nyungwe. Visitors with a vehicle and sufficient interest could easily keep themselves busy for three or four days without significantly retracing their steps. The options for travellers without private transport are more limited, and depend on whether they base themselves at Uwinka Campsite (where the main attraction is the network of Coloured Trails, a good place for colobus and seasonally for chimps) or at the resthouse (the best base for the Waterfall Trail and for visiting the colobus in Gisakura Tea Estate). In the dry season, you need a private vehicle to go chimp-tracking wherever you are based, and at all times of year you need a vehicle to visit the habituated grey-cheeked mangabey troop and to explore the road to Rangiro.

The forest trails are steep and often very slippery. Dress accordingly; jeans, a thick shirt and good walking shoes are the ideal outfit, and a waterproof jacket will be useful during the rainy season.

Uwinka and the Coloured Trails

A network of seven walking trails, each designated by a particular colour, leads downhill from the Uwinka Campsite into the surrounding forested hills. Ranging in length from the 1km Grey Trail to the 10km Red Trail, the footpaths are all well maintained and clearly marked, but don't underestimate the steepness of the slopes or – after rain – the muddy conditions, which can be fairly tough going at this high altitude.

The Coloured Trails are the most popular walks in Nyungwe, not least because they pass through the territory of a habituated troop of 400 colobus monkeys. It is up to the individual visitor to decide whether to go on an ordinary forest walk and leave the colobus sightings to chance, or pay more to go on a specific primate visit, in which case the guides will search for (and almost certainly find) the colobus. During the rainy season, a troop of chimpanzees often moves into this area as well, and once again it is up to individuals to decide whether to pay extra to track them.

Whatever you decide, you can reasonably expect to see some primates along any of the Coloured Trails, as well as a good variety of forest birds – though the latter require patience and regular stops where there are open views into the canopy. Unless you opt for a specific primate visit, chance will be the decisive factor in what you see, though the 2.5km Blue Trail is regarded as especially good for primates and birds, while the 10km Red Trail is good for chimpanzees and passes four waterfalls. For those spending a bit of time in the forest, the Kamiranzovu Trail leads to a quite different ecosystem, a marshy area rich in orchids and swamp-associated birds. This used to be the best place to see Nyungwe's elephants, but none has been sighted here in recent years.

Birdwatchers in particular are advised to explore the main road close to the campsite, as they will probably see a wider variety of birds than from within the forest. About 500m east of the campsite, the road offers some stunning views over the forested valleys, and passes a stand of giant lobelias.

The Waterfall Trail

This superb trail starts at the ORTPN Resthouse and takes between three and six hours to cover as a round trip, depending on how often you stop and whether you drive or walk from the resthouse to the car park about 3km from the resthouse. The first part of the trail – in essence following the road to the car park – passes through rolling tea plantations dotted with relic forest patches which are worth scanning closely for monkeys (we saw a troop of silver monkeys en route). These relic forest patches can also be rewarding for birds; keen ornithologists might well want to take them slowly, and could perhaps view this section of the trail as a worthy birdwatching excursion in its own right.

The trail then descends into the forest proper, following flat contour paths through a succession of tree-fern-covered ravines, and crossing several streams, before a sharp descent to the base of a pretty but small waterfall. Monkeys are often seen along the way (colobus seem to be particularly common) and the steep slopes allow good views into the canopy. I found this trail to be the most rewarding of those we walked for true forest interior birds, with perhaps 20 species identified including Albertine Rift endemics such as Ruwenzori turaco and yellow-eyed black flycatcher.

Gisakura Tea Estate

A relic forest patch in this tea estate, only 20 minutes' walk from the ORTPN Resthouse, supports a resident troop of 38 Ruwenzori colobus monkeys. This troop is very habituated, far more so than the larger troop at Uwinka, and the relatively small territory the monkeys occupy makes them very easy to locate and to see clearly. Oddly, a solitary red-tailed monkey moves with the colobus – some of the guides say that it is treated as the leader. A visit to this forest patch is treated as a primate walk by the ORTPN office and thus costs US$20.

Particularly in the early morning, the relic forest patch is also an excellent birdwatching site, since it lies in a ravine and is encircled by a road, making it easy to see deep into the canopy. Most of what you see are forest fringe or woodland species (as opposed to forest interior birds), but numerically this proved to be the most rewarding spot we visited in Nyungwe, with some 40 species identified in an hour, notably black-throated apalis, paradise and white-tailed crested monarch, Chubb's cisticola, African golden oriole, green pigeon, olive-green cameroptera, three types of sunbird, two greenbuls and two crimson-wings.

Further afield

One monkey, the grey-cheeked mangabey, can only be seen by those who make a special excursion, on a trip which requires a private vehicle. A mangabey troop, resident in a patch of forest along the Banda road, has been habituated by researchers, who normally spend every Monday and Friday with it (consequently, these are the best days to visit the monkeys, as they will already have been tracked down when you arrive). The turn off to Banda, 800m from the Uwinka Campsite towards Butare, is signposted *Eclise Episcopa*

Above Topi in Akagera National Park

Left Ankole bull

Below Red-chested alethe, Nyungwe Forest Reserve

Above Fishing from dugout canoes, Lake Kivu

Right Church, Butare

Below Hills surrounding Lake Burera

de Rwanda. The monkeys are usually found between 5km and 10km along the turn-off. Tracking the mangabeys is regarded to be a formal primate visit, and must be done in the company of a guide. L'Hoest's, silver and colobus monkeys are also often seen in this area.

During the rainy season, chimpanzees are often present in the vicinity of the coloured trails, and chimp tracking can be undertaken on foot from the campsite. During the dry season, however, the chimps tend to move to higher elevations, and tracking them normally entails a drive followed by a hike of up to four hours in either direction. The chimps are not fully habituated, but they are reasonably approachable. You'll have to check the current situation with the guides.

There are no habituated mona monkeys in Nyungwe, but a troop is resident in the vicinity of Karamba, the site of former gold-digging and – immediately before the civil war – a campsite which might yet be reopened. Karamba lies between the campsite and resthouse, but the area can only be explored on foot accompanied by a guide. The troop at Karamba is very large, and reportedly sometimes keeps company with red-tailed monkeys.

The dirt road to Rangiro, which leaves the main tar road about 1.5km east of Uwinka, is regarded as the best excursion for birdwatchers. This is because the road takes passes through both high- and low-elevation forest within a relatively short distance, and affords good views into the canopy in several places. A 4WD vehicle is essential, and a guide recommended. In addition to birdwatching, the Rangiro road offers some stunning views over the mountains, and is a good place to see mangabeys, silver monkeys, and a variety of butterflies.

THE SOUTHERN LAKE KIVU SHORE
Cyangugu

The most southerly of Rwanda's Lake Kivu ports, Cyangugu (pronounced *Shangugu*) is also the most amorphous, sprawling along a 5km road through the green hills that run down to the lake shore. The upper town, more correctly called Kamembe, is a lively business centre, and the site of the main minibus-taxi stand, market, banks and supermarkets, as well as a clutch of local guesthouses and restaurants. Aside from the views of the lake, and a couple of flaking colonial-era buildings, Kamembe is all energy and no character – bustling it may be, but in truth you could be in pretty much any small undistinguished African town anywhere on the continent.

Far more intriguing is the lower town – Cyangugu proper – which has an almost cinematic quality, coming across rather like an abandoned film set used years ago to make a movie about some colonial West African trading backwater. Cyangugu is situated on the lake shore, alongside a bridge across the Rusizi River where it flows out of the lake, which is also the main border crossing between southern Rwanda and the DRC. The town consists of little more than one pot-hole-scored main road, yet within its abrupt confines it does have a decidedly built-up feel, and must once have been rather grand and prosperous. Today, however, many of the old multi-storey buildings have been reduced to shells – victims of one or other war, perhaps, or just decades of neglect – generating an aura of dilapidation underscored by the anomalous Hotel du Lac Kivu, with its freshly painted modern exterior, and the neatly cropped lawn of the Home St François. The outmoded façades of Cyangugu speak of better times past, and while the town's aura of tropical ennui is less than invigorating, it is also somehow rather moving.

While the prefecture of Kibuye (see pages 159–60) has the sad distinction of being the site of the most extensive extermination of Tutsis during the genocide, the prefecture of Cyangugu comes second. Before the French set up their 'safe zone', it was estimated that 85–90% of Tutsis here had died. Many communities were completely wiped out.

Unless you are thinking of crossing into the DRC, Cyangugu has to be classed as something of a dead end in travel terms. It is, however, the closest town to Nyungwe, with far smarter accommodation than anything in the forest, and might therefore make an attractive alternative base for self-drive visitors to Nyungwe. The lake-shore setting is lovely, too, and this atmospheric old town forms a good base from which to explore more off-the-beaten-track destinations such as the Bugarama Hot Springs and Cyamudongo Forest.

Getting there and away
By road
Regular minibus-taxis connect Kigali and Butare to Cyangugu – or more accurately to Kamembe, which is where the main minibus stand for Cyangugu is situated. The fare from Kigali is around US$7, and from Butare around US$4. Direct transport between Kamembe and Kibuye is restricted to one bus daily.

A steady stream of minibus-taxis run back and forth between Kamembe and the border post at Cyangugu, at a cost equivalent to US$0.25 for the 5km trip. The Peace Guesthouse and Hotel des Chutes both lie within 50m of the taxi route, as does the main harbour and port.

By boat
Public lake transport should restart now that the situation with the DRC is calmer; meanwhile two private operators in Kibuye have boats for hire linking Cyangugu to Kibuye and thence to Gisenyi (see page 201). The Guest House Kibuye (reception tel: 568554) has three boats, two seating six and one seating 12; the trip Kibuye–Cyangugu costs US$160 and takes one hour. Telephone Eric on 08683206 or Pascal on 08323555. The Hotel Centre Béthanie (reception tel: 568235) has two boats seating up to 50. Kibuye/Cyangugu costs US$180 and takes five hours. Telephone Omar on 08846826 or Joseph on 08620853. In Cyangugu, the Hotel des Chutes can arrange lake transport; see below.

Where to stay
Near the border post
The **Hotel du Lac Kivu** (tel: 08527709) is about the smartest option in Cyangugu, a beacon of relative prosperity amidst the row of semi-dilapidated buildings that runs along the river immediately south of the border post with

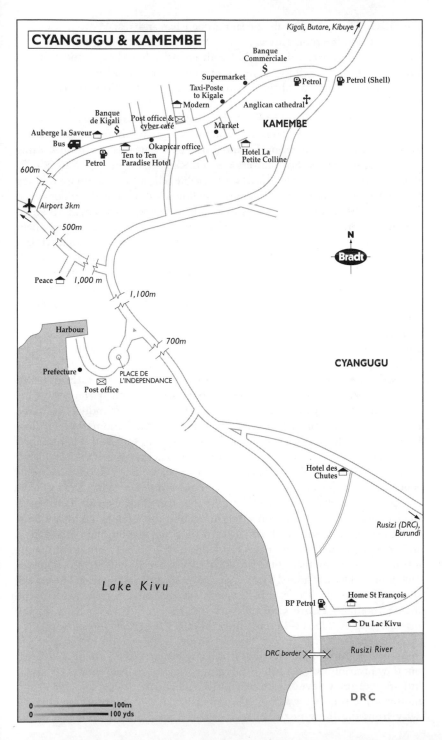

CYANGUGU & KAMEMBE

Kigali, Butare, Kibuye

Banque
Commerciale
$

Supermarket

Taxi-Poste
to Kigale

Petrol

Petrol (Shell)

Banque
de Kigali
$

Modern

Post office &
cyber café

Anglican cathedral

KAMEMBE

Auberge la Saveur

Bus

Petrol

Ten to Ten
Paradise Hotel

Okapicar office

Market

Hotel La
Petite Colline

600m

Airport 3km

500m

N

Bradt

Peace   1,000 m

1,100m

Harbour

700m

CYANGUGU

Prefecture

PLACE DE
L'INDEPENDANCE

Post office

Hotel des
Chutes

Rusizi (DRC),
Burundi

Lake Kivu

BP Petrol

Home St François

Du Lac Kivu

DRC border

Rusizi River

DRC

0   100m
0   100 yds

the DRC. The hotel has an appealing open bar and restaurant area on the riverfront, and the rooms are very comfortable. Prices range from US$10–16 B&B for an ordinary single/double with en-suite hot shower and balcony, through to US$30 B&B for a large suite with television and en-suite hot bath – as well as a big barren volleyball court of a spare room, whose role is difficult to discern.

Opposite the Hotel du Lac Kivu, the church-run **Home St François** (tel: 537915) is easily the best budget option in Cyangugu – in fact as good a deal as you'll find anywhere in Rwanda. Its 24 clean, secure rooms using communal toilets and hot showers cost US$3.50–4.50 single, US$6.50–7.50 double and US$7.50 triple. Meals are available, cheap but otherwise nothing to shout about, and the atmosphere is very homely if not exactly full of cheer. Be warned that unmarried couples are emphatically not accepted, and married couples shouldn't rely on being given the benefit of whatever doubt might exist in the receptionist's mind (all the rooms were 'full' until we shoved our wedding rings under her nose).

Set on a rise about 500m back from the border post, the **Hotel des Chutes** (tel: 537405, 537015, 08323555) boasts an attractive location overlooking the lake, and the balcony is fun for a drink or snack. The rooms are around the same price as those at the Hotel du Lac Kivu but not as nice: comfortable beds and crisp, fresh linen but some bathrooms in need of a face-lift. If you can get a front one with a lake view that makes a big difference. You may be able to fix lake transport to Kibuye from here – ask at reception.

About 1km before you reach Kamembe, the **Peace Guesthouse** (tel: 537799, 08522727; email: mutaben@yahoo.fr) is nicely located overlooking the lake. Constructed by the Anglican Church in 1998, it's a friendly place. Basic rooms with communal hot showers cost US$6–10; small rooms with en-suite hot bath cost US$10–15. There are also five rondavels, each with a lounge, two double bedrooms and en-suite hot bath at US$25 per room or US$50 the unit. Rwandan VIPs – including the president – have stayed here. Good-value meals (but no alcohol) are available in the restaurant, and there are internet facilities.

Up in Kamembe itself, you can't miss the large, new **Ten to Ten Hotel** (tel/fax: 537818). It has 30 rooms (ten on each of three floors, no lift); US$30 with lake views, US$24 without. It has TVs, room service, massage, sauna... and echoey passages which make you vulnerable to noise from other guests. On no account stay there on Friday/Saturday when the nightclub continues loudly until the early hours! The rooms are clean, airy and modern but the en-suite bathrooms need a few small repairs. Another new place in Kamembe is the 18-room **La Petite Colline**: very local, lots of character, close to the market, rooms US$12–14 en suite, US$8 sharing facilities. There are inventive decorations (flower holders made from old car parts...) and a 'museum' of African art. I couldn't find anyone speaking French or English but they probably do exist. Almost opposite the Ten to Ten, the very pleasant little **Auberge la Saveur** (tel: 08623617) has en-suite twins for US$10 and non-en-suite singles for US$7. The rooms are round a quiet courtyard, set away from the lively restaurant and bar. Camping may be possible in the garden – negotiate with the owner. The **Modern Rest Lodge** ($7–10) is pretty scruffy.

Where to eat and drink

The best food overall is probably at the **Hotel du Lac Kivu** and the surroundings are so pleasant; its open-air bar is relaxing, as is the terrace at **Hotel des Chutes** which also has a reasonable menu. Up in Kamembe the **Ten To Ten restaurant** is correct but a bit boring; the **Auberge la Saveur** is good value, organises barbecues by request and has a lively bar. There are also plenty of small places around the market area; and the restaurant at the **Petite Colline** serves a good plateful.

Foreign exchange

The banks provide the usual services but you may find that the independent money-changers around the market offer better rates – however, keep your wits about you. The Bank of Kigali has Western Union.

Excursions

Cyangugu forms the obvious base from which to explore the far southwest of Rwanda, a region which sees very few tourists. The southwest boast a couple of points of interest in the form of the Bugarama Hot Springs and Cyamudongo Forest, though you could argue that these landmarks provide a good pretext to explore a remote corner of Rwanda as much as they rank as worthwhile goals in their own right. With access to a private vehicle, this area could be explored as a day trip out of Cyangugu. Using what limited public transport exists, you're definitely in for an adventure: you should probably plan on spending at least one night out of Cyangugu, and should be prepared for long waits at the roadside, or a lot of walking.

Note that several travel guides refer to the **Rusizi Falls** (*Les Chutes des Rusizi*) on the Rusizi River along the border with the DRC. We spent a morning searching in vain for this, following a variety of confusing directions, only to conclude that whatever waterfall may once have existed has long been submerged beneath the waters of a colonial-era dam (which also serves as an obscure border crossing into the DRC) about 10km south of Cyangugu. My best guess as to the cause of the apparent confusion is that, like the Owen Falls Dam in Uganda, this is referred to locally as the Rusizi Falls Dam. If any readers are able to enlighten me further, we'd be grateful to hear from them.

Another possible excursion from Cyangugu is to the town of **Bukavu** across the border in the DRC. If you do go into DRC, and if you're of a nationality that needs a visa for Rwanda, then unless you have a multiple-entry (rather than a single-entry) Rwandan visa you'll have to pay again – US$60 – to re-enter Rwanda.

Bugarama Hot Springs (Amashyuza ya Bugarama)

Situated slightly less than 60km from Cyangugu by road, the Bugarama Hot Springs lie at the base of a limestone quarry, 5km from the Cimerwa Cement

Factory, in a lightly wooded area dotted by large sinkholes. The springs bubble up into a large green pool which, as viewed from the roadward side, is initially somewhat disappointing. You can, however, follow a path around the edge of the pool, past a large sinkhole to your left, then leap over the outlet stream to the base of the cliff. Here you are right next to the main springs, which bubble into the pool like a freshly shaken and opened fizzy-drink bottle, and are sizzling hot to the touch.

In a private vehicle the springs can be reached in about 90 minutes from Cyangugu, but they are rather more inaccessible using public transport. The first part of the trip involves following the partially surfaced road that connects Cyangugu to Ruha (a border post with Burundi) for approximately 40km to the junction town of Bugarama. You need to turn left at this junction, along a dirt road that passes through Bugarama and a series of small villages, until after 11km you reach the strip of tar outside the Cimerwa Cement Factory. Here you must turn right, passing the factory gate. After another 5km, immediately past a signpost reading *Secteur Nyamaranko*, you'll see a hillside quarry and three-way fork to your left. Follow the leftmost fork for about 100m, then turn right on to a small dirt track, and after 100m or so you'll see the pool in front of you. If in doubt, ask for directions to the *Amashyuza* (aka *Amahyuza*).

Using public transport, one (very slow) bus and several minibus-taxes cover the Ruha road daily, leaving from Kamembe rather than Cyangugu proper, and taking up to two hours to reach Bugarama town. Bugarama itself isn't much to shout about – a hot, dusty small town ringed by plantations of plantains and pines – but accommodation is available at the **Tripartite Bar**, 50m from the main junction in the direction of the cement factory, where basic single rooms cost US$6 each. There is no regular public transport along the 16km road between the town and the springs, but we noticed quite a few pick-up trucks, so finding a lift – at least as far as the cement factory – shouldn't present a major problem. From there, the 5km walk is along flat terrain, and shouldn't take longer than an hour in either direction.

Cyamudongo Forest

Covering an area of about 6km^2, this isolated patch of montane forest is bisected by a rough dirt road, making it very accessible in a 4WD vehicle, and a realistic goal for some off-the-beaten-track hiking. Despite its small size, Cyamudongo harboured populations of chimpanzee and l'Hoest's monkey prior to the civil war, and, while no research has taken place subsequently, the consensus is that these endangered primates are probably still present in small numbers. The forest is also an important ornithological site, as one of the few true high-altitude forests left in Rwanda, and it may well hold a few rare forest species that are no longer found in Nyungwe. Although Cyamudongo is currently afforded no official protection, my impression (based on comparison with old survey maps) is that it has not shrunk significantly in area over the last couple of decades. There is some talk of protecting it as an isolated annexe of the mooted Nyungwe National Park.

The closest town to the forest is Nyakabuye, a sprawl of traditional homesteads and a few tall concrete buildings centred around a bustling marketplace. Nyakabuye lies about 20km from Bugarama town, and 5km past the hot springs, in an area of plantation and bamboo forest. From the town, a steep road leads uphill for 8km, past traditional homesteads (evidently totally unused to tourists), before it winds through the indigenous forest for 2km. The forest ends at a T-junction in front of a large pine plantation, where a left turn along a 15km road, through rolling hills planted with tea, emerges on the surfaced Butare–Cyangugu road at the Shagasha Tea Estate. If you are driving to the forest directly from Cyangugu or the Butare road, it would probably be preferable to approach it via this tea estate, which is signposted from the main road. Either way, there are several forks along the road between the tea estate and the forest, so keep asking directions (bearing in mind that the forest is known locally as Nyirandakunze after a deceased queen).

It isn't easy to reach Cyamudongo Forest without private transport. With patience, it should be possible to catch a lift as far as Nyakabuye on the back of a truck from Bugarama. According to locals, Nyakabuye is also serviced by some sort of public transport direct from Kamembe (Cyangugu) on Wednesdays and Fridays. You'll almost certainly have to walk the 8km from town to the forest boundary, a steep but attractive trail, along which you are bound to attract a lot of friendly attention from curious children (and adults, for that matter). No formal accommodation exists in the area, but it is difficult to imagine that anybody would refuse permission to pitch a tent at one of the homesteads which line the road up to the forest, or that any significant risk would be attached to doing so. But the reality, as with any truly off-the-beaten-track travel, is that this trip should only be attempted by adventurous, flexible travellers who are prepared to deal with a total absence of tourist facilities.

Kibuye

The most conventionally pretty of the lake ports, Kibuye sprawls across a series of hills interwoven with the lagoon-like arms of the lake. Now that the new road from Kigali has been completed, it is the lakeside town most quickly accessible from the capital, and seems much busier with tourists – both foreign and Rwandan – than Gisenyi or Cyangugu. At weekends you'll find families from elsewhere in Rwanda enjoying the small beaches and the swimming, some of them former exiles who returned after the genocide and are rediscovering their country. Hills planted with pines and eucalyptus give the locale a pristine, almost Alpine appearance, in contrast to the atmosphere of fading tropical languor which to some extent afflicts the other ports. It's a green, peaceful and appealing place, whose sudden views of the lake sparkling amid overhanging trees are true picture-postcard material.

It's hard to believe, amid today's sunlight and tranquillity, that during the genocide the prefecture of Kibuye experienced the most comprehensive slaughter of Tutsis anywhere in Rwanda. Previously there had been around 60,000 in the prefecture, an unusually high proportion of about 20%. When the French troops arrived afterwards they estimated that up to nine out of every ten had been killed. Whole communities were annihilated, leaving no witnesses to the crime. If you alight from your minibus-taxi near the sports stadium you will see just one of the mass graves, with a sign announcing: 'More than 10,000 people were inhumated here. Official ceremony was presided over by H E Pasteur Bizimungu, President of the Republic of Rwanda. April 26th 1995.' Now birds chirp on the surrounding wall and the laughter of children in the nearby primary school echoes across the enclosure. Here and throughout Rwanda, memories of the genocide remain acute but daily life carries on determinedly around them. As does tourism.

Getting there and away
By road
There are two minibus-taxis daily from Gisenyi, charging around US$2.50. Apparently no minibus-taxis run regularly between Cyangugu and Kibuye, but there's one bus daily in either direction, leaving at 08.00 and taking up to five hours. The main access is by an excellent road from Kigali via Gitarama, started by the Chinese in 1990. On some stretches it's a considerable feat of engineering, cutting through hillsides and teetering around steep valleys. The journey from Kigali's Nyabugogo bus station takes around two and a half hours. When you arrive by minibus-taxi, alight at the crossroads at the entry to town if you want the Kibuye Guesthouse or the Home St Jean; continue to the final stop by the sports stadium for the Béthanie. There are sometimes some bicycle-taxis around if your bags are heavy.

By boat
Public lake transport should restart now that the situation with the DRC is calmer; meanwhile the Kibuye Guesthouse and the Hotel Centre Béthanie in Kibuye have boats for hire linking Kibuye to Cyangugu and Gisenyi. See under *Gisenyi* (page 201).

Where to stay
The **Kibuye Guesthouse** (BP 1982 Kigali; tel: 568554/568555; mobile: 08300954; fax: 577278; email: gsthouse@rwanda1.com; web: www.kibuyeguesthouse.co.rw), with 22 simply furnished, self-contained rondavel-style rooms at US$24 single/$36 double, isn't cheap. But the beds and bedding are comfortable and good quality, the water is hot, and the location – beside a small beach on the grassy lake shore, with great views and technicoloured sunsets – is idyllic. A campsite with permanent tents is planned: US$10 per tent approx. The restaurant (indoor and outdoor) is excellent, with meals in the US$4–6 range (or more expensive dishes if you feel like a treat), and the place is popular with holidaying Rwandans at weekends. If you had a tough gorilla-trek and you don't mind the cost, you could well relax here for a couple of days – swimming is safe and there are boat trips and waterskiing (for a price) on the lake, as well as tennis and ping-pong.

The **Hotel Centre Béthanie** (tel: 568235) has a beautiful position, also overlooking the lake. It's a lively, friendly place. It has 42 rooms, mostly en-

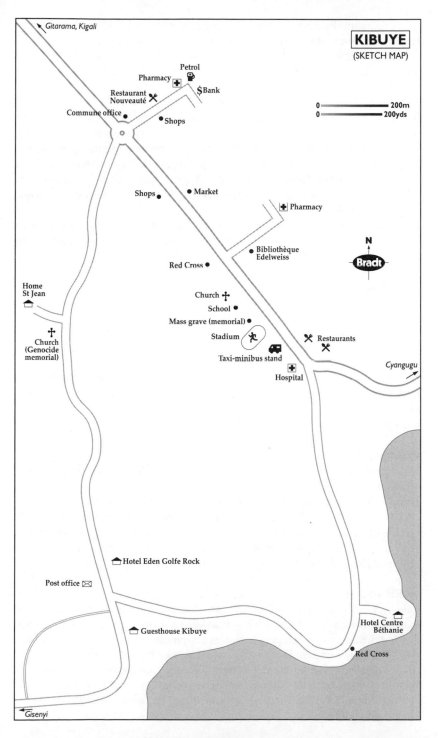

KIBUYE
(SKETCH MAP)

↖ Gitarama, Kigali

Petrol
Pharmacy
Restaurant Nouveauté
Commune office
Shops
$ Bank

0 ——— 200m
0 ——— 200yds

N
Bradt

Shops
Market
Pharmacy

Bibliothèque Edelweiss

Red Cross

Home St Jean

Church (Genocide memorial)

Church
School
Mass grave (memorial)
Stadium
Taxi-minibus stand
Hospital

Restaurants

Cyangugu →

Hotel Eden Golfe Rock

Post office ⊠

Hotel Centre Béthanie

Guesthouse Kibuye

Red Cross

← Gisenyi

suite, thoughtfully built to give views of the lake: from US$16 to US$24. The restaurant, overlooking the lake, provides all meals. And the lakeside location is beautiful; it is more wooded than around the Kibuye Guesthouse so there are more birds. Normally there is plenty of space but the rooms can fill up if there's a religious gathering or seminar, so it's safer to book in advance.

Finally, the cheapest accommodation option is the **Home St Jean** (tel: 568193), tucked away down a lane to the right-hand side of the large church that you'll see on a hill as you enter Kibuye from the east. It is signposted from near the church but rather indistinctly. It took a battering during the genocide but reopened in 1996: ten clean doubles at US$6.50 per person with shared facilities.

The **Hotel Eden Golfe Rock** may look promising, but in fact it has been bought by a Chinese road-building company and is now used to house Chinese personnel.

I have just heard – but too late to check it out – that some nuns are opening up simple, cheap accommodation near the roundabout (see town plan). Let us know for the next edition!

Where to eat/drink

The restaurant at the **Kibuye Guesthouse** is excellent, either for a full meal or just for a drink sitting out at a lakeside table admiring the view. When I checked it out for this edition, a new chef had arrived two months before – and he's great! See details in *Where to stay*, above. The restaurant at the **Béthanie** is also fine, with a standard menu. In town, two small restaurants near the hospital serve traditional *mélanges* of rice, meat and vegetables, as does the fancifully named **Restaurant Nouveauté** (also good for a snack or drink) at the northern end of town. There are plenty of places for a quick beer or fruit juice when you're strolling.

Practicalities

The **post office** down near the Kibuye Guesthouse has international telephone and fax facilities and the staff are endlessly helpful. In town, the **Banque Continentale Africaine Rwanda** can change cash – I suspect US dollars may be easier than other currencies. There's a **pharmacy** down a side road to the right of the market as you face it; follow the sign to it and you'll pass the **Bibliothèque Edelweiss**, a tiny lending library with a stock of children's and adults' literature in French.

What to see

Kibuye is such a relaxed, pleasant town that it's enjoyable just strolling and watching life unfold. There's a big **market** on Fridays, in an open area just beyond the hospital, when people come in from outlying villages and across the lake from Idjwi Island. The week-long market in the centre of town hasn't a huge range but is still worth a browse. You'll come across work parties of prisoners quite often in Kibuye, as elsewhere in Rwanda, in their silly pink uniforms and Bermuda shorts – without them, far less reconstruction would have been completed.

As the sketch map shows, you can do a **circular walk** around Kibuye. This offers some beautiful views across the lake and can be stretched to fill a couple of hours or so, depending on how often you stop to photograph, birdwatch or just enjoy the surroundings. Views are slightly better going clockwise rather than anticlockwise. Once you've passed the hospital on your way up to the Béthanie there's nowhere to get a drink until you're back down by the Kibuye Guesthouse, so you may want to carry some water.

Boat trips from Kibuye
Apart from longer trips to Cyangugu and Gisenyi (see page 201) there are possibilities for trips on Lake Kivu and to nearby islands: Napoleon's Island (it's shaped like his hat) which has a colony of fruit bats, and Amahoro Island where there is a restaurant, volleyball and camping (bring your own tent as the ones offered are rather tatty). The Guest House Kibuye has boats for hire, as does the Hotel Centre Béthanie (see both under hotel listing, above); also an independent operator, Jean-Baptiste, has two 30-seater boats; tel: 08482315; email: rugijean2003@yahoo.fr.

The genocide memorial
As you enter Kibuye from the east, you'll see a large church perched on a hill above the town. During the genocide, over 4,000 died there. Lindsey Hilsum describes it with powerful economy of words in *Granta* issue 51:

> The church stands among trees on a promontory above the calm blue
> of Lake Kivu. The Tutsis were sheltering inside when a mob, drunk
> on banana beer, threw grenades through the doors and windows and
> then ran in to club and stab to death the people who remained alive.
> It took about three hours.

For some time the church remained empty and scarred. Then gradually work started – new mosaics were sketched out and new stained glass filled the broken windows. New hangings adorned the altar. A memorial has been built outside by the relatives of those who died there and nearby. During the week it is still empty, for anyone who wants to go to reflect peacefully on the past, but on Sundays now it is filled with worshippers and their singing wafts out across Lake Kivu. For me, a memorial of this kind is far more evocative and far more moving than the skulls of Nyamata or the corpses of Murambi. Here there is an echoing beauty, which is no bad accompaniment to thoughts of death. Try to find time for a few reflective minutes in this deeply memorable place.

Ndaba Falls
On your way back by minibus-taxi along the road to Gitarama, look out for this waterfall some distance away on your right about 20km out from Kibuye. Passengers will point it out to you if you warn them beforehand – in French it's the *Chutes de Ndaba*. In the rainy season it's an impressive 100m cascade, in the dry season a fairly unimpressive straggle. You can ask for the minibus to drop you at the viewpoint. Going in the other direction it's harder to spot.

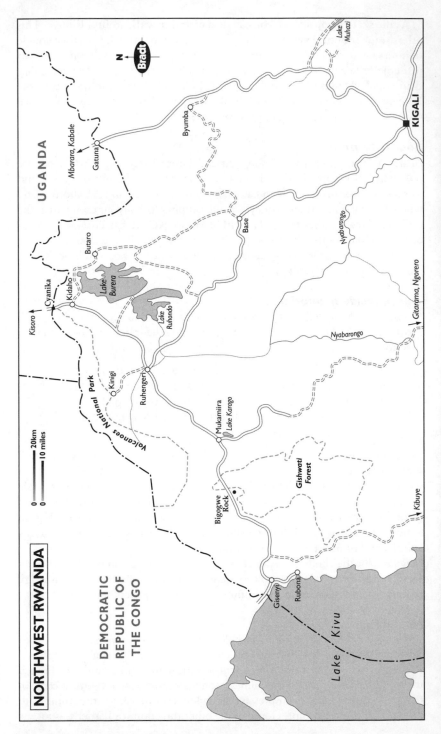

NORTHWEST RWANDA

UGANDA

DEMOCRATIC
REPUBLIC OF
THE CONGO

KIGALI

Byumba

Mbarara, Kabale

Gatuna

Base

Nyabarongo

Butaro

Cyanika

Kidaho

Lake
Burera

Lake
Ruhondo

Kisoro

Gitarama, Ngorero

Nyabarongo

Kinigi

Ruhengeri

Volcanoes National Park

Mukamiira

Lake Karago

Gishwati
Forest

Bigogwe
Rock

Kibuye

Gisenyi

Rubona

Lake Kivu

Lake
Muhazi

0   20km
0   10 miles

Northwest Rwanda

The far north of Rwanda is the focal point of the country's tourist industry. The main point of interest for most travellers is the Volcanoes National Park (*Parc des Volcans*), which protects the Rwandan section of the Virunga volcanoes, and harbours approximately half of the world's mountain gorillas. The Volcanoes Park is currently the best place anywhere in Africa to go gorilla-tracking, while also supporting a number of other localised mammal, bird and plant species.

Only 90 minutes' drive from Kigali, the modestly sized town of Ruhengeri is the most important tourist centre in the north, situated at the base of the Virunga Mountains only 15km from the forest inhabited by the mountain gorillas. Ruhengeri has a good range of tourist facilities, including plenty for budget travellers, and it also forms an excellent base from which to explore a number of less celebrated attractions, notably the stunningly curvaceous Lakes Burera and Ruhondo.

The other important tourist centre in the region is Gisenyi, an attractively faded resort town and active port on the shore of Lake Kivu, 60km west of Ruhengeri. Better equipped for upmarket tourism than Ruhengeri, Gisenyi forms a good alternative base from which self-drive tourists can visit the gorillas, while also offering a seductive tropical ambience that makes it a great place for backpackers to settle into for a few days.

Good roads connect Ruhengeri and Gisenyi to Kigali and southern Uganda, and the region as a whole has an agreeably moderate year-round climate and consistently attractive mountain scenery. Its location close to the Uganda and DRC borders made it an unsettled area both before and for some time after the genocide, because of army and guerrilla activity. From a tourist's perspective, security is no longer a serious concern, but still seek local advice before heading off the beaten track.

RUHENGERI

Location, they say, is everything, and on this score Ruhengeri is privileged indeed. As the closest town to the Volcanoes National Park, it is a most convenient base from which to track mountain gorillas in the Virungas, and is probably the busiest tourist centre in Rwanda (which means that on a busy day you may bump into a few other travellers here). Not only do the Virungas harbour the world's only extant population of mountain gorillas, but their distinctive volcanic outlines provide an otherwise workaday town with a memorably stirring backdrop, at least in clear weather.

For all its strategic importance, Ruhengeri is an unremarkable town, sprawling amorphously from the tight grid of pot-holed roads that surround the central market. But it's a very agreeable travel base: the mood is friendly and free of hassle, and the temperate mid-altitude climate is difficult to fault. The market is lively and worth a visit, and there are some pleasant strolls around town.

Getting there and away
The main minibus-taxi stand is on Avenue de la Nutrition, at the edge of the compact town centre, within five minutes' walk of the cheaper hotels.

To/from Kigali
Kigali and Ruhengeri are linked by a 96km surfaced road. It's in fair condition, though the combination of outrageous bends, the occasional pot-hole, and some seriously manic local drivers requires caution. Even so, you should cover the distance in 90 minutes.

Regular minibus-taxis connect Kigali (Nyabugogo bus station) and Ruhengeri, leaving in either direction when they have a full complement of passengers. Tickets cost about US$2 and the trip takes around 90 minutes.

About 35km out of Kigali, on your left, you'll see a small but ornate cemetery, very different in style from those elsewhere in Rwanda. The graves there are those of Chinese workers who died during the building of this road and others in Rwanda – the excellent Kigali–Kibuye road is also one of theirs.

To/from Gisenyi
The 62km drive between Ruhengeri and Gisenyi follows a fairly good (and by Rwandan standards unusually straight) surfaced road, and should take no longer than an hour and a quarter. Minibus-taxis between the two towns leave regularly and cost US$1.50.

Driving from Ruhengeri to Gisenyi, you pass (on the left) a surfaced road that goes first to Lake Karago (see page 172) and then continues southwards to join the Gitarama–Kibuye road, as shown on the map inside the front cover. It winds high up into the hills and the views are breathtaking – and you've plenty of time to admire them because the middle stretch (about 35km) is unsurfaced and so full of pot-holes that you can only drive very slowly. It passes through hamlets and beside tea plantations, so there is human interest too, but the main attraction has to be the wonderfully panoramic landscape. You could consider it as an alternative way of returning to Kigali from either Ruhengeri or Gisenyi. Hikers can probably get lifts as transport goes to and from the tea plantations – and I passed one bus, although I can't imagine how its suspension survives the jolting.

To/from Uganda

The border crossings between Uganda and Rwanda are covered more fully on page 27. Coming to Ruhengeri straight from Kampala, the most efficient option is to catch a bus or minibus heading directly to Kigali, where you can pick up a minibus-taxi to Ruhengeri.

Coming from the west of Uganda, you will have to pass through Kabale, from where you can either cross directly into Rwanda at the Katuna border post, or else continue within Uganda to Kisoro and cross at the Cyanika border post. If you have private transport, or are visiting Kisoro anyway, then the Cyanika route is the better option. Kisoro and Ruhengeri lie approximately 40km from each other along a mostly tarred road. On public transport, you'll have to change vehicles at the border, and can expect to pay around US$1 for each leg.

Otherwise, given the poor state of the road between Kabale and Kisoro (as well as the limited amount of public transport), the most circuitous route between Kabale and Ruhengeri on paper is almost certainly the most efficient in practice: that is to catch a minibus-taxi from Kabale to Kigali (you might need to change vehicles at the border), from where you can pick up another to Ruhengeri. A variation on this would be to stop at Byumba on the Kabale–Kigali road, then travel along the back road to Base on the Ruhengeri–Kigali road, but this will almost certainly entail spending a night in Byumba (see pages 195–6).

Where to stay

Ruhengeri boasts an unusually good selection of affordable accommodation. The most upmarket option is the **Hotel Muhabura** (BP 118; tel/fax: 546296), which lies on the outskirts of town along Avenue du 5 Juillet in the direction of Gisenyi. Set in compact green grounds, this is a very pleasant and reasonably priced hotel, with ten rooms: large self-contained doubles with hot bath and shower for US$14 and larger suites, also with hot shower and bath, for US$20. A good bar and restaurant are attached to the hotel.

Of the cheaper places scattered around the town centre, the pick is the **Home d'Accueil Moderne** (BP 121, tel: 546525; fax: 546904), situated on Avenue du 5 Juillet diagonally opposite the market and only two minutes' walk from the minibus stand. Its eight clean, freshly painted double or twin rooms with nets and en-suite toilet and hot shower cost US$6 single, US$8 double. The staff here are very friendly and helpful, safe parking is available, and it's no problem if you arrive with US dollars only.

Not quite so central, but still only a few minutes on foot from the minibus stand, the **Centre d'Accueil de l'Eglise Episcopale** is set in large church grounds on Avenue du 5 Juillet near the junction with Rue de Pyrèthre. Basic but clean rooms, some with nets, cost US$6 per person. There are also dormitory beds at US$2. The welcome is friendly, the communal ablutions are clean and have hot showers, and a limited selection of meals is available. Camping is normally permitted in the church grounds for a nominal charge.

Back in the town centre, on Rue de Muhabura, the new and friendly **Tourist Rest House** (tel: 08520758) is a relative of the popular Skyblue Hotel

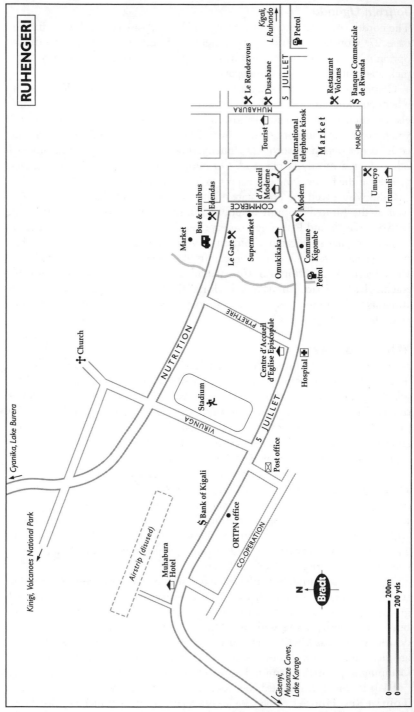

RUHENGERI

Kigali,
L Ruhondo
Petrol

Le Rendezvous
Dusabane

5 JUILLET

Restaurant
Volcans

Banque Commerciale
de Rwanda

MUHABURA

Tourist

International
telephone kiosk

Market

MARCHE

d'Accueil
Moderne

Modern

Umucyo

Urumuli

COMMERCE

Market

Bus & minibus
Edendas

Le Gare

Supermarket

Omukikaka

Commune
Kigombe

Petrol

PYRETHRE

NUTRITION

Centre d'Accueil
d'Eglise Episcopale

Hospital

Stadium

5 JUILLET

VIRUNGA

Church

Cyanika, Lake Burera

Kinigi, Volcanoes National Park

Post office

Bank of Kigali

ORTPN office

CO-OPERATION

Airstrip (disused)

Muhabura
Hotel

N

Bradt

200m
200 yds

Gisenyi,
Musanze Caves,
Lake Karago

in Kabale (Uganda), which means the staff speak English. The five clean but cramped rooms (singles only, en-suite with hot water) are adequate, and at US$6 are reasonably good value.

The **Hotel Urumuli** (aka Hotel Urumuri, tel: 546820), which lies on a back road close to the market, charges US$7 for a small, scruffy self-contained double with flaking paint and no hot water.

About 2–3km out of town (along the Cyanika road past the turning to Kinigi and the park) is the **Hotel Ituze** (tel: 547064, 547014), with nine en-suite rooms (cold water) for US$7–10. The welcome is friendly and it's well away from the bustle of the town but realistically you'd need transport. The restaurant serves good-value basic meals for US$2–6. It's so new that I can't judge how it'll turn out. Ignore signs in town to a **Motel du Mont Nyamagamba**; it's just a bar/restaurant.

In addition to the places listed above, there is accommodation within 20km of Ruhengeri at Kinigi (Volcanoes National Park), Lake Karago and Lake Ruhondo (see pages 182–3, 172 and 176 respectively).

Where to eat and drink

As with hotels, there is plenty of choice when it comes to eating out in Ruhengeri. The most extensive and expensive menu, inevitably, is at the **Muhabura Hotel**. The food is pretty good here – a selection of grills, stews and mild curries at around US$5–7 for a heaped plate – and so is the ambience on the semi-shaded balcony. Beers and other drinks are only slightly more expensive than at the local bars and restaurants in town.

The **Home d'Accueil Moderne** has a popular courtyard restaurant serving a fair selection of grilled and fried meals in the US$2–3 range (great fish and chips). The courtyard restaurant in the **Hotel Urumuli** was our favoured place to eat in Ruhengeri; the whole tilapia (a freshwater fish), chicken and goat kebabs are all recommended and excellent value. The **Tourist Rest House** also has an inviting menu, dominated by stews rather than grills.

Scattered around town are at least a dozen local restaurants serving local food for around US$1 per plate – the **Modern** (roughly opposite the Home d'Accueil Moderne) is a cut above the rest. And there are plenty of grocers with a range of cans, jars, packets, bottles and so forth.

Other practicalities
Foreign exchange
There's a branch of the **Bank of Kigali** close to the Muhabura (it has Western Union too) and a **Banque Commerciale du Rwanda** behind the market. See warnings on page 35 about travellers' cheques – cash is safer.

Travellers fresh across the border from Uganda will probably need to change some foreign currency in Ruhengeri. With US dollars, this shouldn't be a problem: most of the hotels will sort you out at a rate fractionally lower than the street rate in Kigali, which is probably a safer bet than trying to change money on the street or in the market. If you don't have US dollars, you've probably no option but to use one of the banks.

CLIMBING MOUNT KABUYE
Doug Teschner

This 2,643m peak is a pleasant hike, all the more attractive because it can be done easily in a day from Kigali without having to leave before dawn – and you're still back in town before dark. Also, as it's so close to the main road, you can get there by public transport. The hike involves 1,000 metres of ascent and takes two to four hours to the top (a four-to-seven-hour round trip of about 12km) for most people.

The 'mountain' is visible from the Kigali–Ruhengeri road, on the right about an hour out of Kigali. It stands out as a hill that is bigger than the rest. You may wish to obtain a topo map (Gakenke, map number 9) from the Ministry of Public Works in the Gikondo section of Kigali, but it is not necessary as long as visibility is good enough to see the mountain (which it almost always is).

To get there, drive for about 75 minutes out of Kigali. Then look for a village that includes a yellow building named (what else?) Mont Kabuye. Just after this village, a paved road leaves the main road on the right. There is a blue sign marked 'Hospital Nemba 1 km'. Take this road (which quickly becomes dirt) down and loop back left through 'town' to a soccer field on the right and a log bridge. Park here. The total distance from the main road is 0.8 km. The guy in the house across the bridge will probably appear and offer to guard your car. If you like 4-wheeling, you can cross the bridge and go as far as you are comfortable along this steep narrow road (maybe 1,500m at the very most).

Hikers should cross the bridge and follow the road, climbing steadily to its end (about 2 km). After 30 minutes, look for a little shack on the right which (if open) will sell you warm Fantas and you may even be able to arrange for a child to carry some to the top. This is a good way to keep hydrated and support the local economy.

Where the road ends at a pipe, there is an obvious steep section of trail. Above this, there are multiple trails and it is not always easy to pick the best

ORTPN

The ORTPN office in Ruhengeri town is on the first floor of the municipal buildings on Avenue du 5 Juillet; look out for the signpost on the opposite side of the road to the Hotel Muhabura and Centre d'Accueil de l'Eglise Episcopale, and about halfway between them.

The second ORTPN office, in Kinigi, is on the slopes of the Virungas about 12km from Ruhengeri, near the entrance to the park.

Arrangements between these two offices may change before this guide is published; so check with the main ORTPN office in Kigali (see page 53) which – if either – of the two you should approach for last-minute permits or to confirm a booking.

Communications

There are embryonic email and internet facilities in Ruhengeri at the time of one, but you can easily readjust on smaller trails if you lose the main one. The best route goes right at the top of the steep section and stays just to the right of the ridge, passing by the local water supply and eventually passing a school (prominently visible from below) in a big clearing. Above the school, the trail follows the right side of the ridge to a T-Junction. Turn left and enjoy the short flat stretch before turning right and heading steeply back up the very scenic ridge through farmlands and by houses with the mountain prominently visible above. If the sky is very clear, views of the volcanoes will appear off to the left.

After a while, the trail switches over to the left side of the ridge and soon reaches a flattish place on the ridge proper. Turn right after 50m for a scenic rest on rocks in a eucalyptus grove. You're about two-thirds of the way to the top. After your rest, continue up the steepening ridge toward the summit cone. A short steep section up a grassy patch leads to a rocky trail, which slabs off to the left and eventually swings around the peak to reach the pass on the left (north) side of the summit.

At the pass, leave the main trail by turning right on a smaller one. You're now 15 minutes from the top. Follow this vague path up the ridge, through new eucalyptus trees, to nearly the top. The precise but somewhat indistinct summit (visible en route from a prior false top) is reached by leaving the path for the final 20 metres. If it is very clear, you can see all the Virunga volcanoes and Lake Ruhondo to the north. Just down on the other side of the summit, there is a pine forest which offers shade on a sunny day.

As in all places in Rwanda, expect to be followed by a pack of children, although I have found that each time we go (I have done it five times), there are fewer, as they seem to be getting used to visitors.

Descend the same way, or pick another. The valley off to the right (looking down) is very beautiful, but it adds at least an hour to the descent. You are welcome to call me (tel: 08560729) if you have questions or want a hiking companion.

writing, and if the trend elsewhere in Rwanda is anything to go by, more will soon appear. Public phones are in various shops and kiosks.

Excursions from Ruhengeri

Most people who visit Ruhengeri see it purely as a base from which to track gorillas (see the section *Volcanoes National Park*) and very few explore the surrounding area further. But several local points of interest make for worthwhile day or overnight excursions from Ruhengeri, notably the little-visited Lakes Karago, Burera and Ruhondo. If rushed for time, you could conceivably visit Gisenyi (on Lake Kivu) as a day trip from Ruhengeri.

Musanze Cave and Natural Bridge

The impressive Musanze Cave lies in the grounds of a school about 2km from the town centre off the Gisenyi road. The main cave, reportedly 2km long, has an entrance the size of a cathedral, and is home to an impressive bat colony. The large ditch out of which the cave opens is littered with pockmarked black volcanic rubble, and at the opposite end there is a natural bridge which was formed by a lava flow from one of the Virunga volcanoes.

Legend has it that Musanze Cave was created by a local king, and that it has been used as a refuge on several occasions in history. There are plans to develop it as a tourist attraction – but meanwhile it's advisable not to enter. It was the site of a massacre during the genocide; local people consider it a tomb and don't take kindly to tourists scrambling about inside. Please respect this: either view from a distance or go with a local guide.

To get to Musanze Cave from the town, follow Avenue du 5 Juillet past the Hotel Muhabura towards Gisenyi. Just short of 2km from the town centre, you'll see the large steel *Entrepots Opravia Musanze* to your left. Turn right directly opposite this building, following a curved dirt track which after about 100m leads to a football field and school. The cave lies in a ditch on the opposite side of the football field.

Lake Karago

This small lake is less impressive than the two larger lakes which lie to the east of Ruhengeri, but it is also a lot more accessible on public transport, and sufficiently attractive that it served for years as the site of the president of Rwanda's holiday home. Lake Karago makes for a pleasant rustic excursion from Ruhengeri, the main attraction being the characteristically mountainous Rwandan landscape around the lake and a set of rapids along the river that runs into the lake. There were also quite a few birds around when we visited, notably pelicans and herons.

Lake Karago lies 1.5km from Mukamiira, a small junction town on the main road between Ruhengeri and Gisenyi. Regular *matatus* cover the 20km between Ruhengeri and Mukamiira, where you need to turn left at the main junction towards Ngororero. The walk from Mukamiira to the first viewpoint over the lake takes about 15 minutes. From here, several footpaths lead to the shore, a 10–20-minute descent, depending on how muddy it is and which path you use.

Although Lake Karago can easily be visited as a day trip out of Ruhengeri, there is a welcoming but very basic guesthouse in Mukamiira should you feel moved to spend the night. It is signposted *Bar Restaurant Chambres*, and lies alongside the Gisenyi road about 500 from the Ngororero junction. Single rooms cost US$2.50 (a fair reflection of the quality of the accommodation); hot bucket showers are provided, meals are prepared to order, and the fridge is stocked high with beers and sodas.

For the continuation of the road after Lake Karago, see page 166.

Lake Burera

The largest and most beautiful of the lakes in the vicinity of Ruhengeri, Burera (aka Bulera) has until now been almost entirely neglected by travellers. With a private vehicle, however, the dirt road that loops around Burera's eastern shore makes for a superb day outing, while adventurous backpackers could happily spend several days exploring the lake using a combination of motorcycle-taxis, boats, and foot power. No formal accommodation exists anywhere on the lake shore, but the area is dotted with small villages where it shouldn't be a problem to ask permission to pitch a tent.

Lake Burera is visually reminiscent of Uganda's popular Lake Bunyonyi – not too surprising when you realise that these two bodies of water lie no more than 20km apart as the crow flies. Burera's eccentric shape is defined by the incredibly steep hills that enclose it. The slopes which fall towards the lake are densely terraced and intensively cultivated: very little natural vegetation remains among the fields of plantains, potatoes, beans and other crops, while the most common tree is the Australian eucalyptus. The stunning and distinctive scenery around the lake is enhanced by the outlines of the Virunga Mountains, the closest of which towers 10km away on the western horizon.

For travellers with their own transport, the circuit around the lake is straightforward enough. The road is mostly in good shape, and likely to present no problems provided that your vehicle has reasonable clearance (a 4WD would be advisable during the rainy season). The full round trip from Ruhengeri covers about 150km, 90km of which are on dirt, and realistically takes a minimum of five hours to complete. Better, arguably, to leave after breakfast, carry a picnic lunch, and make a day of it, stopping along the way to enjoy the views and rustic villages.

To follow the circuit, head out of Ruhengeri along the road towards Cyanika for about 15km until you reach Kidaho, where you need to turn right into an unsignposted dirt road. After about six relatively flat kilometres along this track, the lake becomes visible to the right: on the shore you'll see a small fishing village (so far as we could ascertain, this is also called Kidaho) and dozens of small boats used to ferry locals around the lake. A few hundred metres past this village, a side road leads around the small Musangabo peninsula, offering stunning views in all directions.

The largest centre on the eastern shore of the lake is Butaro, which maps would suggest is only about 10km from Musangabo. In reality, the two are divided by a spectacular 44km stretch of road which hugs the cultivated contours about 100–200m above the lake shore. En route, the road passes through the small market village of Umugu. Butaro itself lies a couple of kilometres off the main road; about 50m from the junction, the attractive Rusumo Falls (not to be confused with their namesake on the Tanzania border) tumble over a cliff to the fields next to the lake.

After Butaro, the road veers away from the lake, and the views are few and far between, which leaves you with the option of returning the way you came (65km of which 50 are on dirt) or pushing on to complete the circuit (85km of which 41 are on dirt). Assuming that you decide to sally forth, the next main settlement you will reach, after 13km, is Kirambo (also referred to as Cyeru, the district for which it is the headquarters). Here, you can either turn left along a side road which leads to the village of Ruyange in a cultivated river valley at the southern tip of Lake Burera (a 20km round trip), or else continue straight ahead towards Base on the main Kigali–Ruhengeri

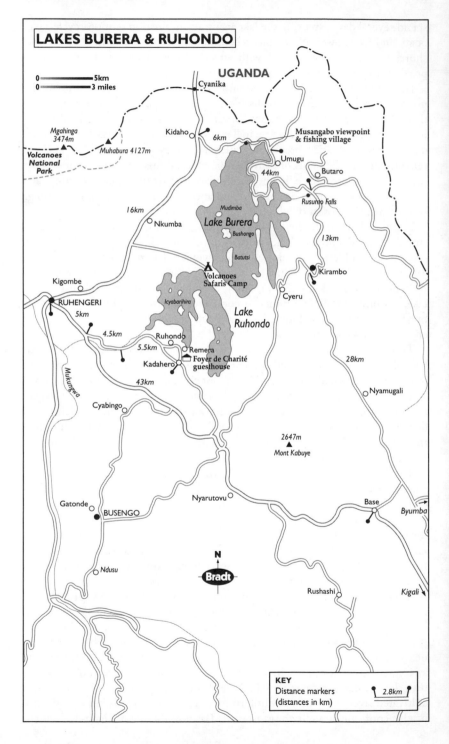

LAKES BURERA & RUHONDO

0 ▬▬▬▬5km
0 ▬▬▬▬3 miles

UGANDA

Cyanika

Mgahinga
3474m
▲
Volcanoes
National
Park
▲ Muhabura 4127m

Kidaho   6km

Musangabo viewpoint
& fishing village

Umugu
44km   Butaro

Rusumo Falls

16km   Nkumba

Mudimba
Lake Burera
❀ Bushongo
Batutsi

13km

Kirambo

Kigombe
RUHENGERI
5km

Volcanoes
Safaris Camp

Icyabarihira

Cyeru

Lake
Ruhondo

4.5km
5.5km   Ruhondo
Kadahero   Remera
□ Foyer de Charité
guesthouse

28km

Mukungwa

43km

Cyabingo

Nyamugali

2647m
▲
Mont Kabuye

Gatonde
BUSENGO

Nyarutovu

Base
Byumba

Ndusu

N

Bradt

Rushashi
Kigali

KEY
Distance markers
(distances in km)   2.8km

road. Base lies 28km past Kirambo, and is almost equidistant between Kigali and Ruhengeri.

For travellers without a vehicle, the absence of public transport along parts of this circuit make it inaccessible or challenging, depending on how you see these things. For a day trip to Burera, it is easy enough to get as far as Kidaho – any Cyanika-bound minibus-taxi can drop you there, though you will probably be expected to pay the full fare of around US$1 – from where a motorcycle-taxi to Musangabo peninsula will cost less than US$1. With an early start, you should also have time to catch a boat-taxi from the fishing village next to the peninsula to the lake shore below Butaro and the Rusumo Falls, and to return the same way. The boat taxi takes 30–60 minutes in either direction, and costs around US$1.25. It should also be straightforward and affordable to hire a boat privately, either to go to the falls, or else just to explore the lake. Beryl Hutchison writes:

> I made the journey to Lake Burera by minibus and got to the
> peninsula by bicycle taxi. It was such a beautiful and tranquil place.
> There were no motorised boats so I hired a pirogue. I was told that
> the journey to Rusumo Falls takes about four hours and although the
> boatman was willing I decided against it. Instead we had a row round
> the lake and then got out of the pirogue and walked through the
> shambas to the Ugandan border.

Keen walkers might also think about exploring the area over a few days. I've not heard of anybody doing this, so it would be uncharted territory, and would probably be practical only if you have a tent and are prepared to ask permission to camp at the many villages and homesteads along the way. It would probably be advisable to carry some food (though fish and potatoes should be easy to buy along the way). It is difficult to imagine that any serious security concerns are attached to hiking in this Uganda border area; you'll come across loads of local pedestrians for company, and travellers are still something of a novelty in this rural area.

The road to the east of the lake can effectively be viewed as an unusually wide hiking trail: it offers great views the whole way, is used by very few vehicles, and follows the contours for most of its length. The most beautiful stretch for hiking is the 44km between Musangabo and Butaro (which can also be covered by boat), and you would be forced to walk the 13km between Butaro and Kirambo. From Kirambo, there is a limited amount of public transport to Base, where it is easy to find a lift on to Ruhengeri or Kigali.

Lake Burera could also be explored more extensively by boat, once again an option suitable only for those with a tent and a pioneering spirit. The obvious place to start a trip of this sort would be Musangabo, though boats are the main form of transport throughout the area, so it should be easy enough to hire a boat and paddler anywhere. In addition to Rusumo Falls, there are at least four large islands in the southern half of the lake: Mudimba, Munanira, Bushongo and Batutsi. In theory, it should be possible to boat to the south of Lake Burera, hike across the narrow strip of hilly terrain that separates it from Lake

Ruhondo, and then pick up another boat to the Foyer de Charité on the southern shore of that lake (see *Lake Ruhondo* below). We've never heard of a traveller who attempted this, so drop us a line to let us know how it goes!

There's a new permanent camp being built between the two lakes and a friend who visited the site recently tells me it 'has probably the best view in Rwanda', overlooking the lakes and the chain of volcanoes. To stay there (and it's likely to be very comfortable) you'll have to book through tour operators Volcanoes Safaris; see contact details on pages 28 and 121. They'll also arrange your gorilla visit and other trips. It's the **Parc National des Volcans** (PNV) **Camp** and should be open by 2004.

Lake Ruhondo

Separated from Lake Burera by a 1km-wide strip of land (thought to be an ancient lava flow from Mount Sabinyo), Lake Ruhondo is, like the more northerly lake, an erratically shaped body of water whose shore follows the contours of the tall, steep hills that characterise this part of Rwanda. In common with Lake Burera, Ruhondo's shores are densely cultivated, and little natural vegetation remains, but it is nevertheless a very beautiful spot, offering dramatic views across the water to the volcanically formed cones of the Virunga Mountains looming on the horizon. Ruhondo is also an easy target for an overnight excursion, since good accommodation is available.

The lake is most accessible from the southwest, where the **Foyer de Charité** guesthouse (BP 53 Ruhengeri; tel: 547024; fax: 547025; mobile: 08510659) has a superb location on a hilltop overlooking the lake, with sweeping views across to the volcanoes in the northwest, and potentially stupendous sunsets. Established as a religious retreat in 1968, the mission was renovated in 1995 after it had been damaged during the genocide, and, although it remains first and foremost a religious retreat, lay visitors are very welcome. More than 40 comfortable guest rooms with wash basins are available, at a charge of US$12/18 single/double (considerably cheaper for church visitors), as are communal hot showers (heated by solar panels), solid meals (around US$1.50 for breakfast and US$5 for lunch or dinner) and cold beers and sodas. It is advisable to phone in advance, as the mission occasionally closes to lay visitors for special religious events.

The best route to the Foyer de Charité starts on the main Kigali road about 5km south of Ruhengeri. Coming from Ruhengeri, you need to turn left along a dirt road signposted for Remera which initially leads through a marshy area dotted with traditional brickmaking urns, before following a cultivated river valley. After 2.8km, take a left fork, then almost 2km after that turn right to cross a bridge over the river. The road is flat until this point, but now it starts to ascend gently, with the lake becoming visible to the left about 2.5km past the bridge. Several footpaths lead from this viewpoint to the lake shore, an easier ascent than the one from the Foyer de Charité. Beyond the viewpoint, the road continues to climb for 3km to the village of Kadahero, where a left turn leads after about 200m to the mission.

This is all straightforward enough provided that you have a vehicle, ideally a 4WD, and that – if driving along the tar from Kigali – you don't inadvertently take an earlier road signposted for Remera (this road does lead to the mission, but it's longer and rougher). There is no public transport, however, and hitching might prove to be frustrating. One option would be to catch public transport towards Ruhengeri as far as the turn-off to Remera, then to walk the final 10km to the mission (the last 6km would be steep going with a rucksack). The alternative is to hire a motorcycle-taxi from Ruhengeri – the going rate is around US$3–4 one-way – and arrange to be collected at a specified time.

There is little in the way of formal entertainment at the mission – the beautiful singing at evening mass in the chapel might qualify I suppose – but it's a lovely place to relax for a couple of days, and there's plenty of room for exploration on the surrounding roads. Several footpaths lead down the steep slopes below the mission to the lake shore, a knee-crunching descent and lung-wrenching ascent. At the lake, it is easy to negotiate a fee to take a pirogue to one of the islands, or to the hydro-electric plant on the opposite shore, where a small waterfall connects Lake Ruhondo with Lake Burera.

THE VOLCANOES NATIONAL PARK

This 13,000-hectare national park (in French *Parc des Volcans*) protects the Rwandan sector of the Virunga Mountains (also known as the Birungas), a range of six extinct and three active volcanoes which straddles the border with Uganda and the DRC. The Volcanoes Park forms a contiguous conservation unit with the Virungas National Park and Mgahinga National Park, which respectively protect the DRC and Ugandan sectors of the Virungas. The three national parks are managed separately today (that's if the word 'managed' can be applied to any park in the DRC at the time of writing). Prior to 1960, however, the Volcanoes and Virungas Parks together formed the Albert National Park.

Under Belgian colonisation, the Albert National Park was established by the decree of April 21 1925, in the triangle (considered a gorilla sanctuary) formed by the Karisimbi, Mikeno and Visoke volcanoes. At the time of its creation it was the first national park in Africa to be known as such. The *Institut du Parc National Albert* was created by decree on July 9 1929. A further decree on November 12 1935 determined the final boundaries of the Albert National Park, then covering 809,000 hectares. About 8% of the park lay in what is now Rwanda and today constitutes the Volcanoes National Park, while the rest was in the Congo. At the time of independence, Rwanda's new leaders confirmed that they would maintain the park (the gorillas were already well known internationally), despite the pressing problem of overpopulation.

Ranging in altitude from 2,400m to 4,507m, the Volcanoes National Park is dominated by the string of volcanoes after which it is named. This chain of steep, tall, free-standing mountains, linked by fertile saddles which were formed by solidified lava flows, is one of the most stirring and memorable sights in East Africa. The tallest mountain in the chain, and the most westerly part of the national park, is Karisimbi (4.507m) on the border with the DRC. Moving eastwards, the other main peaks are Visoke or Bisoke (3,711m), also on the DRC border; Sabinyo (3,634m) at the juncture of Rwanda, Uganda and the DRC; and Gahinga (3,474m) and Muhabura (4,127) on the Uganda border.

The altitudinal vegetation zones of the Virungas correspond closely with those of other large East African mountains, although the Afro-montane forest which once flourished below an altitude of 2,500m has been almost entirely sacrificed to make way for agriculture. Between 2,500m and 3,500m, where an average annual rainfall of 2,000m is typical, bamboo forest is interspersed with stands of tall hagenia woodland. Higher altitudes support a cover of Afro-Alpine moorland, grassland and marsh, a landscape dominated by other-worldly giant lobelia and senecio plants similar to those on Kilimanjaro and the Ruwenzoris.

The Volcanoes National Park is best known to the outside world as the place where, for almost 20 years, the American primatologist Dian Fossey undertook her pioneering studies of mountain gorilla behaviour. It is largely thanks to Fossey's single-mindedness that poaching was curtailed while there were still some gorillas to save. For her dedication, Fossey would pay the ultimate price: her brutal – and still unsolved – murder at the Karisoke Research Centre in December 1985 is generally thought to have been the work of one of the many poachers with whom she crossed swords in her efforts to save her gorillas.

Three years after her death, Fossey's life work was exposed to a mass audience with the release of *Gorillas in the Mist*, a cinematic account of her life filmed on location in the Volcanoes Park. *Gorillas in the Mist* drew global attention to the plight of the mountain gorilla, and generated unprecedented interest in the gorilla tourism programme which had been established in the park some ten years earlier. In 1990, the Volcanoes Park was the best organised and most popular gorilla sanctuary in Africa, and gorilla tourism was probably Rwanda's leading earner of tourist revenue.

The wheels came off in February 1992, when the park headquarters were attacked, two park employees were killed, and the research centre established by Dian Fossey had to be evacuated. The park reopened to tourism in June 1993, but it was evacuated in April 1994 due to the genocide. In late 1995, it once again reopened to tourism, only to close again a few months later. Gorilla tracking was finally resumed on a permanent basis in July 1999, since when the number of tourists visiting the Virungas has increased rapidly. More details of gorillas and gorilla-tracking follow later in this section.

Non-gorilla attractions

The Volcanoes National Park is no longer just about mountain gorillas. Tourists who previously came for just one night can now stay for four or five and still not run out of things to do. Trekking, walking and climbing are now

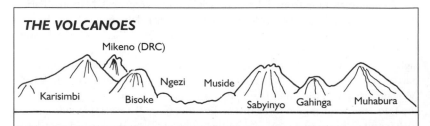

THE VOLCANOES

Mikeno (DRC)

Karisimbi   Bisoke   Ngezi   Muside   Sabyinyo   Gahinga   Muhabura

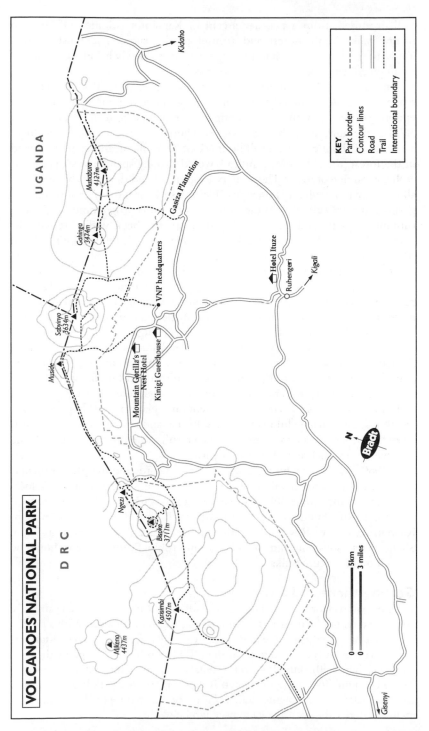

VOLCANOES NATIONAL PARK

DRC

UGANDA

Kidaho

Muhabura
4127m

Gahinga
3474m

Gasiza Plantation

Sabyinyo
3634m

Muside

VNP headquarters

Hotel Ituze

Ruhengeri

Kigali

Mountain Gorilla's
Nest Hotel

Kinigi Guesthouse

Ngezi

Bisoke
3711m

Mikeno
4437m

Karisimbi
4507m

Gisenyi

N

KEY
Park border
Contour lines
Road
Trail
International boundary

5km
3 miles
0
0

well organised, from a two-day ascent of Karisimbi volcano (US$100) to nature walks in the forest and around nearby lakes. The most exciting innovation, however, is that tourists can now visit a newly habituated group of about 40 golden monkeys – see box opposite.

The ascent of Karisimbi is a two-day excursion; ORTPN will provide guides but trekkers should have suitable clothing and equipment. A shorter option (costing US$40) is the ascent of Mount Visoke to its crater lake at 3,711m; the upward climb takes about two hours. For the less energetic, there are walks of about two and a half hours (US$20) to the nearer crater lakes and in the forest; the elder of the authors would happily spend a week going off each day on one of these! The scenery is beautiful and the forest has a quality all of its own. Finally, it is now possible to visit Dian Fossey's tomb and the gorilla cemetery (US$50). At the time of writing this programme hasn't been running for long and will probably develop, so check with ORTPN for current details. All arrangements can be made through the ORTPN offices, whether in Kigali, Ruhengeri or Kinigi.

Gorillas and golden monkeys aside, little information is available regarding the current status of large mammals in the park, but some 76 mammal species have been recorded in Uganda's neighbouring Mgahinga National Park, and it seems reasonable to assume that most of these animals also occur in the larger Rwanda section of the Virungas. Surprisingly, monkeys are poorly represented by comparison with other forests in Rwanda and western Uganda. A small number of silver monkeys, a more widespread race of blue monkey, also occur in the forest of the Virungas. Elephant and buffalo are still quite common, judging by the amount of spoor we encountered, but are very timid and infrequently observed. Also present are giant forest hog, bushpig, bushbuck, black-fronted duiker, spotted hyena, and several varieties of small predator. Recent extinctions, probably as a result of deforestation, include the massive yellow-backed duiker and leopard.

In 1980, roughly 180 bird species had been recorded in the park, though it is possible that several rainforest specialists have since vanished. A local speciality is the vulnerable Grauer's swamp warbler, while at least 13 Albertine Rift endemics are present, including handsome francolin, Ruwenzori turaco, Ruwenzori batis, strange weaver, dusky crimson-wing, Shelley's crimson-wing and Archer's ground robin. Some of these should be spotted on the nature walks.

Getting there and away

The normal base for visiting the Volcanoes Park is Ruhengeri, which can easily be reached on public transport from Gisenyi, Kigali or Uganda. With a private vehicle, it is perfectly possible to drive to Ruhengeri from Gisenyi or Kigali on the day you track (you need to be at the ORTPN office in Kinigi, by the park entrance, by 07.30), but this isn't a reliable option using public transport. There is no public transport between Ruhengeri and the park headquarters at Kinigi. Details of arranging transport to tie in with gorilla-tracking are included under the gorilla-tracking section below.

GOLDEN MONKEYS IN VOLCANOES NATIONAL PARK

The little-known golden monkey (*cercopithecus kandti*) is listed as 'endangered' by the World Conservation Union, so it's a rare treat for visitors to be able to view a newly habituated group of about 40 in the Volcanoes National Park. Visits can be arranged through any ORTPN office; they last for one hour and are for a maximum of six people; the cost in 2004 is likely to be around US$80.

The golden monkey is characterised by a bright golden body, cheeks and tail, contrasting with its black limbs, crown and tail-end. It is endemic to the Albertine Rift. It was previously found in the Gishwati Forest, which since the return of the post-genocide refugees has become too degraded; and there may be a small population somewhere in the Nyungwe Forest; but it is thought that the only viable population is here in the area of the Virunga volcanoes. Researchers are only now assembling a detailed picture of its lifestyle.

In early 2002, ORTPN approached the Dian Fossey Gorilla Fund International (DFGFI) to discuss the possibility of habituating the golden monkeys for purposes of tourism. The DFGFI welcomed the chance to learn more about this little-studied monkey and to help promote tourism in the park. First, two possible groups were selected for habituation – they are in areas of the park that would be suitable as part of a nature trail for tourists. Field assistants were then trained in habituation and data collection techniques, and work could begin.

The first few months were terribly frustrating. Dense vegetation (bamboo) made approaching the groups very difficult and the monkeys would flee at the first sight of humans. In time, the researchers were able to refine their techniques and determine at what time of day the monkeys were most active, which made them easier to locate. Gradually the monkeys came to accept the presence of the observers for longer and longer periods. Meanwhile the researchers were gathering more and more data about their diet, habitat use, social structure and behavioural ecology, all of which must be understood if the project is to succeed in the long term.

The first group was 'opened to the public' in summer 2003 and has delighted visitors. It's a very different experience from gorilla-viewing, where the huge creatures are entirely visible as they react and interact; the golden monkeys in their bamboo thicket are smaller, nimbler and can be harder to spot. However, they will become bolder with time, and eventually the second (and larger) group should also be habituated for tourism. The benefits of this project are mutual; for tourists, the pleasure of observing a rare species of monkey; for researchers, the satisfaction of learning more about a little-known species; and for the endangered golden monkeys, far less threat of extinction, as they are studied, protected and better understood.

ASOFERWA

If you spend the night close to the entrance to Rwanda's Volcanoes National Park prior to gorilla-tracking, you may choose to stay at the attractive and friendly Kinigi Guest House – which is run by the non-profit women's association ASOFERWA or Association de Solidarité des Femmes Rwandaises. Profits from the Guest House are ploughed back into ASOFERWA's programme.

This body was set up in August 1994 to help those left vulnerable and struggling as a result of the genocide, of whom many were women and children: widows, orphans, teenage mothers, traumatised women, victims of AIDS (through rape) and other forms of physical and moral violence, the old and handicapped, women in detention centres with their babies, and minors in re-education centres accused of genocide. All of these feature in ASOFERWA's work.

Among the multiple and urgent needs in 1994, ASOFERWA's first task was to provide shelter and other basic requirements for widows and for children being cared for by an older sibling. This was carried out within the framework of the 'Peace Villages' constructed throughout Rwanda under

Where to stay and eat

Most travellers stay in Ruhengeri, and some in Gisenyi, on the night before they go gorilla-tracking. There's now a smart new lodge much closer to the park entrance, the **Mountain Gorilla's Nest** (BP 79 Ruhengeri; tel/fax: 546331; mobile: 08625318, 08538218; email: gorillanest@yahoo.fr), which has 20 smallish but well-equipped and comfortable rooms ($80 single, US$100 double) with water heaters, verandas, phone, etc, in bungalows around a central lawn and surrounded by trees. It's an idyllic location. There are also two apartments: US$100 single, US$120 double. Room rates are reduced for longer stays and include the biggest pre-gorilla-trek breakfast I've ever seen! The lodge is too new for me to judge how it will turn out – but so far it's promising. The restaurant is good too: three-course dinner US$7. Another option is the **Kinigi Guest House** run by the charity

the national resettlement and rehousing programme. A village consists of 100 to 150 houses and a population of 600 to 1,200. Widows rehoused under this scheme were asked, in return, to take in orphans and care for them; while ASOFERWA helped them to set up income-generating schemes (agriculture, handicrafts, livestock, small kiosks or boutiques...). These also benefit the surrounding community, as do the villages' educational and medical facilities.

The work quickly expanded and international funding agencies gave support and sponsorship. Orphans have been rehomed, women's groups set up, schools and training centres opened, young people given practical skills, a tannery, a modern dairy farm and a literacy training centre established. ASOFERWA also still works with mothers in prison and with minors accused of genocide, whether in prison, during their re-education or after their return to their community. In one area a mobile medical team cares for the psycho-social needs of rape victims.

The needs are still great. But speak to any of ASOFERWA's active and dedicated team and you'll be in no doubt that they're equal to the task. Kigali office tel: 86394; fax: 84413; email: asoferwa@rwanda1.com.

ASOFERWA (BP 565 Kigali; tel: 546984; mobile: 08533606; email: kinigi-guesthouse@rwanda1.com; web: www.rwanda-gorillas.com). Kinigi's wooden chalets, mostly en suite, have an almost Swiss appearance: single US$20, double US$25, apartment US$30, all including continental breakfast. There are comfortable public areas, good food and – a view of the volcanoes. See advertisement opposite and box above. Finally, there is a **campsite** close to the park office – arrange camping via ORTPN (contact details on page 53).

Gorillas and gorilla-tracking

The most celebrated resident of the Virunga Mountains is the mountain gorilla, distinguished from other forms of gorilla by several adaptations to its high-altitude home, most visibly a longer and more luxuriant coat. Approximately 300 mountain gorillas live in the Virungas, with their total range of 420km^2 spread across three countries: Rwanda, Uganda and the DRC. Current estimates place Rwanda's gorilla population at around 140–150, about half of which move in two large groups of between 30 and 40 individuals, and the remainder in five or six groups of between five and 15 animals.

While the lowland races of gorilla were first described by European biologists in the mid-18th century, the mountain gorilla was unknown to Western science until October 1902, when two individuals were shot in the Virunga Mountains by Oscar van Beringe. The first detailed study of wild mountain gorilla behaviour was undertaken in the 1950s by George Schaller, whose pioneering work formed the starting point for the more recent and better publicised study by the late Dian Fossey in Rwanda.

THE DISCOVERY OF THE MOUNTAIN GORILLA

The mountain gorilla was first discovered on October 17 1902, on the ridges of the Virunga Mountains, by German explorer Captain Robert von Beringe, then aged 37. Captain von Beringe, together with a physician, Dr Engeland, Corporal Ehrhardt, 20 Askaris, a machine gun and necessary porters set off from Usumbura on August 19 1902 to visit the Sultan Msinga of Rwanda and then proceed north to reach a 'row of volcanoes'. The purpose of the trip was to visit the German outposts in what was then German East Africa in order to keep in touch with local chiefs and to confirm good relations, while strengthening the influence and power of the German Government in these regions. On arriving at the volcanoes, an attempt was made to climb Mount Sabyinyo.

Captain von Beringe's report of the expedition (below) is adapted from *In the Heart of Africa* by Duke Adolphus Frederick of Mecklenburg (Cassell, 1910).

From October 16th to 18th, senior physician Dr. Engeland and I together with only a few Askaris and the absolutely necessary baggage attempted to climb the so far unknown Kirunga ya Sabyinyo which, according to my estimation, must have a height of 3,300 metres. At the end of the first day we camped on a plateau at a height of 2,500 metres; the natives climbed up to our campsite to generously supply us with food. We left our camp on October 17th taking with us a tent, eight loads of water, five Askaris and porters as necessary.

After four and a half hours of tracking we reached a height of 3,100 metres and tracked through bamboo forest; although using elephant trails for most of the way, we encountered much undergrowth which had to be cut before we

Mountain gorillas are on average bulkier than other races of gorilla, weighing up to 200kg, though the heaviest individual gorilla on record is a 210kg eastern lowland gorilla measured in Zaire. Like other gorillas, they are highly sociable, moving in defined troops of anything from five to 50 animals. A troop typically consists of a silverback male (the male's back turns silver when he reaches sexual maturity at about 13 years old), his three or four wives and several young animals. Unusually for mammals, it is the male who forms the focal point of a troop; when he dies, the troop normally disintegrates. A silverback will start to acquire his harem at about 15 years of age, normally by attracting a young sexually mature female from another troop. He may continue to lead a troop well into his forties.

Female gorillas reach sexual maturity at the age of eight, after which they often move between troops several times. However, once a female has successfully given birth, she will normally stay with the same silverback until he dies, and she will even help defend him against other males (if a male takes over a troop, he will kill any nursing infants which are not his, a could pass... After two hours we reached a stony area with vegetation consisting mainly of blackberry and blueberry bushes. Step by step we noticed the vegetation becoming poorer and poorer, the ascent became steeper and steeper, and climbing became more difficult – for the last one and a quarter hours we climbed only over rock. After covering the ground with moss we collected, we erected our tent on a ridge at a height of 3,100 metres. The ridge was extremely narrow so that the pegs of the tent had to be secured in the abyss. The Askaris and the porters found shelter in rock caverns, which provided protection against the biting cold wind.

From our campsite we were able to watch a herd of big, black monkeys which tried to climb the crest of the volcano. We succeeded in killing two of these animals, and with a rumbling noise of falling rocks they tumbled into a ravine, which had its opening in a north-easterly direction. After five hours of strenuous work we succeeded in retrieving one of these animals using a rope. It was a big, human-like male monkey of one and a half metres in height and a weight of more than 200 pounds. His chest had no hair, and his hands and feet were of enormous size. Unfortunately I was unable to determine its type; because of its size, it could not very well be a chimpanzee or a gorilla, and in any case the presence of gorillas had not been established in the area around the lakes.

On the journey back to Usumbura, the skin and one of the hands of the animal that von Beringe collected were taken by a hyena but the rest (including the skull) finally arrived safely at the Zoological Museum in Berlin. It was classified as a new form of gorilla and named Gorilla beringei in honour of the Captain. Later it was considered rather to be a subspecies and renamed *Gorilla gorilla beringei*.

strong motive for a female to help preserve the status quo). A female gorilla has a gestation period similar to that of a human, and if she reaches old age she will typically have raised up to six of her offspring to sexual maturity. A female's status within a troop is based on the length of time she has been with a silverback: the longest-serving member of the harem is normally the alpha female.

Mountain gorillas have a primarily vegetarian diet, and are known to eat 58 different plant species. Gorillas also eat insects, with ants being a particularly popular protein supplement. A gorilla troop will spend most of its waking hours on the ground, but it will generally move into the trees at night, when each member of the troop builds itself a temporary nest. Gorillas are surprisingly sedentary creatures, typically moving less than 1km in a day, which makes tracking them on a day-to-day basis relatively easy for experienced guides. A troop will generally move a long distance only after a stressful incident, for instance an aggressive encounter with another troop.

Gorillas have few natural enemies and they often live for up to 50 years in the wild, but their long-term survival is critically threatened by poaching, deforestation and increased exposure to human-borne diseases. Unlike their lowland cousins, mountain gorillas have never been reared successfully in captivity. Dian Fossey's *Gorillas in the Mist* (see *Further Reading*) is a good starting point for anybody who wants to know more about mountain gorilla behaviour.

Conservation and tourism

Until recently lumped together as one race (see box *Gorilla taxonomy*, pages 190–1), the mountain gorilla and Bwindi gorilla are the only representatives of the world's largest primate to occur east of the Albertine Rift. Although both races number about 300 in the wild, the Bwindi gorilla is probably the more secure of the two, since it is confined to one forest in Uganda where it is protected in the Bwindi-Impenetrable National Park. The mountain gorilla, by contrast, has a range that straddles three countries. While national parks in all these countries afford some protection to the mountain gorilla, the volatility of this area in recent years has repeatedly forced researchers and rangers to evacuate one or other of the parks.

Poaching and deforestation have certainly taken a heavy toll since 1902, but it is difficult to say how many mountain gorillas lived in the Virungas before that – given their restricted range, it seems unlikely that the total population would have exceeded a couple of thousand. During the two decades following the 'discovery' of mountain gorillas, it is known that at least 50 gorillas were captured or killed in the Virungas, prompting the Belgian government to create Africa's first national park there.

The gorilla population of the Virungas is thought to have been reasonably stable in 1960, when the gorilla researcher George Schaller estimated it to be around 450. By 1980, however, that number had plummeted to 250, a decline caused by several factors: the splitting of the Albert National Park into its current Rwandan and Congolese components, the ongoing political instability caused by fighting between local Hutus and Tutsis, the handing over of more than 40% of the gorillas' habitat to local farmers in 1957 and to a European-funded agricultural scheme in 1968, and a grisly but profitable tourist trade in poached gorilla heads and hands – the latter used by some sad individuals as ashtrays!

In 1978, the first gorilla tourism project was initiated in the Volcanoes Park; it integrated tourism, education and anti-poaching measures with remarkable success. By the middle of the 1980s, gorilla tourism was raising up to US$10 million annually, making it Rwanda's third highest earner of foreign revenue. At the end of that decade, the Virunga gorilla population had increased by almost 30% to 320 animals. The mountain gorilla had practically become Rwanda's national emblem, and it was considered by the government to be the country's most important renewable natural resource. To ordinary Rwandans, the gorillas were a source of great national pride: living gorillas ultimately create far more work and money than poaching had ever done.

Gorilla tourism in Rwanda came to an abrupt halt in 1991, when the country erupted into a civil war which culminated in the genocide of 1994. The civil war also raised considerable concern about the survival of the gorillas. Researchers and park rangers were twice forced to evacuate the Volcanoes Park, land mines were planted by various military factions, and the Virungas were used as an escape route by thousands of fleeing refugees. Remarkably, however, when researchers were finally able to return to the park, it was discovered that only four gorillas could not be accounted for. Two of the missing gorillas were old females who most probably died of natural causes; the other two might have been shot, but might just as easily have succumbed to disease. It is also encouraging to note that the war has had no evident effect on breeding activity, a strong indication that it was less disruptive to the gorillas than had been feared.

While concern about the fate of a few gorillas might seem misplaced in the context of a war which claimed a million human lives, it is these self-same gorillas which give Rwanda a real chance of rebuilding the lucrative tourist industry that was shattered by the war. It will do this in an environment in which increasing concern is being voiced about the ramifications of habituating gorillas for tourists. There is, for instance, the issue of health: humans and gorillas are genetically close enough for there to be a real risk of a tourist passing a viral or bacterial infection to a habituated gorilla, which might in turn infect other members of its group, potentially resulting in all their deaths should they have no resistance to the infection.

Another concern is that habituating gorillas to humans increases their vulnerability to poachers. During 1995, seven habituated gorillas died as a result of poaching: four members of Bwindi's Kyaguliro Group were speared to death, while in what was then Zaire, the famous silverback Marcel was shot dead, together with one adult female. In both cases, an infant was removed: the one captured at Bwindi is now assumed to be dead; the one taken from the Volcanoes Park was confiscated at the Ugandan border and returned to the troop from which it was taken. These incidents were thought to be linked to one dealer's attempts to acquire an infant gorilla, and did not appear to signal the start of a trend. Then, in May 2002, two females were shot and two babies stolen in Rwanda's Volcanoes Park; in October 2002 an infant was taken by – but subsequently rescued from – poachers.

Given the above, a reasonable response might be to query the wisdom of habituating gorillas in the first place. The problem facing conservationists is that gorillas cannot be conserved in a vacuum. At current prices, the authorities can potentially earn US$12,000 daily in tracking permits alone, much of which can be pumped back into the protection and management of the Volcanoes Park. There are also the broader benefits of job creation through tourism in and around the Virungas. And even in terms of pure conservation, habituation has many positive effects, allowing researchers and rangers to monitor the gorillas on a daily basis, and to intervene when one of them is ill, injured or in a snare. As one gorilla researcher based in Ruhengeri put it, tourism for all its negatives is probably the only thing that will save the Volcanoes Park – and by default save the gorillas.

For post-genocide Rwanda, struggling to re-establish a reputation as a viable tourist destination, things would be ten times worse without the mountain

MOUNTAIN GORILLA CONSERVATION
Dr Liz Williamson, Scottish Primate Research Group, University of Stirling
Mountain gorillas are the focus of several conservation organisations. The six international organisations currently working in Rwanda are listed alphabetically with a summary of their activities.

Dian Fossey Gorilla Fund Europe
The London-based DFGFE manages 20 projects designed to integrate traditional conservation and research with economic development and education. These include:

- Beekeepers, who are supported to develop modern sustainable honey farms at the edge of, rather than inside, the park boundary
- Fresh water in village schools using local engineering technology to provide water cisterns. Water collection is one of the main causes of encroachment in the gorilla habitat, and children living close to the forest often miss school to collect water for their families
- Training in Sustainable Agriculture for farmers in areas adjacent to gorilla habitat
- Tree Planting to alleviate environmental degradation, since most fuel used in households comes from wood
- Virunga Wildlife Clubs in schools, which organise field trips, tree planting and environment week activities, and a Conservation Network that links local organisations in the Virunga region

For more details, see website www.dianfossey.org/projects/

Dian Fossey Gorilla Fund International – Karisoke Research Centre
The Atlanta-based DFGFI funds and operates 'Karisoke', originally established by Dr Dian Fossey in 1967. Although the research centre was destroyed during the 1990s, staff continue to monitor three gorilla groups and carry out daily anti-poaching patrols from a base outside the park. DFGFI aims to further strengthen research and protection efforts through education, local capacity building, the addition of staff and equipment resources, and support to a Geographic Information Systems unit based within the National University.
For information on the DFGFIU, see www.gorillafund.org.

International Gorilla Conservation Programme
IGCP is a joint initiative of three organisations, the African Wildlife Foundation, Fauna and Flora International and the World Wide Fund for Nature. IGCP's overall goal is the sustainable conservation of the world's remaining mountain gorillas and their habitat. IGCP aims to enhance communication and co-operation between protected-area authorities through regional meetings, training programs, cross-border patrols and

communications networks, and advises governments on environmental policy and legislation enforcement. IGCP provides training and support for park staff, and has established a Ranger Based Monitoring programme throughout the Virunga region.

Websites: AWF: www.awf.org; FFI: www.fauna-flora.org; WWF: www.panda.org

Morris Animal Foundation – Mountain Gorilla Veterinary Project

MGVP provides veterinary care to the mountain gorillas. The project's vets monitor the health of individual gorillas in both the research and tourist groups, and are able to intervene in emergency situations, such as a gorilla becoming trapped by a life-threatening snare. Since disease transmission from humans is a serious threat to the gorillas' survival, MGVP also monitors the health of government and project staff working in the park, and organises seminars addressing health and hygiene issues.

Web: www.morrisanimalfoundation.org/animalnews/gorillas.asp

Mountain Gorilla Conservation Fund

Recently established as a breakaway from the Mountain Gorilla Veterinary Project, MGCF will address conservation issues in Rwanda via:

* Natural Treasures Curriculum: a school-based programme using a hands-on approach to teach students about gorillas, benefits gained from protecting them and the rainforest where they live, and the steps the students can take to live in harmony with the gorillas and their habitat
* Student Connections: a programme connecting local schools with schools throughout the world. International students write letters and create posters, books or gifts about their own communities and ecosystems to share with students in Rwanda.

Web: www.mgcf.net/15-Projects.html

Wildlife Conservation Society

With strong historic links to the mountain gorillas, WCS's major programme in Rwanda is now the Nyungwe Forest Conservation Project. WCS is also implementing training programmes in monitoring and research with its partners, including ORTPN in Rwanda.

Web: http//wcs.org/home/wild/Africa/gorillas/

In addition, the volcanoes fall within the focus of WCS's Albertine Rift Project. The objective of this programme is to improve conservation by providing information for park managers, building capacity to better manage these areas, and encouraging collaboration across national boundaries. Biological and socio-economic surveys are used to identify priority conservation areas and to plan measures to alleviate poverty in the communities that border them.

Website: http://wcs.org/home/wild/Africa/Albertinerift/

gorillas. It is the gorillas that will bring back the tourists, who will also spend money in other parts of the country, thereby providing foreign revenue and creating employment well beyond the immediate vicinities of the mountain gorilla reserves. Tourism is probably integral to the survival of the mountain gorilla; the survival of the mountain gorilla is certainly integral to the growth of Rwanda's tourist industry. This symbiotic situation motivates a far greater number of people to take an active interest in the fate of the gorillas than would be the case if gorilla tourism were to be curtailed.

Visiting the gorillas

Mountain gorilla-tracking in the Virungas is a peerless wildlife experience, and one of Africa's indisputable travel highlights. It is difficult to describe the simple exhilaration attached to first setting eyes on a wild mountain gorilla. These are enormous animals: the silverbacks weigh about three times as much as the average man, and their bulk is exaggerated by a shaggily luxuriant coat. And yet despite their fearsome size and appearance, gorillas are remarkably peaceable creatures, certainly by comparison with most primates – gorilla-tracking would be a considerably more dangerous pursuit if these gentle giants had the temperament of vervet monkeys, say, or baboons (or, for that matter, humans).

GORILLA TAXONOMY

The gorilla is a widespread resident of equatorial East and Central African rainforest. Recent estimates indicate a global population of perhaps 100,000 wild gorillas, mainly concentrated in the Congo Basin (Gabon and the DRC). Until recently, all gorillas were classified as one species (*Gorilla gorilla*), with three races recognised: the western lowland gorilla (*G. g. gorilla*) of the Congo Basin, the eastern lowland gorilla (*G. g. graueri*) of the DRC immediately west of the Albertine Rift, and the mountain gorilla (*G. g. beringei*) of the Virunga and Bwindi ranges on the eastern side of the Albertine Rift.

This conventional classification of gorillas has recently been shattered by advances in DNA tests and fresh morphological studies. It is now known that the western and eastern gorilla populations have almost as many genetic differences as humans and chimpanzees, which means they should almost certainly be regarded as distinct species tentatively assigned as *G. gorilla* (west) and *G. beringei* (east).

The status of the western gorilla is reasonably secure, since it is far more numerous in the wild than its eastern counterpart, and has a more extensive range. DNA research has, however, resulted in the Cross River gorilla *G. g. dielhi* of the Cameroon–Nigeria border area being recognised as a distinct race of western gorilla. The Cross River gorilla has the dubious distinction of being placed on a shortlist of the world's 25 most endangered primate morphs, and it fulfils the IUCN criteria for a listing of 'Critically

More impressive even than the gorillas' size and bearing is their unfathomable attitude to their daily human visitors, which differs greatly from that of any other wild animal. Anthropomorphic as it might sound, almost everybody who visits the gorillas experiences an almost mystical sense of recognition: we regularly had one of the gorillas break off from chomping on bamboo to study us, its soft brown eyes staring deeply into ours, as if seeking out some sort of connection.

Equally fascinating is the extent to which the gorillas try to interact with their visitors, often approaching them, and occasionally touching one of the guides in apparent recognition and greeting as they walk past. A photographic tripod raised considerable curiosity in several of the youngsters and a couple of the adults – one large female walked up to the tripod, stared ponderously into the lens, then wandered back off evidently satisfied. It is almost as if the gorillas recognise their daily visitors as a troop of fellow apes, but one too passive to pose any threat – often a youngster would put on a chest-beating display as it walked past us, safe in the knowledge that we'd accept its dominance, something it would never do to an adult gorilla. (It should be noted here that close contact with humans can expose gorillas to fatal diseases, for which reason the guides try to keep their tourists at least five metres away – but the reality is that there is little anybody can do to stop the gorillas from flouting rules of which they are unaware.)

Endangered', as it lives in five fragmented populations, only one of which is protected, and which together total no more than 200 individuals.

Although at least 15,000 eastern gorillas remain in the wild, all but 600 of them are assigned to the lowland race. The remaining 600 are generally classified as mountain gorillas, which – like their Cross River counterparts – are listed among the world's 25 most endangered primate morphs. There is, however, growing consensus among primate researchers that this conventional assignation needs to be revised. It was previously thought that the approximately 300 gorillas resident in Uganda's Bwindi-Impenetrable Forest, though they live at a lower altitude and have a thinner coat, were racially identical to the mountain gorillas of the Virungas – a not unreasonable assumption given that the montane forests of the Virungas and Bwindi were linked by a corridor of mid-altitude forest until about 500 years ago. But DNA tests indicate that the Bwindi and Virunga gorillas are discrete races, and that the two montane forests have supported isolated breeding populations of gorillas for many millennia.

Esoteric stuff, perhaps, but the bottom line is that a mere 300 mountain gorillas remain in the wild, the entire population is confined to the Virunga Mountains, and approximately half of them are resident in Rwanda's Volcanoes Park. Neither the mountain gorilla nor the Bwindi gorilla has been bred successfully in captivity, and both races should probably be regarded as 'Critically Endangered' – one criterion for this classification being that fewer than 250 mature adults remain in the wild.

The magical hour with the gorillas is relatively expensive and getting there – have no illusions – can be hard work. The hike up to the mountain gorillas' preferred habitat of bamboo forest involves a combination of steep slopes, dense vegetation, slippery underfoot conditions after rain, and high altitude. For all that, the more accessible gorilla groups can be visited by reasonably fit adults of any age, and in 15 years of African travel we have yet to meet anybody who has gone gorilla-tracking and regretted the financial or physical expense.

Permits

A gorilla-tracking permit costs US$250 (cash), and can be bought in advance through the ORTPN office or tour operators in Kigali. Depending on availability, permits can also normally be bought in Ruhengiri and Kinigi; but procedures may change and you are strongly advised to check this beforehand with ORTPN in Kigali – details on page 53. Either way, it is advisable to visit or ring the ORTPN office in Ruhengeri on the afternoon before you intend to go tracking in order to confirm arrangements.

Eight permits per day are issued for each of the four habituated groups in the Volcanoes Park. At the time of writing, two habituated groups stay within tracking range on a permanent basis, while two others spend most of their time in the Volcanoes Park but occasionally cross the border into Uganda or the DRC. Depending on the movement of the gorillas, this means that between 16 and 32 permits can be issued daily.

The more difficult to reach of the two permanent groups is the **Susa Group**, which lives on the slopes of Mount Karisoke. Consisting of 35 individuals, including three silverbacks and several youngsters, this is the second-largest group of mountain gorillas in the world (there is a larger research group) and it was the one originally studied by Dian Fossey. A visit to the Susa Group is delightfully chaotic and totally unforgettable, with gorillas seemingly tumbling out of every bush and bamboo stand. The Susa Group is the first choice of most fit visitors, but be under no illusions about the severity of the hike. The ascent from the car park to the forest boundary is gaspingly steep, and will take the best part of an hour. On a good day, it will take no more than 20 minutes to reach the gorillas from the boundary; on a bad day you might be looking at two hours or more in either direction (the record from the previous day will give an indication of how deep in the gorillas are, as they generally don't move too far in one day).

A far less strenuous prospect is the **Sabinyo Group**, whose permanent territory lies within the Volcanoes Park, on a lightly forested saddle between Mount Sabinyo and Mount Gahinga. Depending on exactly where the gorillas are, the walk from the car park to the forest boundary is flat to gently sloping, and will typically take 20–30 minutes. Once in the forest, the gorillas might take anything from ten minutes to an hour to reach, but generally the slopes aren't too daunting. The Sabinyo Group consists of nine individuals, again with two silverbacks. Although it is less numerically impressive than the Susa Group, the Sabinyo Group does seem more cohesive and one gets a clearer impression of the group structure and interaction.

Group Thirteen spends most of its time on the same saddle as the Sabinyo Group, but its territory does cross into neighbouring countries, so it is not permanently in the Volcanoes Park. When it is around, however, it is normally just as easy to reach as the Sabinyo Group. Group Thirteen's name dates to when it was first habituated, and numbered 13 gorillas, but today it is a smaller group of ten. As with the Sabinyo Group, this means you get a good feel for group structure and interaction. Group Thirteen seems to be a favourite of many of the guides, probably because its silverback is more relaxed and approachable than those in other groups.

Finally there is the **Amahoro Group**, numbering 13, generally to be found on the slopes of Mount Visoke. The hike is intermediate in difficulty between those of Susa and Sabinyo.

Transport

No public transport connects Ruhengeri to any of the points where one enters the forest to start tracking, all of which lie about 10–15km from town. Individuals may be able to beg lifts with other trackers, but for larger transport-less groups the only option is to hire a vehicle and driver for the morning. ORTPN in Ruhengeri can advise on this. In the rainy season you'll probably need a 4WD; in the dry season an ordinary *taxi-voiture* should be adequate and will cost far less. The going rate for a 4WD from/to Ruhengeri is around US$50 for the round trip; tour operators in Kigali can organise it as a day trip from Kigali for around US$125, less if several of you share a vehicle. If you spend the night beforehand at the Mountain Gorilla's Nest, the Kinigi Guest House or the ORTPN Campsite, all quite close to the Kinigi park office, you stand a reasonable chance of hitching a lift up there from the main road; but you'll still need transport in the morning to reach the start of the trek. Whatever method you choose, make sure that it's reliable – if you don't turn up at the appointed time you risk invalidating your permit and having to pay again.

Physical preparation

Depending on which group you visit, and your own level of fitness, the trek to see the gorillas will be at best taxing and at worst exhausting (the guides told us they have on occasion had to carry tourists down, and we met one Dutch woman who was too exhausted by the hike up to the forest to continue on to see the gorillas). One reason for this is the steep slopes that characterise the Virungas, particularly en route to the Susa Group. Once in the forest, the slopes aren't as steep, and the pace is slower, but bending and crawling through the thick vegetation can be tiring, particularly after rain when everything is muddy underfoot.

Don't underestimate the tiring effects of being at high altitude. The trekking takes place at elevations of between 2,500m and 3,000m above sea level, not high enough for altitude sickness to be a concern, but sufficient to knock the breath out of anybody – no matter how fit – who has just flown in from a low altitude. For this reason, visitors who are spending a while in Rwanda might think seriously about leaving their gorilla-tracking until they've been in the country a week or so, and are better acclimatised. Most of Rwanda lies at above 1,500m, and much of the country is higher – a couple of days at Nyungwe, which lies above 2,000m, would be good preparation for the Virungas. Likewise, if you are coming from elsewhere in Africa, try to plan your itinerary so that you spend your last pre-Rwanda days at medium to high altitude: for example, were you flying in from Kenya, a few days in Nairobi (2,300m) or even the Masai Mara (1,600m) would be far better preparation than time at the coast.

If you are uncertain about your fitness, don't visit the Susa Group, but rather opt for Group Thirteen or the Sabinyo Group, both of which are reached by reasonably easy hikes on flattish terrain. Once on the trail, take it easy, and don't be afraid to ask to stop for a few minutes whenever you feel tired. Drink plenty of water, and carry some quick calories – biscuits and chocolate can both be bought at supermarkets in Ruhengeri. The good news is that in 99% of cases, whatever exhaustion you might feel on the way up will vanish with the adrenalin charge that follows the first sighting of a silverback gorilla!

What to wear and take

Whichever group you visit, you may have to walk a long distance in steep, muddy conditions, possibly with rain overhead, before you encounter any gorillas. Put on your sturdiest walking shoes. Ideally, wear thick trousers and a long-sleeved top as protection against vicious stinging nettles. It's often cold when you set out, so start off with a sweatshirt or jersey (which also help protect against nettles). The gorillas are thoroughly used to people, so it makes little difference whether you wear bright or muted colours. Whatever clothes you wear to go tracking are likely to get very dirty as you slip and slither in the mud, so if you have pre-muddied clothes you might as well wear them. When you're grabbing for handholds in thorny vegetation, a pair of old gardening gloves are helpful.

Carry as little as possible, ideally in a waterproof bag of some sort. During the rainy season, a poncho or raincoat might be a worthy addition to your daypack, while sunscreen, sunglasses and a hat are a good idea at any time of year. You may well feel like a snack during the long hike, and should certainly carry enough drinking water – at least one litre, more to visit the Susa Group. Bottled water is sold in Ruhengeri. Especially during the rainy season, make sure your camera gear is well protected – if your bag isn't waterproof, seal your camera and films in a plastic bag (for further details about photographing gorillas see the box *Photographic tips* on pages 70–1).

Binoculars are not necessary to see the gorillas. In theory, birdwatchers might want to carry binoculars, though in practice only the most dedicated are likely to make use of them – the trek up to the gorillas is normally very directed, and walking up the steep slopes and through the thick vegetation tends to occupy one's eyes and mind.

Regulations and protocol

Tourists are permitted to spend no longer than one hour with the gorillas, and it is forbidden to eat or smoke in their presence. It is also forbidden to approach within less than 5m of the gorillas, a rule that is difficult to enforce with curious youngsters (and some adults) who often approach human visitors.

Gorillas are susceptible to many human diseases, and it has long been feared by researchers that one ill tourist might infect a gorilla, resulting in the possible death of the whole troop should they have no immunity to that disease. For this reason, you should not go gorilla-tracking with a potentially airborne infection such as flu or a cold, and are asked to turn away from the gorillas should you need to sneeze in their presence.

To the best of my knowledge, no tourists have ever been seriously hurt by habituated gorillas, but there is always a first time. An adult gorilla is much stronger than a person, and will act in accordance with its own social codes. Therefore it is vital that you listen to your guide at all times regarding correct protocol in the presence of gorillas.

BYUMBA

The small but sprawling town of Byumba lies about 3km off the main road between Kigali and Kibale (Uganda), and is likely to be visited only by travellers who want to cut across from the Kibale–Kigali road to Base on the Ruhengeri road. Byumba has nothing in the way of tourist attractions, though the surrounding countryside is rather pretty (Byumba lies at the heart of a major tea-growing area) and the dirt road to Base is one of the most scenic in the country.

There is plenty of transport to Byumba from Kigali and the Gatuna border with Uganda. The 42km road between Byumba and Base, notable for spectacular views of the tea estates around Base, is serviced by at least one bus daily, leaving Byumba in the early morning and returning from Base later in the day. There don't seem to be any minibus-taxis along this route, but hitching isn't impossible. On the Kigali–Byumba road about 10km outside Kigali is the rather surprising Highland Flowers Rose Farm, growing high-quality roses for sale locally and for export to Europe.

There's a good hotel in Byumba: the **Hotel Urumuli** (tel: 564322, 564323). It's at the top of the long main street, about 2km from the public minibus stop but served by private minibuses – Okapicar, Gasabo, Atraco, etc. Opened in 2000 and under the same management as the Jali Club in Kigali, it has eight solidly built, semi-circular rooms in bungalows set in a cared-for garden, with small en-suite bathrooms (hot water) and comfortable beds: US$16 single, US$20 double excluding breakfast. It's used by (among others) German tour groups. The surrounding countryside is beautiful and very green; you could well spend a couple of days here just walking and enjoying the expansive views. The **Centre Diocésain de Formation et de Conférence** (tel: 564375) also has self-contained rooms – US$8–12 – but can get busy with church guests. An alternative is the **Ikaze Bagenzi Bar Restaurant Amacumbi** (tel: 08528047), which has basic singles for around US$3, a room sleeping four in bunk beds for US$8 and an en-suite double for US$10. There are showers, running water and flush toilets. It's about 300m from the minibus station and can be reached by walking downhill past the bakery, turning right when you reach an open area used as a market and then left at the next junction. The **Banque Commerciale du Rwanda**, 100m from the minibus station, changes US cash and theoretically travellers' cheques; it also has Western Union.

GISENYI

The most northerly port on the Rwandan part of Lake Kivu, Gisenyi is well worth a visit, especially as it lies little more than an hour by road from the gorilla-tracking base of Ruhengeri. Gisenyi is split into an upper and lower town, the former an undistinguished grid of busy roads centred around a small market area, the latter a more spacious and atmospheric conglomeration of banks, government buildings, old colonial homesteads and hotels lapped by the waters of Rwanda's largest lake. The waterfront, with its red sandy beaches, pleasing mismatch of architectural styles, and shady palm-lined avenues, has the captivating air of a slightly down-at-heel tropical beach resort. Indeed, Gisenyi could easily be mistaken for a sweaty West African or Indian Ocean backwater, except that the relatively high altitude of 1,500m means it has a refreshing climate at odds with its tropical appearance.

In 1907, the Duke of Mecklenburg wrote:

> Kissenji possesses an excellent climate, for by virtue of its 1,500 metres above sea level all enervating heat is banished. The natural coolness prevalent in consequence makes a visit there a very agreeable experience. The man who has this place allotted to him for his sphere of activity draws a prize. In front are the swirling breakers of the most beautiful of all the Central African lakes, framed in by banks which fall back steeply from the rugged masses of rock; at the rear the stately summits of the eight Virunga volcanoes.

Gisenyi today offers little in the way of formal sightseeing, but its singular atmosphere, combined with an excellent range of affordable accommodation, makes it the sort of town which you could easily settle into for a few days. It's an interesting place to wander around, too, whether your interest lies in the prolific birds that line the lake shore, the fantastic old colonial buildings that dot the leafy suburban avenues, lazing around on the beach, or mixing in to the hustle and bustle of the market area. Further afield, the 6km walk or *matatu* drive to Rubona port offers some lovely lake views, while at Rubona itself you can easily arrange to explore the immediate vicinity in a dugout canoe or pirogue.

A touching genocide story lingers in the mind. There was a Catholic lay worker, a Hutu, who helped many hunted people to flee across the border even when she knew the military were aware of her action. When the *interahamwe* finally came to her house, 30 refugees were there. One by one they were shot in front of her, after which she asked to be killed too, so that they might stay together in death as in life. Before shooting her, the militia leader asked her to pray for his soul.

Gisenyi is home to the Imbabazi orphanage (tel: 540740), originally started in December 1994 by Rosamond Halsey Carr at her plantation in nearby Mugongo to shelter some of the many genocide orphans and displaced children, and shifted

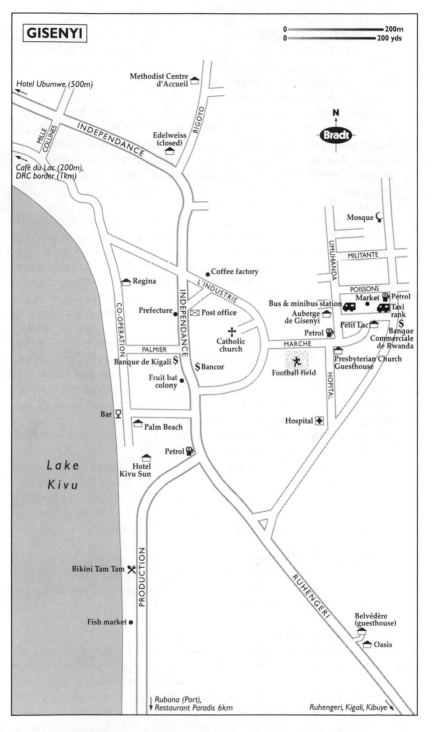

GISENYI

0 ———————— 200m
0 ———————— 200 yds

Hotel Ubumwe (500m)

Methodist Centre
d'Accueil

BIGOYO

MILLE COLLINES

INDEPENDANCE

Edelweiss
(closed)

N

Bradt

Café du Lac (200m),
DRC border (1km)

Mosque ☾

UMUHANDA

MILITANTE

Coffee factory

L'INDUSTRIE

POISSONS

Regina

CO-OPERATION

Prefecture

INDEPENDANCE

Post office

Bus & minibus station   Market   Petrol
Taxi
rank
Auberge
de Gisenyi   Petit Lac $
Banque
Commerciale
de Rwanda

Petrol

Catholic
church

MARCHE

PALMIER

Banque de Kigali $

$ Bancor

Fruit bat
colony

Football field

Presbyterian Church
Guesthouse

HOPITAL

Bar ☖

Palm Beach

Hospital

Lake
Kivu

Petrol

Hotel
Kivu Sun

PRODUCTION

Bikini Tam Tam ✕

RUHENGERI

Belvédère
(guesthouse)

Oasis

Fish market ●

Rubona (Port),
Restaurant Paradis 6km

Ruhengeri, Kigali, Kibuye

IMBABAZI ORPHANAGE

Since Mrs Rosamond Halsey Carr founded the Imbabazi Orphanage in 1994, she and her staff have cared for more than 400 orphans and currently have 102, aged from two years upwards.

As a young fashion illustrator in New York City, Rosamond Halsey married an adventurous hunter-explorer, Kenneth Carr, and journeyed with him to the Congo in 1949. After their eventual divorce, Kenneth left; Rosamond stayed on. In 1955 she moved to northwest Rwanda to manage a flower plantation, Mugongo; and later bought it. For the next 50 years she witnessed the end of colonialism, celebrated Rwanda's independence and became one of Dian Fossey's closest friends. (In the film *Gorillas in the Mist*, the role of Roz Carr is played by Julie Harris.)

During periods of violence and upheaval, Mrs Carr always stayed fast at her home in Mugongo, while others fled. But with the outbreak of the genocide in April 1994 the American Embassy finally insisted that she leave. After several months in the US, she received word that Sembagare, her friend and plantation manager of 50 years, had survived what turned out to be three attempts on his life. In August 1994, aged 82, she returned in a cargo plane, to find her home in ruins and 50 years' worth of possessions either stolen or destroyed. At Mugongo, she and Sembagare did the only thing that made sense to them: they converted an old pyrethrum drying-house and set up the Imbabazi Orphanage, to care for the genocide orphans.

In 1997 the orphanage was forced to move from Mugongo for security reasons, and, having changed locations four times, is now based in Gisenyi. Mrs Carr lives in a house nearby and is at the orphanage every day, managing its affairs. She has kept the Mugongo farm – which continues to provide the orphanage with fresh vegetables and is the sole source of income for the 15 families who work there.

Imbabazi receives funds from various friends and organisations, many of

to its present site in 1998. This is a positive and heartwarming project. See *Appendix 3*, page 241, and box above.

Getting there and away

All buses and minibus-taxis leave from the bus station next to the market in the old town centre. The main port for Gisenyi is at Rubona, about 6km south of town; the two are connected by regular minibuses.

To/from Kigali and Ruhengeri

Gisenyi lies approximately 60km from Ruhengeri by road, and 160km from Kigali. The road is sealed and mostly in good condition, though there are some pot-holed stretches. The direct drive from Kigali should take no longer than three hours. Regular minibus-taxis connect the three towns: the fare from Gisenyi to Ruhengeri is around US$1.50 and to Kigali US$3.

them in the US. (Search 'Imbabazi Orphanage' on the internet and you'll find links to some.) A novel fundraising scheme, 'Through the Eyes of Children', began in 2000, originally as a photographic workshop conceived by photographer David Jiranek. Using disposable cameras, the children at the orphanage took photos of themselves and their surroundings, both for themselves and to share with others, exploring their community and finding beauty as Rwanda struggled to rebuild after the genocide.

At first the photos were developed locally, displayed on the orphanage walls and put into photo albums by the children. A year later, the children were invited by the US Embassy to exhibit their work in Kigali, with all proceeds going towards their education. In the 2001 Camera Arts Magazine Photo Contest, eight-year-old Jacqueline won First Prize for portraiture; and the project has won Honourable Mention in an international competition featuring professional and non-professional photographers from around the world.

Unicef invited the Imbabazi children to participate in its 2003 *State of the World's Children Report*. This resulted in the cover photograph being taken by Umuhoza of her friend, Murakete, at the orphanage. Also published inside are other photos of the children using their disposable cameras, as well as a description of the project as it relates to Unicef's mission.

In addition, New York University invited the project to be exhibited at the Gulf & Western Gallery at the NYU Tisch School for the Arts in New York City in December 2002 and January 2003. The photos were also displayed at the premiere of the Human Rights Watch International Film Festival in New York in June 2003. For more information, check the comprehensive website www.rwandaproject.org.

Rosamond Carr is the author of *Land of a Thousand Hills: my life in Rwanda* (she wrote the book with her niece, Ann Howard Halsey), chronicling her love affair with Rwanda; see *Further Reading*, page 241.

To/from Kibuye and Cyangugu

To drive from Gisenyi to Kibuye, you first need to head out along the Ruhengeri road for 10km, before turning right at a poorly signposted junction on to a 78km dirt road which brings you out at Commune Mabanza on the surfaced road between Kigali and Kibuye. It's a drive of about 110km in all, and the dirt stretch is in variable condition, so three to four hours should be allowed. Although the dirt road runs parallel to Lake Kivu, it offers disappointingly few glimpses of the lake, though this is compensated for by some spectacular mountain scenery and relic patches of Gishwati Forest.

In the early 20th century, Gishwati was the second-largest tract of indigenous forest in Rwanda, stretching along the western rift escarpment from the Virungas halfway down Lake Kivu. The forest has since become heavily fragmented: by 1989 it consisted of two main stands covering a

CONSEQUENCES OF FOREST DEGRADATION AND POSITIVE ACTION TOWARDS FOREST MANAGEMENT IN RWANDA

Ugirashebuja Emmanuel (lawyer at the Constitutional Commission in Rwanda and researcher in Environmental Law)

It has become unarguably clear that people who live in rural areas or in close proximity to forests are suffering as a consequence of their degradation. The suffering is in the form of floods and landslides, both resulting from the destruction of forests. The shock and fury expressed by Rwandans in the aftermath of such calamities is as much a response to forest degradation and poor forest management. People in different parts of the country have been buried alive and others drowned. Whole farms and homesteads have been swept away, with great loss of life and property.

Landslides in Rwanda are linked to excessive deforestation, as well as to active settlement and farming on steep slopes without adequate anti-erosion measures.

The Government has declared that it will minimise the risks by ensuring that there is no settlement in areas prone to floods and landslides. However, we all have our own contribution to make.

What should we do?

As Rwandans, we must stop degrading what is left of our patrimony of natural resources and at the same time establish a sustainable re-afforestation programme. After that, for the sake of future generations, we must create adequate mechanisms to ensure that the forests remain protected.

We must work together, bringing on board all sectors: water, settlements, agriculture, lands, environment, the private sector, the civil society and all other interest groups who would like to make a contribution.

The question frequently asked is, where shall we obtain land to plant trees? Firstly, people who have encroached forest land (such as Gishwati) in the recent past must surrender it to the Forest Department. Secondly, an innovative approach, which involves incentives to farmers to encourage them to convert part of their land to forest, should be applied.

combined 28,000 hectares, about a quarter of its extent 100 years earlier, and today little of Gishwati remains.

Katot Meyer writes:

> The road is in fairly good condition. Very twisty but with lovely views of tea plantations and the lake at some times. It passes a small patch of indigenous forest to the east exactly 40 km from Gisenyi. I went for a

Above Byumba tea plantation
Left Tea picker on the tea estate, Byumba
Below Traditional brick-making site

Above Street store selling crafts, Kigali
Below Market, Byumba

walk there. Very few people were on the road and luckily I could slip into the forest without any kids following me. There are a lot of trails, most of them with cattle tracks on, but I saw not a soul.

Peace and quiet in Rwanda? I thought it to be impossible. There were birds singing in the trees, frogs at the river crossing, an absolute feast. At some places the undergrowth is very thick but as long as you stay on the paths this is an incredible hiking area. It must be part of what once was Gishwati Forest. I could see the forest stretching over quite a few hills but in some places on the horizon cultivators had already invaded it.

I would have thought that the areas closest to the main road would be in the greatest danger, yet I found many trees that had fallen from natural causes and were just left to rot.

As in all Rwandan Forest areas, wear long trousers for walking.

From Kibuye, it's another 100km to Cyangugu, a three-to-four-hour drive, mostly along dirt roads.

Public transport along the road between Gisenyi and Kibuye is rather less frequent than along the surfaced road heading east from Gisenyi, but minibus-taxis cover the route daily at a fare equivalent to US$2.50. At present they leave Gisenyi at 06.00 and 14.00 but this could vary. You'll need to change vehicles at Kibuye if you are heading on to Cyangugu.

Boat transport on Lake Kivu lapsed while relations with the DRC were volatile but is now picking up. At the time of writing there is no scheduled public transport between the lake ports, but individuals have boats for hire. It's possible to get by boat from Gisenyi to Kibuye and Cyangugu (see under Oasis Guesthouse, below); and the Hotel Ihusi in Goma (DRC) has a fast, 22-seater boat for transport to Kibuye ($400) and Cyangugu ($1,000). Advance booking is necessary: phone Vincent (085137736) or Vani (08313108). The Kibuye Guesthouse (see page 160) also offers boat transport between Gisenyi and Kibuye. By the time you read this there will certainly be more operators, so ask around – but, in every case, be aware that safety standards may not be 100% and check what is available.

Where to stay
Gisenyi has a range of accommodation to suit most tastes and budgets, and prices are generally very reasonable for what you get. Most of the accommodation is on the lake front, about 15 minutes on foot from the bus and minibus-taxi stand; travellers who don't want to walk down will find a few taxis lined up at the petrol station next to the bus stand. There are a couple of cheap guesthouses close to the bus station, but on the whole it is more pleasant to stay by the lake.

Upper and mid-range
The **Palm Beach Hotel** (BP 347; tel: 08500407) is a somewhat idiosyncratic set-up with an art-deco façade, stylish décor and a light airy ambience to the interiors. Large self-contained doubles with private balcony and en-suite hot bath cost

MY LIFE IN GISENYI...

Catherine Simmons

My day usually begins with an early wake-up call from the local mosque at around 04.30. Not to be outdone, the church across the road starts early morning mass, complete with drumming and joyful singing, at 05.30. Just as I am drifting off to sleep again, my alarm goes off at 06.00. So I stagger into the bathroom where I am soon wide awake due to the effects of a vigorous cold shower. At least I'm out quickly, which is good for my two flatmates! Coffee is a must so I pop the kerosene stove on in the kitchen. It's accompanied by the BBC World Service if reception is good (BBC is on shortwave only in Gisenyi), or some rousing Rwandan music and the news in French on Radio Rwanda if not.

The school bus arrives at 07.20 and we all pile in, along with some other teachers who live locally. We then drive around Gisenyi, picking up teachers and other staff members as we go. Those who miss the bus get picked up second time around, as with nearly 50 teachers we can't all fit in. These bus rides are a lively mix of gossip, jokes and chat between the teachers in Kinyarwanda and Swahili. We usually screech into school about 10–15 minutes before lessons start, just enough time to straighten up and double-check the staffroom notice board for any last-minute meetings. I teach nearly 500 students so every day something unexpected happens and life in the classroom is never boring.

Any hours when I'm not teaching I spend in the English club room

US$30 single/$40 double including breakfast; smaller and scruffier rooms US$25. The restaurant is very atmospheric, with a distinctly European feel in pleasing contrast to the equally likeable beachfront bar.

The **Oasis Guesthouse** (tel: 08513922) lies about 500m out of town along the Ruhengeri road. This is a pleasant little place, with a variety of rooms, ranging from spacious self-contained doubles with sofa, balcony, TV and hot bath at US$30 to self-contained singles at US$15 and a four-roomed villa. The restaurant is good and affordable, but service is slow when it's full. Negatives are the distance from the beach and town centre, and the lack of character by comparison with several other hotels in Gisenyi.

The owners have a five-seater boat which you can hire to go to Kibuye ($100), Cyangugu ($300) or nearby Gishamwana island ($6), where there is a coffee plantation, restaurant and camping. For details phone 08305961 or 08322223; or email kagimaggie@yahoo.fr.

Just downhill from the Oasis, on the same side, is a track leading to the **Belvédère** (BP 252 Gisenyi; tel/fax: 540349; mobile: 08322777), a pleasant new place with eight rooms from US$18 to US$33 according to size and facilities, and a lovely view over the lake. The restaurant is good too.

The top hotel in this class, the old Izubu Meridien (next to the Palm Beach), is due to reopen as the very smart 60-bed **Hotel Kivu Sun** early in preparing lessons or doing marking. When I've finished for the day I catch the local minibus back into the centre of Gisenyi. These bus rides give me a chance to practise my Kinyarwanda: everyone wants to know who I am and what I am doing on the bus.

In town I may do some shopping in the market, go to the bank or use the internet. Being able to speak even basic Kinyarwanda really helps, as does taking the time to stop and talk to people. I also check out the newest bootleg tapes and explain to the tape man that I still don't want to buy that special *Greatest Hits of Don Williams* (although I did succumb to the *Kenny Rogers Christmas Album*). A bit of retail therapy!!

As I walk on home, people always greet me or ask my name or where I'm going, or ask for sweets or biscuits. It's not unusual for someone to walk home with me just for the conversation and because they are interested.

Evenings in Gisenyi are quite low key. Doing dinner can take longer than you would imagine, especially if the electricity goes off or if the stove runs out of kerosene. We spend the time chatting to each other and talking about our days at school. We might listen to some music, or read a bit. At the weekend we often make a pizza in our special home-made 'oven', scoff home-made cake, go swimming in beautiful Lake Kivu and sunbathe. Sometimes we even treat ourselves to the occasional dinner out!!

Cat has been teaching in Gisenyi for Voluntary Service Overseas; see pages 80–1.

2004; it's part of the Southern Sun group so details should eventually appear on website www.southernsun.com.

Budget

Situated on the beachfront, the **Hotel Regina** (tel: 08502226) would easily make my nomination list for Africa's best budget hotel. Built in the colonial era, and still largely fitted in period style, the Regina exudes tropical languor, being sufficiently run-down to fit in the budget category, but not so much that you could fairly describe it as run-down. The wide veranda overlooks a tangled garden and the lake, while the bar and restaurant, with their high ceilings and wooden floor, could be a movie set. Large, airy self-contained rooms cost US$20 single, US$25 double, while rooms using communal hot baths and toilets cost US$15/20 single/double. The food is acceptable and affordable, but the service is appropriately lethargic. A big programme of refurbishment and staff training is currently under way.

A few hundred metres further from the town centre, also overlooking the lake, the **Café du Lac** (tel: 08521326) is another atmospheric and affordable gem. It consists of a well-maintained old colonial house in which two upstairs double rooms are rented out at around US$12 per night (shared bathroom). The wooden floors, slatted windows and whitewashed appearance create

CLIMBING NYIRAGONGO (DRC)

Katot Meyer

We were eight people in total, ranging in age from a 12-year-old boy to about 45 years. On Saturday morning we were at the Rwanda–DRC border in Gisenyi at 08.00. After all the custom procedures to enter DRC, we met up with one of the vulcanologists and our guide. They accompanied us to the foot of the volcano where we negotiated a price of US$30 per person and US$20 for the guide. Some of the people hired a porter for US$10.

We left the base office at exactly 10.00. The first bit of the trail goes through beautiful rainforest. It is amazing to see all the indigenous trees and hear the different bird songs. After a while we left the forest to walk on old lava from the 2002 eruption. We followed the lava to our lunch spot, which was about halfway up the volcano. When the volcano erupted in 2002 the lava came out of the side of the mountain and not the top. We saw the place where it emerged and there was still some smoke coming out. The lava flowed down the path we had come up, then stopped before it reached the town. But it then found another way under the volcano and came out of the side of the mountain at another place, near the airport, from where it went through the town and ended up in Lake Kivu.

After lunch we went through rainforest again. The path was now much steeper and we also had some ran. We reached the 'huts' at about 16:30. There used to be three metal huts – one is now down completely, half of the second one is still standing and the third one is still OK. We pitched one tent inside hut number 2 and the other two tents outside.

The guide, guard and porter slept in hut number 3. They also carried up a bag of charcoal and we could warm ourselves up and get our clothes dry. We also used this hut for doing all our cooking. Outside it was quite chilly but the amazing view over the other volcanoes, lake and town made up for it.

After a rest and dinner we climbed for a final 30 minutes to the summit. It was dark so we used torches and head lamps. We could only see a red glowing mist in the big volcano pot. We could hear the lava bubble down under. It sounded like the waves of the sea. We could see the lights of the two towns and all the fishing boats down on the lake.

We were back on the summit the next morning just after sunrise. We traversed for about half an hour around the volcano rim. All the mist lifted out of the huge pot and we could see the lava down at the bottom. What an amazing sight. We were standing on top of a live volcano!

On the way down we investigated the crater at our lunch spot more closely and then followed the lava back to the base. It was an amazing weekend!

plenty of period character, and the interior has a spacious, airy feel. Meals and drinks are served in the ground-floor restaurant or on the large lawn.

By comparison with all the above, the **Hotel Ubumwe** (BP 39; tel: 540530) is a bit of a non-starter: reasonably comfortable but otherwise undistinguished rooms with en-suite hot showers and toilets at an uncompetitive US$16/20 single/double. The location, too, is less than ideal: a good 20-minute walk from the town centre, and set back a block from the lake. It can get noisy with traffic to/from the border.

Near the market, the **Presbyterian Church's Centre d'Accueil** (tel: 540397) is a pleasant place, bright and fresh, with rates from US$2.50 (dormitory) up to US$10 (self-contained double). It's spaciously laid out and the restaurant is good value. The downhill walk to the beach takes 10–15 minutes. Nearer the market and much grubbier is the **Logement du Petit Lac**, at US$4/$7 single/double. The **Auberge de Gisenyi**, near the minibus stand, is a standard local guesthouse and bar/restaurant with small en-suite rooms (cold water, hot buckets by request) for US$8/10 single/double. Away from the centre, there's a friendly welcome at the **Centre d'Accueil of the Methodist Church**: six twin rooms with washbasins and shared shower/toilet (cold water) at US$6 and rooms with three beds (also sharing facilities) at US$3 a bed or US$9 the room. Meals are prepared by request and there's a view of the lake. **Camping** is possible on request at the **Paradis Restaurant** in Rubona (see below) as well as on Gishamwana Island owned by the proprietors of the **Oasis Guesthouse** (see above). You may spot signs to an Edelweiss Hotel but it's closed.

Where to eat and drink

The best places to eat are generally the hotels. The restaurant at the **Palm Beach Hotel** is probably the best in town, with attractive decor and good Belgian cuisine in the US$5–7 range, and the beachfront bar is a great place to indulge in the tradition of sundowners. It may have a rival in the new **Kivu Sun Hotel**, once that opens. You can eat well at the **Hotel Regina** and the **Belvédère** for comfortably under US$6. About 6km from the centre, in the direction of the Bralirwa Brewery, the **Paradis Restaurant** (tel: 08465959) serves wonderfully fresh fish and the view across the bay is superb. Follow the road towards Rubona for about 5km; when you can see the brewery ahead of you, turn sharp right, continue along the lake shore and you'll come to it on your left. Or just come for a drink and enjoy watching the kamikazi pied kingfishers!

Another good spot for sundowners – indeed for a drink at any time of day – is the **Bar-Restaurant Bikini Tam-Tam**, which has a perfect lakefront position marred only slightly by the smell from the fish market next door. A limited selection of snacks and grills is available in the US$2–5 range.

Foreign exchange

Any of the banks marked on the map will change US dollars cash at rates considerably lower than those on the street. The Banque de Kigali also has Western Union. See page 35 for warnings about travellers' cheques.

Excursions from Gisenyi
Rubona
Set on an attractive peninsula 6km from the town centre, Rubona is the main harbour for Gisenyi and the site of Rwanda's largest brewery. It is connected to the town centre by a surfaced road and regular minibus-taxis, a scenic route which would make for a pleasant stroll in one or other direction. Rubona is a bustling little satellite town, and fun to stroll around, but it is mainly of interest to travellers looking for lake transport, or photographers attracted by the hundreds of small fishing pirogues or dugout canoes that dot the harbour.

Goma
An interesting half-day trip is across into Goma (DRC) to see the lava flow from the 2002 volcanic eruption. Although much has been cleared and rebuilt, the seas of craggy lava still lie beside the road with truncated buildings arising from them. Now that the situation with DRC is more stable, operators in Gisenyi will surely start to organise day trips to Goma (there are also walks and scenic drives there) so do ask around. At the time of writing, if you're heading into the countryside around the town, it's advisable to do so in the company of a local person – for reasons not of safety but of hassle.

If you feel like an adventure, see the box on page 204 – but for this you must have proper equipment and be accompanied by a competent guide. Ask around locally, starting in hotels and guesthouses.

You don't need a visa as such but a fee of US$30 is levied at the border. If you're of one of the nationalities that needs a visa to enter Rwanda, then make sure that you have a multiple- rather than a single-entry one otherwise you'll have to pay extra (US$60) to return into Rwanda from DRC. The frontier post normally opens at 08.00 and closes at 18.00 sharp. Goma has taken a beating but was a gracious and attractive town and is well worth a stroll.

Eastern Rwanda

East of Kigali, the highlands of the Albertine Rift descend towards the western rim of the Lake Victoria Basin, a relatively flat and low-lying region marked by a distinctly warmer and more humid climate than the rest of Rwanda. Geographically, the most significant feature of eastern Rwanda is probably the Akagera River, which forms the border with Tanzania, and feeds the extensive complex of lakes and marshes protected within Akagera National Park.

For tourists, Akagera National Park is undoubtedly the most important attraction in eastern Rwanda. Although the park was recently reduced in area and has suffered heavily from poaching during the last decade, it remains Rwanda's only conventional safari reserve. The untrammelled savanna of Akagera is home to typical plains animals such as lion, elephant, buffalo, zebra and giraffe, while its lakes and marshes support large numbers of hippo and crocodile, as well as a multitude of waterbirds. At present, Akagera is not an easily accessible destination for those without private transport, but it makes for a highly alluring overnight safari out of the capital – provided that you have access to a vehicle.

Akagera aside, the east of Rwanda lacks any major tourist attractions. The handful of towns that dot the region are uniformly dull; they are fine to use as a base, but have little inherent charm, although some have lively markets. Other landmarks include the Rusumo Falls on the Tanzania border and Lake Muhazi, both of which are diverting enough if you are in the area, but not really worth making a major effort to reach, although the drive along the northern shore of Lake Muhazi is attractive (see page 209). The area of rolling hills and cattle farming in the far northeast near the Uganda border offers extensive views – but this is an area for strolling and people-watching rather than any great excitement.

The main roads through eastern Rwanda are surfaced and covered by the usual proliferation of minibus-taxis. Accommodation options are limited by comparison with those in other parts of the country, but all the main towns have at least one reasonably comfortable – and reasonably priced – hotel. Because it lies at a lower altitude than the rest of the country, the Tanzania border area is the one part of Rwanda where malaria is a major rather than a minor risk, particularly during the rainy season.

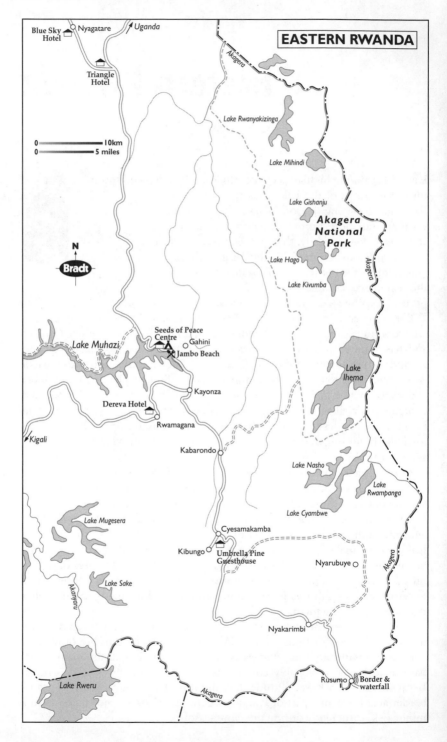

EASTERN RWANDA VIA THE BYUMBA ROAD
Rwanda Na Gasabo

The first substantial right turn off the main Kigali–Byumba road, about 25km out of Kigali, takes you on a winding route to **Rwanda Na Gasabo** or the original Rwanda hill. This is where (allegedly) the first of the ancient kings, travelling to Rwanda from the northeast, stopped at the top and set up his kingdom. It's high, with a flat top and a view in all directions. After leaving the main road, continue for a short distance to a cluster of houses where there's a sharp left turn on to a narrow road that climbs steeply. Just follow this upwards and you'll reach the top of the hill. (A 4WD is advisable, particularly after rain.) People are generally around, so ask directions if you're unsure. The view is spectacular. There are plans to develop this site for tourism (reconstructed dwellings, interpretation boards...) but at present it's peaceful.

Legends abound! The ancient King Gihanga (see box on page 211) is said to have left two of his cows here; their names were Rugira and Ingizi. One day another king went hunting and threw a branch after an animal; the tip sank into the ground and took root, becoming a species found nowhere else in Rwanda. The great trees planted as the gateway to his land are still standing, after many centuries. There was a magic earthenware pot in the court; it would fill with water of its own accord to signify that rain was on the way. The monarch had a very special group of royal drummers, whose drumming awakened him in the morning and sent him to sleep at night. And so on. You may well meet someone up there who will tell you other tales.

The northern bank of Lake Muhazi

About five minutes further up the Kigali–Byumba road after the Gasabo turning, another right turn is the start of a beautiful (but sometimes rough) road that follows the northern bank of Lake Muhazi and emerges on the main road flanking Akagera Park. It crosses some small creeks on rough wooden 'bridges' so is best done in the dry season and certainly in a 4WD. It may well become impassable in a couple of places when the lake rises: ask about this.

Very soon after leaving the main road you cross a small iron bridge; then, after about 25 minutes (or longer if you stop to birdwatch and enjoy the lakeside views), you'll come to three simple places to stay, wonderfully located at the water's edge and within a few hundred metres of each other. In only five minutes (when we stopped at one for a drink) we spotted pied and malachite kingfishers, an otter and a fish eagle! The first place on the right as you come from Kigali – **Café-Resto Hakurya y'i Gasabo** – has a bar/restaurant and two small, en-suite rondavels at US$6. The second, **Rwesero Beach**, has a bar/restaurant, picnic place and camping. The third, **Martin Pecheur**, also has a bar/restaurant and camping area, plus children's swings and volleyball. And even phone numbers: 574745 & 08488318.

All three places have boats, so you can fish on the lake – or cross to the opposite bank and camp there. They're very new at the time of writing so will certainly develop their facilities – and will become busy with Kigali folk at weekends..

From then on it's a succession of tranquil, watery views (and numerous birds) as the road continues alongside the lake. Allow a half-day for this road, including stops – you can do it in less, but it's a shame to hurry and the surface is sometimes quite rutted. Hitching could be difficult; transport comes in from either end but doesn't necessarily go the whole way through.

LAKE MUHAZI

In common with most lakes in Rwanda, Muhazi is an erratically shaped body of water whose shores follow the contours of the surrounding hills. It is a pretty spot, though not as beautiful as the lakes around Ruhengeri, but – at least for travellers dependent on public transport – it has the virtue of being highly accessible. The eastern tip of Lake Muhazi lies beside the surfaced Kagitumba road, about 8km north of Kayonza. Here, opposite the turn-off to the small hillside town of Gahini, is the **Seeds of Peace Centre** (Episcopal Church; office tel/fax: 67422; email: gahini@rwanda1.com) which has got itself well organised for tourism, with boating, swimming, birdwatching, a restaurant offering fresh lake fish, camping, a picnic place and two reconstructed traditional dwellings. It also has rondavels, each with two bedrooms, bathroom, kitchen and lounge: US$40 for four people, US$35 for three, US$24 for two or one. Profits from this and the Gahini Guest House (see below) go back into the diocese for its work in the local community.

Across the road and up a steepish hill is Gahini, an attractive little town set high above the lake. The friendly **Gahini Guest House** (Episcopal Church; office tel/fax: 67422; email: gahini@rwanda1.com) has an en-suite double at US$12, double and single with shared facilities US$10 and US$8; capacious dormitories (bunk beds) US$2; and conference facilities.

Further along the road towards Rwamagana is the **Jambo Pleasure Beach**, a similar (but currently smaller) lakeside resort. with a restaurant and camping space but no rooms.

Back in the olden days, this was a lake much studied by the Germans as they explored their new territory. Writing in 1907, a Doctor Mildbraed rather crossly commented:

> The west end of Lake Mohasi terminates in a papyrus swamp, and therefore promised rich spoils for zoological treasure-hunters. We were all the more keenly disillusioned to find the fauna far more meagre in character in this great water basin – the first we had explored in Africa – than we had been led to suppose in Germany. In spite of the luxurious vegetation at this part of the lake, the most diligent search was needed before we found a few sponges and polypi attached to some characeous plants.

RWAMAGANA

One of several unremarkable small towns in eastern Rwanda, Rwamagana is of interest to travellers primarily as a base from which to explore Lake Muhazi

THE NAMING OF COW
A new variation on a traditional tale

The great King Gihanga ruled a part of Rwanda in the early 12th century – or perhaps the late tenth. Some historians say that he was the first of the royal dynasty, others claim that many kings preceded him. That's the trouble with oral history – the facts are elusive, and who knows whether or not any of this story is true! Anyway, it's certain that Gihanga had many wives and many children.

One day, his favourite daughter Nyirarucyaba lost her temper with a wife who was not her mother, scratching at the woman's face and tearing her hair until she screamed in pain. To lose control was considered very shameful and all the courtiers had seen what happened, so the king had no choice. He banished Nyirarucyaba, sending her to the deep forest where only wild beasts live. She wept pitifully but he would not yield, although his heart was torn.

After many days alone, the girl heard a rustling in the leaves and a snapping of branches – and crouched to the ground in fear. But it was a young man who had, like her, been cast into exile. Now, together, they began to contact the animals around them. There was one that seemed friendly, despite its great size and ugly voice. By day it munched the forest grasses and by night they kept warm against its soft hide.

In time it gave birth to a young one, with wet matted skin and shaky legs, which nuzzled under its mother and sucked at her teats. They saw that it drank a white liquid and learnt that it was milk. Now they had food indeed! They shared the milk with the calf and grew strong and healthy. In time they bore children of their own and the cow had many more calves.

Meanwhile the king had fallen sick with an illness that robbed him of all strength and joy. Doctors could find no cure. Finally three of the court's wisest men, so old that their hair was white and thin upon their heads, recognised it as grief, and took it upon themselves to speak. They told him Nyirarucyaba was still alive – and at once he sprang from his couch and dispatched hunters to the forest to search for her. They found her beside a stream, her children at her side and many cattle grazing nearby. Her return to her delighted father was a time of great celebration at the court.

The cattle came too, with their rich supply of milk. The courtiers gained a taste for it, and grew fat and strong. One day – it was summer, and the grasses around the huts carried much pollen – one of the king's grandchildren asked him the name of the precious beasts. At that moment he sneezed explosively – 'Ha-ha-ha-inkaaah!' – and all heads nodded wisely. The king had spoken. From that time on, the cow has been called 'inka' in Kinyarwanda.

and Akagera National Park, though it does boast a couple of marginally interesting colonial buildings including a large church. The market is currently being rebuilt. The town lies about 60km from Kigali, no more than a hour's drive along a good surfaced road covered by regular minibus-taxis, some of which are 'express' while others also serve villages nearby. In Kigali they leave from the Nyabugogo bus station and call at Remera bus station en route. On your return you may also be dropped off at Kigali's central bus station in Avenue de Commerce.

The **Dereva Hotel** (BP 126; tel: 67244), set in large green grounds alongside the main road, offers what are probably the most commodious lodgings in this part of Rwanda, and is very reasonably priced at around US$10/8 for a suite-sized single/double with hot showers. The attached restaurant serves large meals in the US$3–5 range. If the Dereva is full you could try the much shabbier **Ikambere** (tel: 67372), where an en-suite double (cold water) costs US$5.

As you pass through Rwamagana coming from Kigali, look out for some new buildings on the left of the main road at the Kigali end of town. These are part of a project run and financed by Projet Rwa/020 of Lux-Development (for information phone 67380); it includes the development and promotion of local handicrafts and trains young people to produce them. It also markets the work of craftspeople throughout Kibungo province. You can generally watch the items (patchwork, tie & dye, beadwork, bags made from sisal and – improbably! – from bottle-tops, leatherwork and so on) being made. The young trainees are helped to work together in groups after their training. The crafts shop on the premises is run by the association 'IAKI', meaning *Inter-Association des Artisans de Kibungo*, so carries a range of local objects.

KAYONZA
This small, rather scruffy settlement is situated 78km from Kigali, at the junction of the main north–south road connecting Kagitumba on the Rwanda border to Rusumo on the Tanzania border. Kayonza is, if anything, even less remarkable than Rwamagana, though once again it serves as a possible base for exploring Lake Muhazi and Akagera National Park and is readily accessible from Kigali on public transport (minibuses leave from Nyabugogo bus station).

The few basic hotels at the Kayonza junction (Buganza, Iraba, Greenland Guesthouse…) were either closed for renovations or barely open when I checked – there certainly is cheap accommodation there but not ready to be included in this edition! At present you'd do better to continue to the Umbrella Pine at Kibungo (see below).

NYAGATARE
The far northeastern tip of Rwanda is a wide-open area of rolling landscapes and cattle, stretching to the hills of Uganda in the distance. The vegetation is much the same as that of Akagera National Park: fresh and gently green at moister times of year, parched and tinder dry just before the rainy season, with weary cattle – mostly the long-horned Ankole – plodding from clump to

clump of bristly scrub. There's a pioneering feel about the hamlets and villages here; they squat defiantly, surrounded by the empty plains. As you drive up from Kigali you'll also notice patches of new housing, built (often with foreign funds) to accommodate the returning refugees. These are the houses of a child's pictures, plain and single-storeyed, with a small square window on either side of the front door. In fact they're dotted all over Rwanda, but the open landscapes here make them more visible.

Nyagatare is a small, scattered town and administrative centre and, if you want a wholly un-touristy experience, you could consider spending a night there. Minibuses run from Kigali's Nyabugogo bus station, and it's handy for the Uganda border if you're travelling on.

The **Blue Sky Hotel** (BP108 Nyagatare; tel: 65244) has five en-suite doubles/twins with mosquito nets for around US$13, and 20 more rooms with shared facilities (clean) at US$5 single, US$8 double. Electricity is from a generator so don't plan too much reading in bed. In the evenings the bar is companionably busy with local people and the restaurant isn't bad – although breakfast is a touch Spartan. There are also two church places. The **Seeds of Hope Guest House** (Episcopal Church; office tel/fax: 67422; email: gahini@rwanda1.com), not far from the Blue Sky, has an en-suite double for US$10; non-en-suite twin US$8 and dormitory bed US$2. The **Centre Spirituel Amizero** (Presbyterian Church) has an en-suite double for US$11 and dormitory beds (bunks) for US$2. There are a couple of small restaurants in the main street serving the usual *mélanges* of meat, rice and vegetables. Also, 5km or so from Nyagatare as you turn off from the main Kigali–Uganda road, there's the **Triangle Hotel** (20 small bare rooms, mosquito nets, US$8 double, basic shared facilities, no phone or restaurant but probably OK if you're stuck or broke).

The tiny main street offers – surprisingly – a photo laboratory, post office, dry cleaners, barber, general store and a sign-writer who also sells local paintings (rather gaudy, judging by the selection I saw).

What you can do from Nyagatare is walk – ask (and take note of) local permission and advice, fill up your water bottle and then just stroll off across fields, plains, hillsides… It's a wonderfully clear, open panorama (unlike in much of the rest of Rwanda with its jutting hills and intensive cultivation) and local farmers told me that they often find antelope and zebra grazing peacefully among their cattle. Also, in Nyagatare as in all of Rwanda, you can while time away pleasantly by people-watching and engaging in conversation. (Have you remembered how to ask 'What's your name'? I'll remind you. It's *Witwandé*?)

KIBUNGO

The largest town in the southeast of Rwanda, Kibungo lies about 25km south of Kayonza junction and 100km from Kigali. It is a convenient base from which to explore Akagera National Park (though Rwamagana, only slightly further from the park entrance, does have a smarter hotel) and the obvious springboard for a half-day trip to the Rusumo Falls. Otherwise, it is no more distinguished than other towns in this part of Rwanda: a small grid of roads lying 3km west of the altogether more bustling junction town of Cyesamakamba. Regular minibus-taxis connect Kibungo to Kigali and Rusumo.

It's the administrative centre of Kibungo prefecture, in a region suffering not only from the aftermath of the genocide (much still needs to be reconstructed, both physically and mentally) but also from the unkindness of nature; at the time of writing it depends on external food aid, as the autumn rains were both too late and yet again too little.

Located in Cyesamakamba (aka Cyamakamba) on the main road towards Rusumo about 200m past the turn-off to Kibungo proper, the **Motel Umbrella Pine** (tel: 66269, 572567) is a simple but attractive, friendly and hard-working little place. There are shortcomings – dodgy plumbing, water shortages during the dry season – but the staff are so willing that it's worth a try. The restaurant serves good, inventive meals (under US$5) and can rustle up a picnic if you need it for visiting Akagera. If the canned music drifts through to your bedroom, ask them to turn it off! (They plan to install TV in the rooms, which may not be an asset.) En-suite rooms (hot water) are US$12 single, US$17 double including breakfast. It can be hard to spot – coming from Kigali, directly after the turning off to Kibungo there's a petrol station on the right and it's just beyond that, set back a little from the road.

The alternative in Kibungo is the **Centre St Joseph** (tel: 566303) near the Stella Taxi Express office. En-suite rooms (cold water) are US$5 single, US$10 double including breakfast; dormitory beds US$2.50; suites US$14. There's a restaurant (but no alcohol).

A couple of other bars and restaurants are dotted around the junction, serving chilled beers, goat kebabs and other local fare – the food isn't comparable to that of the Umbrella Pine, but it is a lot cheaper.

RUSUMO FALLS

The Rusumo border with Tanzania, 60km southeast of Kibungo, is also the site of Rwanda's most impressive waterfall. Rusumo Falls isn't particularly tall, and it couldn't be mentioned in the same breath as the Victoria or Blue Nile Falls, but it is a voluminous rush of white water nevertheless, as the Akagera River surges below the bridge between the two border posts. The Rwandan officials don't appear to have any objection to tourists wandering on to the bridge to goggle at the spectacle, though it's a moot point whether the falls actually justify the two-hour round trip from Kibungo. At present you can photograph the falls from the bridge, but nothing else. It's best to ask permission anyway.

At the Rusumo border there's a basic hotel: the **Amarembo Hotel**, with two doubles ($6) and seven singles ($4) sharing facilities. The small restaurant has all the usual drinks and the buffet lunch looked tasty. It gets busy with cross-border traffic. There's also an 'Anarembo Taxi Express' running between the hotel and Kigali: US$3.50 one way.

It's here at Rusumo that the German Count von Götzen, later to become Governor of German East Africa, entered Rwanda in 1894. He then travelled across the country to Lake Kivu, visiting the Mwami at Nyanza en route. Later, in 1916, when the Belgians were preparing to wrest the territory from the Germans, Belgian troops dug a trench and mounted artillery at the spot where one can see the falls today, in order to dislodge the German troops ensconced on the other bank who were guarding the only negotiable crossing.

If you are heading this way, it's definitely worth stopping at **Nyakarimbi**, a large village straddling the Kibungo road about 20km from the Rusumo border crossing. This part of Rwanda is noted for its distinctive cow-dung 'paintings' – earthy, geometric designs which are mostly used to decorate the interiors of houses. In Nyakarimbi, however, a couple of the houses have cow-dung paintings on their outer walls, and about 2km south of the town there's a craft co-operative. This is where most of the geometric paintings and pottery you see in Kigali originate from, but it's more fun (and cheaper) to buy them at source, especially as the people who run the co-operative aren't at all pushy. The sign outside reads 'Ishyirahamwe Association Kakira – Art "Imigongo"' and shows geometric patterns. A small brochure, available in the workshop, explains (in more or less these words):

In olden times, there was Kakira, son of Kimenyi, King of Gisaka in Kibungo province (southeastern Rwanda). Kakira invented the art of embellishing houses and making them more attractive. To decorate the inside walls, cow dung was used, in patterns with prominent ridges. Then the surfaces were painted, in red and white colours made from natural soil (white from kaolin, red from natural clay with ochre), or else in shining black made from the sap of the aloe plant – *ikakarubamba* – mixed with the ash of burned banana skins and fruits of the *solanum aculeastrum* plant. It was the art of mixing together the soil, fire, raw materials from the cow and medicinal art that is the source of this work.

Kakira's knowledge was disappearing, due to the increasing use of industrial materials (paint); and so a women's association was created to maintain Kakira's work. After the 1994 genocide, most of the women, now widows, restarted their work together. Since 2001, the association has benefited from better promotion. Previously the women made no more than 20 pieces a month; now it is much more as orders have increased. Today, the Kakira Association makes 'Imigongo' art: modelled and painted tiles, panels, tables and other objects.

Coloured tiles cost US$16; black-and-white tiles US$6 – and they're beautiful, with very intricate patterns. Working hours are Monday to Saturday, 07.30–12.30 and 14.00–18.00. Kakira products can be ordered from the workshop or via Mr Emmanuel Bugingo, tel: 08594372; email: bugingemmanuel@yahoo.fr.

So far as travel practicalities go, the surfaced road between Kibungo and Rusumo is in reasonable condition, and can be covered in an hour. Regular minibus-taxis service the route.

AKAGERA NATIONAL PARK

Named after the river which runs along its eastern boundary, Akagera National Park is Rwanda's answer to the famous savanna reserves of anglophone East and southern Africa. In contrast to the rest of the country, Akagera is relatively warm and low-lying, and its undulating plains support a cover of dense, broad-leafed woodland interspersed with lighter acacia woodland and patches of rolling grassland studded evocatively with stands of the superficially cactus-like *Euphorbia candelabra* shrub. To the west of the plains lies a chain of low mountains, reaching elevations of between 1,600m and 1,800m. The eastern part of the park supports an extensive network of wetlands: a complex of a dozen lakes linked by extensive papyrus swamps and winding water channels fed by the mighty Akagera River.

In terms of game-viewing, it would be misleading to compare Akagera to East Africa's finest savanna reserves. Poaching has greatly reduced wildlife populations in recent years, and what was formerly the north of the park has been settled by returned refugees. The intense human pressure on Akagera is reflected in the fact that much of the northern and western territory was de-gazetted in 1998, reducing its total area by almost two-thirds from 250,000 to 90,000 hectares. Even after this concession to local land requirements, the lakes that remain within the national park are dotted with local fishing camps, and routinely used to water domestic cattle (the

AKAGERA'S HISTORY

The Belgian colonisers were concerned about nature conservation. From 1920 onwards (and earlier, in the Congo) conservation measures were put into practice and became the object of various legislative and administrative decrees. It was the decree of November 26 1934 that created the *Parc National de la Kagera*, on about 250,000 hectares. The park included – which was extremely rare before 1960 – a Strict Natural Reserve and an adjoining area where certain human activities were tolerated. It came under the jurisdiction of the *Institut des Parcs Nationaux du Congo Belge et du Ruanda-Urundi*, which was also responsible for the three parks (Albert, Garamba and Upemba) in the Belgian Congo. (In fact 8% of the Albert Park was also in Rwanda; now representing the Volcanoes Park in the northwest.) Kagera was renamed Akagera after independence, when the new Republic's leaders announced their intention of maintaining the park (and the Volcanoes Park) despite population pressure. Akagera's borders were altered – a few thousand hectares were retroceded to local communities while almost 20,000 hectares of the lacustrine zone to the south were incorporated. Several dozen elephants were transported, first by helicopter and then by truck, from Bugesera, which was to be developed for agriculture. In November 1984, Rwanda held an official celebration of the park's 50th anniversary.

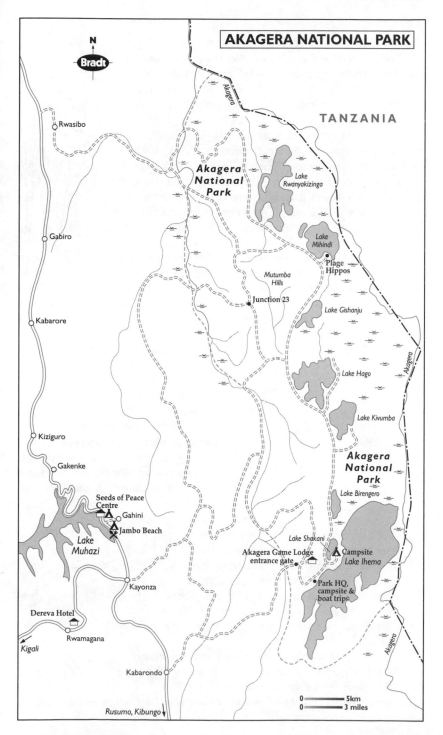

AKAGERA NATIONAL PARK

N

Bradt

Rwasibo

Akagera

*Akagera
National
Park*

Lake
Rwanyakizinga

TANZANIA

Gabiro

Lake
Mihindi

Plage
Hippos

*Mutumba
Hills*

Junction 23

Lake Gishanju

Kabarore

Lake Hago

Akagera

Lake Kivumba

Kiziguro

Gakenke

*Akagera
National
Park*

Lake Birengero

Seeds of Peace
Centre

Gahini

Jambo Beach

Lake Shakani

Akagera Game Lodge
entrance gate

Campsite
Lake Ihema

*Lake
Muhazi*

Park HQ,
campsite &
boat trips

Kayonza

Dereva Hotel

Kigali

Rwamagana

Kabarondo

Akagera

Rusumo, Kibungo

0 ▬▬▬ 5km
0 ▬▬▬ 3 miles

ANTELOPE OF AKAGERA

The 11 antelope species in Akagera range from the eland, the world's largest antelope, through to the diminutive common duiker. The most common, however, is the **impala** *Aepeceros melampus*, a slim handsome antelope which bears a superficial similarity to the gazelles, but belongs to a separate family. Chestnut in colour, the impala has diagnostic black and white stripes running down its rump and tail, and the male has large lyre-shaped horns. It is one of the most widespread antelope species in East and southern Africa, normally seen in large herds in woodland habitats, and common in the woodland around and between the lakes of Akagera.

The **Defassa waterbuck** *Kobus ellipsiprymnus defassa* is a large, shaggy brown antelope with a distinctive white rump. The male has large lyre-shaped horns, thicker than those of the impala. Waterbuck inhabit practically any type of woodland or grassland provided that it is close to water, and they are probably the most common large antelope after impala in the far south of Akagera.

Very common in the north of the park and in the Mutumba Hills, the **topi** or **tsessebe** *Damaliscus lunatus* is a large, slender dark-brown antelope with striking yellow lower legs. It has a rather ungainly appearance, reminiscent of the hartebeest and wildebeest, to which it is closely related, and is often seen using an anthill as a sentry point. Oddly, the herds of topi we saw in northern Akagera are far larger than those found in the Serengeti ecosystem.

Similar in size to a topi, but far more handsome, the **roan antelope** *Hippotragus equinus* has, as the Latin name suggests, a horse-like bearing. The uniform fawn-grey coat is offset by a pale belly, and it has short decurved horns and a light mane. Recent reports suggest that roan are now rare in Akagera.

Much larger still is the **common** or **Cape eland** *Taurotragus oryx*, which attains a height of up to 1.75m and can weigh as much as 900kg. The common eland is light-brown in colour, with faint white vertical stripes, and a somewhat bovine appearance accentuated by the relatively short horns and large dewlap. In Akagera, small herds are most likely to be seen on the open grassland of the Mutumba Hills, where is it quite common.

A trio of smaller antelope are also mainly confined to the Mutumba Hills. The largest of these is the **Bohor reedbuck** *Redunca redunca*, a light-fawn animal with moderately sized rounded horns; reedbucks are almost always seen in pairs, and in Akagera are rather skittish. The smaller **oribi** *Ourebia ourebi* is a tan grassland antelope with short straight horns and a small but clearly visible circular black glandular patch below its ear. It is the commonest antelope on the Mutumba Hills, typically seen in parties of two or three, and has a distinctive sneezing alarm call. The **klipspringer** *Oreotragus oreotragus* is a goat-like antelope, normally seen in pairs, and easily identified by its dark, bristly grey-yellow coat, slightly speckled appearance and unique habitat preference. Klipspringer means 'rockjumper' in Afrikaans and it is an apt name for an antelope which occurs exclusively in mountainous areas and rocky outcrops.

The only small antelope found in thicker bush is the **common duiker** *Sylvicapra grimmia*, an anomalous savanna representative of a family of 20-plus small hunchbacked antelopes associated with true forests. Generally grey in colour, the common duiker has a distinctive black tuft of hair sticking up between its small straight horns. It is common in all bush areas, though it tends to be very skittish.

A widespread resident of thick woodland and forest, the pretty **bushbuck** *Tragelaphus scriptus* is a medium-sized, rather deer-like antelope. The male is dark brown or
continued overleaf

ANTELOPE OF AKAGERA continued

chestnut, while the much smaller female is generally pale red-brown. The male has relatively small, straight horns, while both sexes have pale throat patches, white spots and sometimes stripes. The bushbuck tends to be secretive, but might be seen anywhere in Akagera except for open grassland.

Similar in appearance to the bushbuck, and a close relation, the semi-aquatic **sitatunga** *Tragelaphus spekei* is a widespread but infrequently observed inhabitant of west and central African swamps. The male, with a shoulder height of up to 125cm (much taller than a bushbuck) and a shaggy fawn coat, is unmistakable, while the smaller female might be mistaken for a bushbuck except for its more clearly defined stripes. The status of the sitatunga within Akagera is uncertain; they are almost certainly still present, but uncommon and restricted to inaccessible swampy areas.

distinctive long-horned Ankole cow is far and away the most commonly seen large mammal in Akagera). And the man-made litter around tourist areas in the park has to raise serious concerns. We retrieved two jagged-edged tin cans and a plastic bag, all potentially dangerous to wildlife.

For all that, Akagera is emphatically worth visiting. There are plenty of animals around, and they aren't as skittish as one might expect. To give some idea, over the course of three game drives, we saw a total of 20 mammal species, ranging from elephant and buffalo to the tiny elephant-shrew and bushbaby. The lakes support some of the highest concentrations of hippo you'll find anywhere in Africa, as well as numerous large crocodiles, while lion, leopard and possibly black rhino are still present in small numbers. And the birdlife is phenomenal: not only the sort of rarities that will have ardent birdwatchers in raptures, but also some of Africa's most impressive concentrations of big waterbirds.

As big an attraction as the animal life is the sensation of being in a genuinely off-the-beaten-track chunk of bush: this is one African game reserve where you can still drive for hours without passing another vehicle, never knowing what wildlife encounter might lie around the next corner. Akagera is also among the most scenic of savanna reserves, with its sumptuous forest-fringed lakes, tall mountains and constantly changing vegetation.

Akagera is a good game reserve. It could, with improved management and a bit of time, once again become a truly great one. Equally, it could well be that Akagera will simply not be able to withstand the clamour for land from outside its already reduced boundaries. Which way it goes, one senses, will depend largely on its ability to generate serious tourist dollars and employment opportunities. Rwanda's population has doubled in the last 20 years and it is set to double again over the next 20. The pressure on Akagera will only increase with time, yet in the context of this rapid population growth, forsaking 90,000 hectares of not particularly arable game reserve to cultivation and grazing will at best alleviate a short-term problem. It will not address the heart of the land issue, even though new legislation on grazing has just been introduced.

The survival of Akagera is not simply an esoteric conservation concern, but one that has implications for the country's development as a whole. Prior to the civil war, Rwanda's fledgling tourist industry was one of its three main sources of foreign revenue. If Rwanda is to rebuild that industry, and to develop a self-contained tourist circuit of its own, then it desperately *needs* Akagera. For, without a savanna reserve of Akagera's ilk, the country seems destined to attract nothing but pit-stop cross-border gorilla tourism, tourists spending one or two nights in one small part of the country as an extension of a safari elsewhere in East Africa. It's to be hoped that the facilities of the very new Akagera Game Lodge inside the park may help to rebuild Akagera's tourism.

If you visit Akagera, you won't regret it – it's a lovely, untrammelled slice of African bush. No less important, perhaps, you'll be doing Rwanda a favour.

Natural history
Akagera is notable for protecting an unusually wide diversity of habitats within a relatively small area. Prior to the civil war, it was regarded as one of the few African savanna reserves to form a self-sustaining ecological unit, meaning that its resident large mammals had no need to migrate seasonally outside of the park boundaries. Whether that is still the case today is an open question, as roughly two-thirds of the original park was de-gazetted in 1998, and, while some of this discarded territory is still virgin bush today, it is probably only a matter of time before it will all be settled, putting further pressure on Akagera's diminished wildlife populations.

The modern boundaries of the park protect a 90,000ha area, which stretches from north to south along the Tanzania border for approximately 60km, and is nowhere wider than 30km from east to west. The eastern third of the park consists of an extensive network of wetlands, fed by the Akagera River, and dominated by a series of small-to-medium-sized lakes. Lake Ihema, the most southerly of the lakes to lie within the revised park boundaries, is also the largest body of open water, covering about 100km^2. The lakes are connected by narrow channels of flowing water and large expanses of seasonal and perennial papyrus swamps. The eastern wetlands are undoubtedly the most important of the habitats protected within the park: not only do they provide a permanent source of drinking water for the large mammals, but they also form an important waterbird sanctuary while harbouring a number of localised swamp dwellers.

Akagera's dominant terrestrial habitat is broad-leafed woodland, though pockets of acacia woodland also exist within the park, while some of the lake fringes support a thin belt of lush riparian woodland. Ecologically, the savanna of Akagera is in several respects unique, a product of its isolation from similar habitats by the wetlands to the east and mountainous highlands of central

Rwanda to the west. The flora shows strong affinities with the semi-arid zones of northern Uganda and Kenya, but the fauna is more typical of the Mara-Serengeti ecosystem east of Lake Victoria. Akagera's geographical isolation from similar habitats is emphasised by the natural absence of widespread plains animals such as rhino and giraffe, both of which were subsequently introduced and (at least until the civil war) have thrived in their adopted home. Much of the bush in Akagera is very dense, but there are also areas of light acacia woodland and open grassland, notably on the Mutumba Hills and to the northeast of Lake Rwanyakizinga.

Mammals

While Akagera's considerable scenic qualities and superb birdlife are largely unaffected by the recent years of turmoil, the large mammal populations have suffered badly at the hands of poachers. Having said that, we arrived at Akagera expecting the worst, and were pleasantly surprised at how much wildlife there still is. It is the classic 'bad news, good news' scenario. The populations of all large mammals (except perhaps hippo) are severely depleted by comparison with ten years ago, while a few high-profile species, if not already locally extinct, appear to be heading that way. The good news, however, is that most large mammals are still sufficiently numerous to form a viable breeding population; furthermore, with adequate protection, these numbers are likely to be supplemented by animals crossing into the park from unprotected parts of neighbouring Tanzania which still support plenty of big game. Akagera, in short, is a damaged but salvageable game reserve.

Extirpated species include the **African wild dog**, probably a victim not of poaching but, in common with many other African reserves, of a canine plague which would have been introduced into the population through contact with domestic dogs. **Black rhino**, introduced in 1954, might well be extinct and are certainly very vulnerable, though it would not be surprising if the thick bush still held a few individuals (two unverified rhino sightings were reported by visitors over the year before we visited the park).

Of the larger predators, **spotted hyena** and **leopard** are still around, but infrequently observed (though you might well come across hyena spoor, particularly the characteristic white dung). The future of the park's **lion** – many of which have been poisoned by cattle herders – hangs in the balance. A solitary female was seen in the north of the park in early 2000, and a few months later a female with three cubs was sighted in the same area. Probably this was the same female, and she must have found a male lion somewhere – given the tenacity of these regal felines, and their tendency to

Spotted hyena

Leopard

wander long distances, this is one species which could naturally replenish itself through individuals crossing over from Tanzania.

Smaller predators are well represented. Most likely to be encountered by day are various **mongooses** (we saw dwarf, banded and black-tailed mongooses), while at night there is a chance of coming across viverrids such as the lithe, heavily spotted and somewhat cat-like **genet**, and the bulkier black-masked **civet**. Also present, but rarely seen, are the handsome spotted **serval cat** and the dog-like **side-striped jackal**.

Banded mongoose

One of the most common terrestrial mammals is the **buffalo**, and while the population is nowhere near the estimated 8,000 that roamed the park in the 1980s, it is probably still measurable in thousands. **Hippo**, too, are present in impressive numbers: we saw pods of between 40 and 50 animals on all of the lakes, and on some of the lakes there must be at least a dozen pods. The park's formerly prodigious **elephant** herds have suffered badly from poaching, but a viable population estimated at around 60 survives, centred around Lake Hago. There is talk of importing more. Small herds of **Burchell's zebra** are regularly encountered in open areas, while the population of 30 **Masai giraffe**, descendants of a herd introduced from Kenya in 1975, tend to stick to patches of acacia woodland.

African buffalo

The handsome **impala** is probably the most common and habitat-tolerant large mammal in the park, and of the 11 antelope species which occur in Akagera (see box *Antelope of Akagera* on pages 202–5), only the aquatic **sitatunga** is immediately endangered and unlikely to be seen by visitors. Also very common are three savanna primates: the dark, heavily built **olive baboon**, the smaller and more agile **vervet monkey**, and the tiny wide-eyed **bushbaby** (the latter a nocturnal species likely to be seen only after dusk). The forest-dwelling **silver monkey**, although listed for Akagera, is probably now very rare, possibly even extirpated, due to habitat loss following the reduction in the park's area. For the same reason, it is debatable whether Africa's largest swine, the **giant forest hog**, still occurs in Akagera. The smaller **bushpig**, a secretive nocturnal species, is present but rarely encountered, while the **warthog**, a bolder diurnal pig, is very common throughout.

Warthog

Birds

Akagera is, after Nyungwe, the most important ornithological site in Rwanda. What's more, these two fine birding destinations complement each other to such an extent that our lists for them probably had less than 20% of species in common. In addition to being the best place in Rwanda to see a good selection of savanna birds and raptors, Akagera is as rich in waterbirds as anywhere in East Africa, and one of the few places where papyrus endemics can be observed.

Among the more colourful and common of the savanna birds are the gorgeous lilac-breasted roller, black-headed gonalek (easily picked up by its jarring duets), little bee-eater, Heuglin's robin-chat and brown parrot. Less colourful, but very impressive, are the comical grey hornbill and noisy bare-faced go-away bird. The riparian woodland around the lakes hosts a number of specialised species, of which Ross's turaco, a bright-purple, jay-sized bird with a distinctive yellow mask, is the most striking.

A notable feature of Akagera's avifauna is the presence of species such as crested barbet, white-headed black chat and Souza's shrike, all of which are associated with the *brachystegia* woodland of southern Tanzania and further south, but have colonised the mixed woodland of Akagera at the northernmost extent of their range. Also worthy of a special mention is the red-faced barbet, a localised endemic of savannas between Lake Victoria and the Albertine Rift. Finally, the savanna of Akagera is one of the last places in Rwanda where a wide range of large raptors is resident: white-backed and Ruppell's griffon vultures soar high on the thermals, the beautiful bataleur eagle can be recognised by its wavering flight pattern and red wing markings, while brown snake eagles and hooded vultures are often seen perching on bare branches.

Most of the savanna birds are primarily of interest to the dedicated birder, but it is difficult to imagine that anybody would be unmoved by the immense concentrations of water-associated birds that can be found on the lakes. Pelicans are common, as is the garishly decorated crowned crane, the odd little open-bill stork and the much larger and singularly grotesque marabou stork. Herons and egrets are particularly visible and well-represented, ranging from the immense goliath heron to the secretive black-capped night heron and reed-dwelling purple heron. The lakes also support a variety of smaller kingfishers and shorebirds, and a prodigious number of fish eagles, whose shrill duet ranks as one of the most evocative sounds of Africa.

On a more esoteric note, the papyrus swamps are an excellent place to look for a handful of birds restricted to this specific habitat: the stunning and highly vocal papyrus gonalek, as well as the more secretive and nondescript Caruthers's cisticola and white-winged warbler. Akagera used to be regarded as one of the best places in Africa to see the shoebill, an enormous and unmistakable slate-grey swamp-dweller whose outsized bill is fixed in a permanent Cheshire-cat smirk. Placed in a monospecific genus, the secretive and localised shoebill is among the most sought-after of African birds, and its continued presence in Akagera would do much to boost Rwanda's status as an avi-tourism destination. Unfortunately, we were unable to establish whether the civil war and subsequent reduction in the park's area had any impact on the shoebill's habitat – judging by the blank looks that our questioning and frantic pointing at the field guide drew from everybody we spoke to, the prognosis is less than fantastic!

Reptiles

The **Nile crocodile**, the world's largest reptile and a survivor from the age of the dinosaurs, is abundant in the lakes. Some of the largest wild specimens you'll encounter anywhere are to be found sunning themselves on the mud-banks of Akagera, their impressive mouths wide open until they slither menacingly into the water at the approach of human intruders. Not unlike a miniature crocodile in appearance, the **water monitor** is a type of lizard which often grows to be more than a metre long and is common around the lakes, tending to crash noisily into the bush or water when disturbed. Smaller lizards are to be seen all over, notably the colourful rock agama, and a variety of snakes are present but, as ever, very secretive.

Dangerous animals

Although it is technically forbidden to leave your vehicle except at designated lookout points, the guides in Akagera seem to enforce this rule somewhat whimsically. Bizarrely, the guides we used were very nervous about approaching elephant and buffalo in a vehicle (the former might sometimes go for a car, the latter only in freak instances), but were in our opinion dangerously blasé about trying to sneak up on elephants by foot. So it's probably worth noting that, whatever your guide might say, it is extremely foolhardy to leave the vehicle in the presence of elephant, buffalo or lion.

Hippo and crocodile are potentially dangerous, and claim far more human lives than any terrestrial African animal. For this reason, you should be reasonably cautious when you leave the car next to a lake, particularly at dusk or dawn or in overcast conditions, when hippos are most likely to come out of the water to graze. The danger with hippos is getting *between* them and the water; you have nothing to worry about when they are actually in the water. Special caution should be exercised if you camp next to a lake – don't wander too far from your site after dark, and take a good look around should you need to leave your tent during the night (if there are hippo close by, you'll almost certainly hear them chomping at the grass). Crocs are a real threat only if you are daft enough to wade into one of the lakes.

The most dangerous animal in Akagera is the malaria-carrying anopheles mosquito. Cover up after dark – long trousers and thick socks – and smear any exposed parts of your body with insect repellent. Many tents come with built-in mosquito netting. This will protect you when you sleep, provided that you don't hang a light at the entrance to your tent, which will ensure that a swarm of insects enter it with you. Incidentally, never leave any food in your tent: fruit might attract the attention of monkeys and elephants, while meat could arouse the interest of large predators.

Not so much a danger as a nuisance are tsetse flies, which are quite common in dense bush and can give a painful bite. Fortunately, the pain isn't enduring (though people who tend to react badly to insect bites might want to douse any tsetse bite in antihistamine cream) and there is no risk of contracting sleeping sickness during a short stay in Akagera. Insect repellents have little effect on these robust little creatures, but it's worth noting that they are attracted to dark clothing (especially blue).

Further information
A useful fold-out colour map is sold at the ORTPN office in Kigali. This map was accurate before the civil war, and it remains so for the southern part of the park. However, it does still show the old park boundaries, and details in the north are rather historical. The numbered junctions shown on the map help with navigation, though only about half of the junctions are still numbered on the ground. The map costs around US$2.50 and includes some descriptive material about the park on the flip.

Getting there and away
In a private vehicle, Akagera can be reached from Kigali in a long two hours, and from Kibungo or Rwamagana in about one hour. The only usable entrance gate, 500m from the new Akagera Game Lodge, is reached via a 27km dirt road which branches from the main surfaced road at Kabarondo,15km north of Kibungo. This dirt road is in fair condition, passable in any vehicle except perhaps after rain. Within the park, however, a 4WD is advisable, though any vehicle with good clearance should be OK in the dry season.

Reaching Akagera on public transport is more problematic. Any minibus-taxi travelling between Kayonza and Kibungo can drop you at the junction, from where the only realistic option is a motorbike-taxi (assuming that you can find one). Inside the park, unless you're staying at the Game Lodge, no walking is permitted with or without a guide, and no vehicle is available for game drives.

Where to stay
At last there's accommodation right inside Akagera Park! The smart, new **Akagera Game Lodge** (BP 2288 Kigali; tel/fax: 83250) opened at the end of 2003 (on the site of the old Akagera Hotel, closed since the genocide), with 58 en-suite double studios (two double beds in each) and two suites. Studio rates: B&B US$100 single, US$72pp double; half board US$115 single, US$85pp double. It's managed by the South African company GBD Hospitality & Leisure Managements Services; email: gbd@corpdial.co.za; web: www.goldenleopard.co.za. There's an à la carte/buffet restaurant, pool, conference facilities and tennis courts. Walks and game drives accompanied by guides can be arranged: game drive (two hours) US$25 per person; game trail (three hours) US$15 per person.

There's also a **small bungalow** with three rooms (two double, one twin, shared facilities) beside Lake Ihema – make arrangements via ORTPN (see page 53). Next to it is a restaurant, which was closed when I checked – but food is available and there's a small sitting room.

Finally, for the self-sufficient, **camping** (US$3 per person) is allowed at various locations in the park; again, contact ORTPN.

Fees

An entrance fee equivalent to about US$7 per person is charged, plus US$3.50 for a car and US$4.50 for a 4WD. So far as we could establish, this is a genuine entrance fee as opposed to a daily fee – in other words, you only pay when you enter, no matter how long you spend in the park.

Boat trips

Boat trips are generally available on Lake Ihema, and are worthwhile. Book in advance via ORTPN in Kigali – see page 53. Close encounters with outsized crocodiles and large pods of hippo are all but guaranteed, and you'll also pass substantial breeding colonies of African darter, cormorant and open-bill stork. Other waterbirds are abundant: the delicate and colourful African jacana can be seen trotting on floating vegetation, fish eagles are posted in the trees at regular intervals, jewel-like malachite kingfishers hawk from the reeds, while pied kingfishers hover high above the water to swoop down on their fishy prey. Of greater interest to enthusiasts will be the opportunity to spot marsh specialists such as blue-headed coucal and marsh flycatcher. On a less positive note, you won't fail to notice the thick, dirty foam that laps the lake's shores (evidence of a high level of pollution).

Game drives

Unless you're staying in the Game Lodge, game drives are available only if you have a private vehicle, ideally a 4WD. Guides can be provided at no extra charge (though a tip will be expected) and, while most of them have limited knowledge, they will help you to find your way around and will probably be better at picking up game in the thick bush. The game-viewing circuit is in essence limited to one main road running northwards from the park headquarters at Lake Ihema. Most of the lakes are passed by this road, or can be approached using a short fork. North of Lake Hago, the road branches into two main forks, one of which heads west into the Mutumba Hills, the other continuing along the lake route. These roads reconnect at Lake Rwanyakizinga.

The possibilities for game drives are restricted by the fact that the park can only be entered near Lake Ihema and the Game Lodge. In a long half-day, you could realistically travel from the entrance as far north as the Mutumba Hills and back. To head further north requires the best part of a day, with the option of using the exit-only route north of Lake Rwanyakizinga emerging on the main tar road to the Uganda border. The tracks in the far north are very indistinct, and should be attempted only in the company of a guide. Once back on the main road, the guide can be dropped at Kayonza or Kabarondo junctions with enough money to make his way back to the headquarters by motorbike-taxi.

Starting from the entrance gate, a hilly road through very thick scrub leads over about 5km to **Lake Ihema**. Defassa waterbuck are resident in this area, as are some reportedly aggressive buffaloes. The park headquarters at the lake are worth stopping at to look for hippos, crocodiles and waterbirds. Baboons hang around the headquarters, and a pair of the localised white-headed black chat is resident. This is also where boat trips can be arranged.

About 4km north of Lake Ihema, a road forks through more thick scrub to the small **Lake Shakani**, a scenic camping spot and home to large numbers of hippo. The bush here is rattling with birdlife (look out for the brilliant red chest of the black-headed gonalek) and impala are rather common. Unfortunately the lake is also a popular place to water cattle. About 8km north of this, **Lake Birengiro** is a shallow, muddy body of palm-fringed water which supports huge numbers of waterbirds, notably pelicans, storks and the odd long-toed plover. The best of the lakes for general game viewing, however, is **Lake Hago**, about 15km further north and encircled by a decent track. This is where elephant are most likely to be seen, as well as small herds of buffalo and zebra, and it must support several hundred hippo.

South of Lake Hago, the vegetation is mostly very dense, and animals are difficult to spot, though you can be reasonably confident of seeing baboons, vervet monkeys and impala. This all changes when you turn left at Junction 23, to ascend towards the **Mutumba Hills** through an area of park-like woodland whose large acacias are favoured by giraffe. Eventually the woodland gives way to open grassland and easily the best game viewing in the park. Here, you can be certain of seeing the delicate oribi and reedbuck, as well as the larger topi. With luck, you'll also encounter eland, zebra and (in the wet season) large herds of buffalo.

North of the Mutumba Hills, the vegetation is again very thick, and animals can be difficult to spot, though impala, buffalo and zebra all seem to be present in significant numbers. The papyrus beds around **Lakes Gishanju** and **Mihindi** form the most accessible marshy areas in the park, and are worth taking slowly by anybody who hopes to see papyrus-dwellers. The **Plage Hippos** (Hippo Beach) on Lake Mihindi was, oddly, about the one place in Akagera where we stopped next to open water and *didn't* see any hippos, but it's a pretty spot, and would make for an ideal picnic site.

Heading further north, **Lake Rwanyakizinga** is another favoured spot with elephants, and the open plains to the west of the lake are excellent for plains animals such as warthog, zebra and herds of 50-plus topi. This little-visited part of Akagera is one that is inhabited by lion – and possibly rhino. Having looked around this area, your options are either to head back the way you came, or (more popular) to head cross-country out of the park along the route mentioned earlier in this section.

Appendix 1

LANGUAGE

Words in Kinyarwanda are spelt phonetically here, to make their pronunciation easy. The letters 'r' and 'l' (and their sounds) are often interchanged, also sometimes 'b', 'v' and 'w'. When a word ends in 'e', pronounce it as the French 'é'. Pronounce 'i' as 'ee' rather than 'eye'.

English	French	Kinyarwanda
Courtesies		
good day/hello	*bonjour*	*muraho*
good morning	*bonjour*	*mwaramutse*
good afternoon	*bonjour*	*mwiriwe*
good evening	*bonsoir*	*mwiriwe*
sir	*monsieur*	*bwana*
madam	*madame*	*mubyeyi*
how are you?	*ça va?*	*amakuru?/bitese?*
I'm fine, thank you	*ça va bien, merci*	*amakuru/meza/égo*
please	*s'il vous plaît*	*mubishoboye*
thank you	*merci*	*murakoze*
excuse me	*excusez moi*	*imbabazi*
goodbye (morning)	*au revoir*	*mwiliwe*
goodbye (afternoon)	*au revoir*	*mwilirwe*
goodbye (evening)	*au revoir*	*muramukeho*
goodbye (for ever)	*au revoir/adieu*	*murabeho*
Basic words		
yes	*oui*	*yégo*
no	*non*	*oya*
that's right	*c'est ça*	*ni byo*
maybe	*peut-être*	*ahali*
good	*bon*	*byiza*
hot	*chaud*	*ubushyuhe*
cold	*froid*	*ubukonje*
and	*et*	*na*
Questions		
how?	*comment?*	*bite?*

English	French	Kinyarwanda
how much?	*combien?*	*angahe?*
what's your name?	*quel est votre nom?*	*witwande?*
when?	*quand?*	*ryali?*
where?	*où?*	*hehe?*
who?	*qui?*	*nde?/bande?*

Food/drink

beans	*haricots*	*ibihyimbo*
beer	*bière*	*byeri*
butter	*beurre*	*amavuta*
bread	*pain*	*umugati*
coffee	*café*	*ikawa*
eggs	*oeufs*	*amagi*
fish	*poisson*	*amafi*
meat	*viande*	*inyama*
milk	*lait*	*amata*
potatoes	*pommes de terre*	*ibirayi*
rice	*riz*	*umuceli*
salad	*salade*	*salade*
soup	*potage*	*isupu*
sugar	*sucre*	*isukali*
tea	*thé*	*icyayi (chai)*
tomatoes	*tomates*	*inyanya*
drinks	*boissons*	*ibinyobura*
water	*eau*	*amazi*

Shopping

bank	*banque*	*ibanki*
bookshop	*librairie*	*isomero*
chemist	*pharmacie*	*farumasi*
shop	*magazin*	*iduka*
market	*marché*	*isoko*
battery	*pile/batterie*	*bateri*
film	*filme*	*filime*
map	*carte*	*ikarita*
money	*argent*	*amafaranga*
soap	*savon*	*isabuni*
toothpaste	*dentifrice*	*umuti w'amenyo*

Post

post office	*poste (PTT)*	*iposta*
envelope	*enveloppe*	*ibahasha*
letter	*lettre*	*urwandiko*
paper	*papier*	*urupapuro*
postcard	*carte postale*	

English	French	Kinyarwanda
stamp	*timbre*	*tembri*

Getting around

English	French	Kinyarwanda
bus	*bus*	*bisi*
bus station	*gare routière*	*aho bisi ihagarara*
taxi	*taxi*	*tagisi*
car	*voiture*	*imodoka*
petrol station	*station d'essence*	*aho kunyweshereza essence*
plane	*avion*	*indege*
far	*loin*	*kure*
near	*près*	*hafi*
to the right	*à droit*	*i buryo*
to the left	*à gauche*	*i bumoso*
straight ahead	*tout droit*	*imbere*
bridge	*pont*	*ikiraro*
hill	*colline*	*agasozi*
lake	*lac*	*ikiyaga*
mountain	*montagne*	*umusozi*
river	*fleuve*	*uruzi*
road	*route*	*umuhanda*
street	*rue*	*inzira*
town	*ville*	*umudugudu*
valley	*vallée*	*umubanda*
village	*village*	*akadugudu*
waterfall	*chute*	*isumo*

Hotel

English	French	Kinyarwanda
bed	*lit*	*igitanda*
room	*chambre*	*icyumba*
key	*clef/clé*	*urufunguzo*
shower	*douche*	*urwiyu hagiriro*
bath	*baignoire*	*urwogero*
toilet/WC	*toilette*	*umusarane*
hot water	*l'eau chaude*	*amazi ashushye*
cold water	*l'eau froide*	*amazi akonje*

Miscellaneous

English	French	Kinyarwanda
dentist	*dentiste*	*umuganga w'amenyo*
doctor	*médecin*	*umuganga*
embassy	*ambassade*	*ambasade*
tourist office	*bureau de tourisme*	*ibiro by ubukererarugendo*

Time

English	French	Kinyarwanda
minute	*minute*	*idakika*
hour	*heure*	*isaaha*

English	French	Kinyarwanda
day	*jour*	*umunsi*
week	*semaine*	*icyumweru*
month	*mois*	*ukwezi*
year	*an/année*	*umwaka*
now	*maintenant*	*ubu/nonaha*
soon	*bientôt*	*vuba*
today	*aujourd'hui*	*none*
yesterday	*hier*	*ejo hashize*
tomorrow	*demain*	*ejo hazaza*
this week	*cette semaine*	*iki cyumweru*
next week	*semaine prochaine*	*icyumweru gitaha*
morning	*matin*	*igitondo*
afternoon	*après-midi*	*ni munsi*
evening	*soir*	*umugoroba*
night	*nuit*	*ijoro*
Monday	*lundi*	*ku wa mbere*
Tuesday	*mardi*	*ku wa kabili*
Wednesday	*mercredi*	*ku wa gatatu*
Thursday	*jeudi*	*ku wa kane*
Friday	*vendredi*	*ku wa gatanu*
Saturday	*samedi*	*ku wa gatandatu*
Sunday	*dimanche*	*ku cyumweru*
January	*janvier*	*Mutarama*
February	*février*	*Gashyantare*
March	*mars*	*Werurwe*
April	*avril*	*Mata*
May	*mai*	*Gicuransi*
June	*juin*	*Kamena*
July	*juillet*	*Nyakanga*
August	*août*	*Kanama*
September	*septembre*	*Nzeli*
October	*octobre*	*Ukwakira*
November	*novembre*	*Ugushyingo*
December	*décembre*	*Ukuboza*

African English

Philip Briggs

Although a high proportion of Rwandans were raised in Kenya, Uganda or Tanzania and so speak English as a second language, not all get the opportunity to use it regularly, and as a result they will not be as fluent as they could be. Furthermore, as is often the case in Africa and elsewhere, an individual's pronunciation of a second language often tends to retain the vocal inflections of their first language, or it falls somewhere between that and a more standard pronunciation. It is also the case that many people tend to structure sentences in a second language similar to how they would in their home tongue. As a result, most Rwandans, to a greater or lesser extent, speak English with Bantu inflections and grammar.

The above considerations aside, I would venture that African English – like American or Australian English – is over-due recognition as a distinct linguistic entity, possessed of a unique rhythm and pronunciation, as well as an idiomatic quality quite distinct from any form of English spoken elsewhere. And learning to communicate in this idiom is perhaps the most important linguistic skill that the visitor to any African country where English is spoken can acquire. If this sounds patronising, so be it. There are regional accents in the UK and US that I find far more difficult to follow than the English spoken in Africa, simply because I am more familiar with the latter. And precisely the same adjustment might be required were, for instance, an Australian to travel in the American south, a Geordie to wash up in my home town of Johannesburg, or vice versa.

The following points should prove useful when you speak English to Africans:

- Greet simply, using phrases likely to be understood locally: the ubiquitous sing-song 'How-are-you! – I am fine', or if that draws a blank try the pidgin Swahili 'Jambo!' It is important always to greet a stranger before you plough ahead and ask directions or any other question. Firstly, it is rude to do otherwise; secondly, most Westerners feel uncomfortable asking a stranger a straight question. If you have already greeted the person, you'll feel less need to preface a question with phrases like 'I'm terribly sorry' or 'Would you mind telling me' which will confuse someone who speaks limited English.

- Speak slowly and clearly. There is no need, as some travellers do, to take this too far, as if you are talking to a three-year-old. Speak naturally, but try not to rush or clip phrases.

- Phrase questions simply, with an ear towards Bantu inflections. 'This bus goes to Butare?' might be more easily understood than 'Could you tell me whether this bus is going to Butare?' and 'You have a room?' is better than 'Is there a vacant room?' If you are not understood, don't keep repeating the same question more loudly. Try a different and ideally simpler phrasing, giving consideration to whether any specific word(s) – in the last case, most likely 'vacant' – might particularly obstruct easy understanding.

- Listen to how people talk to you, and learn from it. Vowel sounds are often pronounced as in the local language (see Kinyarwanda pronunciation above), so that 'bin', for instance, might sound more like 'been'. Many words, too, will be pronounced with the customary Bantu stress on the second-last syllable.

- African languages generally contain few words with compound consonant sounds or ending in consonants. This can result in the clipping of soft consonant sounds such as 'r' (important as eem-POT-ant) or the insertion of a random vowel sound between running consonants (so that pen-pal becomes pen-I-pal and sounds almost indistinguishable from pineapple). It is commonplace, as well, to append a random vowel to the end of a word, in the process shifting the stress to what would ordinarily be the last syllable e.g. pen-i-PAL-i.

- The 'l' and 'r' sounds are sometimes used interchangeably (hence Lake

Burera/Bulera and Rue Karisimbi/Kalisimbi), which can sometimes cause confusion, in particular when your guide points out a lilac-breasted roller! The same is to a lesser extent true of 'b' and 'v' (Virunga versus Birunga), 'k' and 'ch' (the Rwandan capital, spelt Kigali, is more often pronounced 'Chigari') and, very occasionally, 'f' and 'p'.

- Some English words are in wide use. Other similar words are not. Some examples: a request for a 'lodging' or 'guesthouse', is more likely to be understood than one for 'accommodation', as is a request for a 'taxi' (or better 'special hire') over a 'taxi-cab' or 'cab', or for 'the balance' rather than 'change'.
- Avoid the use of dialect-specific expressions, slang and jargon! Few Africans will be familiar with terms such as 'feeling crook', 'pear-shaped' or 'user-friendly'.
- Avoid meaningless interjections. If somebody is struggling to follow you, appending a word such as 'mate' to every other phrase is only likely to further confuse them.
- We've all embarrassed ourselves at some point by mutilating the pronunciation of a word we've read but not heard. Likewise, guides working in national parks and other reserves often come up with innovative pronunciations for bird and mammal names they come across in field guides, and any word with an idiosyncratic spelling (eg: yacht, lamb, knot).
- Make sure the person you are talking to understands you. Try to avoid asking questions that can be answered with a yes or no. People may well agree with you simply to be polite or to avoid embarrassment.
- Keep calm. No-one is at their best when they arrive at a crowded bus station after an all-day bus ride. It is easy to be short tempered when someone cannot understand you. Be patient and polite; it's you who doesn't speak the language.
- Last but not least, do gauge the extent to which the above rules might apply to any given individual. It would be patently ridiculous to address a university lecturer or an experienced tour guide in broken English, equally inappropriate to babble away without making any allowances when talking to a villager who clearly has a limited English vocabulary. Generally, I start off talking normally to anybody I meet, and only start to refine my usage as and when it becomes clear it will aid communication.

Appendix 2

WEBSITES AND CONTACT DETAILS
Websites

For up-to-the-minute news reports from Rwanda and elsewhere in Africa the most comprehensive site is probably **www.allafrica.com**. Follow links to Rwanda. The bi-weekly Rwandan newspaper *The New Times* sometimes has news items not picked up elsewhere: **www.newtimes.co.rw**. A good site for checking the latest currency exchange rate (not all of them include the Rwandan franc) is **www.xe.com**. Conditions in Rwanda – as elsewhere in Africa – may change, so as a precautionary measure, before travelling, always check the Foreign Office website **www.fco.gov.uk/knowbeforeyougo**, or that of the US State Department: **http://travel.state.gov/travel_warnings.html**.

Four comprehensive websites on Rwanda are **www.rwandemb.org** (set up by the Rwandan Embassy in Washington, DC); the official Rwanda government website **www.rwanda1.com**; that of the Rwandan Embassy in London: **www.ambarwanda.org.uk**; and that of ORTPN (the Rwanda Tourist Board): **www.visitrwanda.gov.rw**, which provides impressive 'virtual tours' of many of the country's attractions. All have numerous links and cover a wide range of topics, including Rwanda's history, geography, politics, development, genocide trials, economy, business potential and tourism. On the whole they are up to date although some sections haven't been touched for a while at the time of writing. This is a problem with all sites giving information about Rwanda: things are changing so fast that practical details (visa costs, phone numbers, addresses, hotels…) don't get updated regularly. A little tip: Kigali phone numbers now either have six digits and start with 5, or have five digits and start with 8. So, if a website quotes a Kigali number that has five digits and doesn't start with 8, it is out of date: prefix the number with 5.

The website of the National University of Rwanda has useful information about the country as a whole, plus various links: **www.nur.ac.rw**. The KIST site (see pages 108–9) is also helpful: **www.kist.ac.rw**.

The site of the UN International Criminal Tribunal for Rwanda, **www.ictr.org**, has details of the current status of genocide criminals and the trials in progress. Human Rights Watch on **www.hrw.org** carries news of Rwanda, as does the Amnesty International site **www.amnesty.org**.

Finally, just doing a general internet search under 'Rwanda' will throw up a huge range of miscellaneous information, some of it reasonably up to date and some more than a decade old. You really need to aim for something specific, such as 'Rwanda+gorillas', otherwise it's hard to sift the good from the bad.

Contact addresses

Centre Presbytérien d'Amour de Jeunes (see page 89) BP 56 Kigali; tel/fax: 576929

CICODEB (see page 88) BP1579 Kigali; tel: 519043, 08530185; email: cicodeb@yahoo.fr

Communauté des Autochtones Rwandais or **CAURWA** (see pages 77–8) BP 3809 Kigali; tel: 577640 or 08689551; email: CAURWA@rwanda1.com

Engalynx (see page 87) 35 Birch Drive, Brantham, Suffolk CO11 1TG, UK; tel: 01206 395089; email: lantern@cpwpost.com

Forest Peoples' Project (see page 85) 1c Fosseway Centre, Stratford Rd, Moreton-in-Marsh, Glos GL56 9NQ, England; tel: 01608 652893; fax: 01608 652878; email: info@fppwrm.gn.apc.org; web: www.forestpeoples.org

Imbabazi Orphanage (see pages 197–9) BP98 Gisenyi; tel: 540740

Kigali Institute of Science, Technology & Management (see pages 108–9) Av de l'Armée, BP 3900 Kigali; tel: 574696; email: info@kist.ac.rw; web: www.kist.ac.rw

Kigali Public Library (see pages 82–3) tel (part-time Kigali office): 514338, 083128888; email: kigalilibrary@aol.com; web: www.kigalilibrary.com

National Museum of Rwanda (see pages 137–8) Butare; tel: 530586, 530207; fax: 530211; email: museumrwanda@yahoo.fr

National University of Rwanda (see page 136) BP56 Butare; tel: 530122; fax: 530121; email: nurcc@nur.ac.rw; web: www.nur.ac.rw

Nyamata Vocational School Project (see pages 84–5) via RUGO (below)

Office Rwandais du Tourisme et des Parcs Nationaux (see page 53) Bd de la Révolution, BP 905 Kigali; tel: 576514/5, 573396; fax: 576515; email: ortpn@rwanda.com and info@rwandatourism.com; web: www.rwandatourism.com

ORTPN see above

Parrainages Mondiaux see World Sponsorships

PASSEVU (see page 87) BP4261 Kigali; tel: 08534152; fax: 517222; email: passevu@yahoo.fr

Rwanda Investment Promotion Agency (see page 90) BP 6239 Kigali; tel: 510248, 510251; fax: 510249; email: investrw@rwanda1.com

Rwanda United Kingdom Goodwill Organisation or **RUGO** (see pages 83–5) c/o Mike Hughes (chairman) tel (UK): 01252 861059 or Ernest Sagaga (Secretary) 26 Thurlby Close, Harrow, Middx HA1 2LZ, UK; tel: 020 8427 3186; web: www.rugo.org

Send a Cow UK (see pages 85–7) Unit 4, Priston Mill, Priston, Bath BA2 9EQ, UK; tel: 01225 447041; email: info@sendacow.org.uk; web: www.sendacow.org.uk

Voluntary Service Overseas (see pages 80–1) 31 Putney Bridge Rd, London SW15 2PN; tel: 020 8780 7200; web: www.vso.org.uk

World Sponsorships/Parrainages Mondiaux (see page 89) 33 rue du Marché, 4500 Huy, Belgium; tel: 085 613520; fax: 085 230147; email: asbl.adpm.huy@belgacom.net

Appendix 3

FURTHER READING
Historical background

Reader, John *Africa: A Biography of the Continent* Hamish Hamilton, 1997
This award-winning book, available as a Penguin paperback, provides a compulsively readable introduction to Africa's past, from the formation of the continent to post-independence politics – the ideal starting point for anybody seeking to place their Rwandan experience in a broader African context.

Fegley, Randall (compiler) *Rwanda – World Bibliographical Series volume 154* Clio Press, 1993
This selective, annotated bibliography contains over 500 entries covering a wide range of subjects including Rwanda's history, geography, politics, literature, travellers' accounts, flora and fauna. Its preface and introduction give a condensed but useful (although somewhat dated) overview of Rwanda from early times until just before the genocide.

Kagame, Alexis *Un abrégé de l'ethno-historie du Rwanda* and *Un abrégé de l'histoire du Rwanda de 1853 à 1972*, Editions Universitaires du Rwanda, Butare, 1972 and 1975.
These works are now out of print (and there are no English translations) but the seriously interested should try to track down secondhand copies. Drawing on oral tradition, Kagame describes the country and its people from several centuries before the arrival of the Europeans (in the first book) through to the first decade of colonisation (in the second).

Natural history
Field guides (mammals)

Kingdon, Jonathan *The Kingdon Field Guide to African Mammals* Academic Press, 1997
This is my first choice: the most detailed, thorough and up-to-date of several field guides covering the mammals of the region. The author, a highly respected biologist, supplements detailed descriptions and good illustrations of all the continent's large mammals with an ecological overview of each species. Essential for anybody with a serious interest in mammal identification.

Stuart, Chris & Tilde *The Larger Mammals of Africa* Struik, 1997
This useful field guide doesn't quite match up to Kingdon's, but it's definitely the best of the rest, and arguably more appropriate to readers with

a relatively casual interest in African wildlife. It's also a lot cheaper and lighter!

Stuart, Chris & Tilde *Southern, Central and East African Mammals* Struik, 1995
This excellent mini-guide, compact enough to slip into a pocket, is remarkably thorough within its inherent space restrictions. Highly recommended for one-off safari-goers, but not so good for forest primates, which limits its usefulness in Rwanda.

Dorst, J & Dandelot, P *Field Guide to the Larger Mammals of Africa* Collins, 1983
Haltenorth, T & Diller, H *Field Guide to the Mammals of Africa including Madagascar* Collins, 1984
Formerly the standard field guides to the region, these books are still recommended in many travel guides. In my opinion, they have largely been superseded by subsequent publications, and now come across as very dated and badly structured – with mediocre illustrations to boot.

Estes, Richard *The Safari Companion* Green Books (UK), Russell Friedman Books (SA), Chelsea Green (USA)
This unconventional book might succinctly be described as a field guide to mammal behaviour. It's probably a bit esoteric for most one-off visitors to Africa, but a must for anybody with a serious interest in wildlife.

Field guides (birds)

Stevenson, Terry & Fanshawe, John *Field Guide to the Birds of East Africa* T & A D Poyser, 2002
The best bird field guide, with useful field descriptions and accurate plates and distribution maps. It covers every species found in Rwanda as well as in Uganda, Kenya, Tanzania and Burundi. For serious birdwatchers, this is *the* book to take.

Van Perlo, Ber *Illustrated Checklist to the Birds of Eastern Africa* Collins, 1995
This is the next best thing to the above (and is cheaper and lighter), since it illustrates and provides a brief description of every species recorded in Uganda and Tanzania, along with a distribution map. I don't know of any bird found in Rwanda but not in Tanzania or Uganda, and I found that distribution details can normally be extrapolated from the maps of neighbouring countries. Be aware that the descriptive detail is very succinct and many of the illustrations are misleading

Williams, J & Arlott, N *Field Guide to the Birds of East Africa* Collins, 1980
As with the older Collins mammal field guides, Williams' was for years the standard field guide to the region, and is still widely mentioned in travel literature. Unfortunately, it feels rather dated today: less than half the birds in the region are illustrated, several are not even described, and the bias is strongly towards common Kenyan birds.

Zimmerman et al *Birds of Kenya and Northern Tanzania* Russell Friedman Books, 1996
This monumentally handsome hardback tome is arguably the finest field guide to any African territory in print. The geographical limitations with

regard to Rwanda are obvious, but its wealth of descriptive and ecological detail and superb illustrations make it an excellent secondary source. A lighter and cheaper but less detailed paperback version was published in 1999.

Others

Fossey, Dian *Gorillas in the Mist* Hodder & Stoughton, 1983
Enjoyable and massively informative, Fossey's landmark book is recommended without reservation to anybody going gorilla-tracking in the Parc des Volcans.

Goodall, Jane *Through A Window* Houghton Mifflin, 1991
Subtitled *My Thirty Years with the Chimpanzees of Gombe*, this is one of several highly readable books by Jane Goodall about the longest ongoing study of wild primates in the world. Set in Tanzania, this is nevertheless obvious pre-trip reading for anybody intending to track chimps in Nyungwe.

Kingdon, Jonathon *Island Africa* Collins, 1990
This highly readable and award-winning tome about evolution in ecological 'islands' such as deserts and montane forests is recommended to anybody who wants to place the natural history of Nyungwe and the Virungas in a continental context.

Mowat, Farley *Woman in the Mists* Futura, 1987
An excellent biography of the controversial Dian Fossey, one which leans so heavily on her own journals that parts are almost autobiography.

Stuart, Chris & Tilde *Africa's Vanishing Wildlife* Southern Books, 1996
An informative and pictorially strong introduction to the endangered and vulnerable mammals of Africa, this book combines coffee-table production with an impassioned and erudite text.

Background to the genocide

Prunier, Gérard *The Rwanda Crisis – History of a Genocide* Hurst & Company, 1998
This painstakingly researched history of the Rwandan genocide, full of personal anecdotes and individual stories, describes with icy clarity the composition of the time bomb that began ticking long before its explosion in 1994. Prunier presents the genocide as part of a deadly logic, a plan hatched for political and economic motives, rather than the result of ancient hatred. He helps the reader to understand not only Rwanda's genocide but also the complexities of modern conflict in general.

Melvern, L R *A People Betrayed – the Role of the West in Rwanda's Genocide* Zed Books, 2000
Linda Melvern's investigative study of the international background to Rwanda's genocide contains a full narrative account of how the tragedy unfolded. Documents held in Kigali, and previously unpublished accounts of secret UN Security council deliberations in New York, reveal a shocking sequence of events, and the failure of governments, organisations and individuals who could – had they opted to do so – have prevented the

genocide. Melvern also recounts the all-too-often forgotten heroism of those who stayed on in Rwanda and did what they could in deteriorating conditions.

Gourevitch, Philip *We wish to inform you that tomorrow we will be killed with our families* Picador, 1998
Subtitled 'Stories from Rwanda', this winner of the *Guardian* First Book Award is war reporting of the highest order. Blending starkly factual narrative with human anecdotes and observations, Gourevitch paints on a broad canvas and the picture he creates is unforgettable. He shows us 'little people' caught up in unstoppable horrors – and reaching great heights of heroism.

Rwanda – Death, Despair and Defiance African Rights, London, 1995
This 1,200-page compilation by the UK organisation African Rights is a painfully thorough and detailed account of the genocide and its effect on Rwanda's people – the careful preparations, the identities of the killers and their accomplices, the massacres, the attacks on churches, schools and hospitals, and the aftermath. Victims tell their own stories and those of their families, and the horror and immensity of the slaughter are highlighted by the simplicity of their narratives. The impact is powerful, sometimes overwhelming. The index enables the reader to discover easily what happened in any particular area or village.

Leave None to Tell the Story African Rights Watch, 1999
Another painfully comprehensive account, full of personal testimonies based on Rwandan government records, this shows how ordinary administrative structures and practices were turned into mechanisms of murder. It describes the opposition to the killing and how it was crushed, while survivors relate how they resisted and escaped. Using diplomatic and court documents, the survey shows what might have been the result had the international reaction been swifter and more determined.

Barnett, Michael *Eyewitness to a Genocide: The United Nations and Rwanda* Cornell University, 2002
Tracing the history of the UN's involvement with Rwanda, Barnett argues that it did bear some moral responsibility for the genocide. A clear and factual study, also covering the warnings raised by the genocide and the question of whether it is possible to build wholly moral institutions.

Berkeley, Bill *The Graves are not yet Full* Basic Books, 2001
Pulling no punches, Berkeley focuses on the individuals, scholar-diplomats as well as Africans, whose greed and obsession with power fuel the conflicts devastating so much of Africa. He shows that behind apparently random slaughter lies a method that serves the powerful and power-hungry.

Keane, Fergal *Season of Blood – a Rwandan Journey* Penguin, 1995
Keane's prose – sometimes so precisely balanced that it verges on poetry – is always impeccable. Here he blends factual narrative and analysis with spontaneous emotion in such a way that the reader is both moved and informed in a single phrase. As a BBC correspondent, he was travelling around Rwanda – among the killers and among the victims – as the genocide spread countrywide.

His reports at the time brought home the extent of the human tragedy and their essence is preserved in this book, which won the 1995 Orwell Prize.

Sibomana, André *Hope for Rwanda* Pluto Press, 1999
In this very personal account, subtitled *Conversations with Laure Guilbert and Hervé Deguine*, the speaker describes the unfolding of the genocide, and his own experiences, with impressive fairness, clarity and lack of accusation. A touching and informative book by a remarkable man.

Miscellaneous
Lewis, Jerome & Knight, Judy *The Twa of Rwanda* World Rainforest Movement (UK), 1996
The Twa are the smallest 'ethnic' group in Rwanda. This report, published by the World Rainforest Movement in co-operation with the International Work Group for Indigenous Affairs (Denmark) and Survival International (France), traces their history, highlights their current impoverished situation, quotes their opinions about their past and future, and allows them to express their fears and aspirations. It also shows the dilemma faced by African governments as they try to build national unity while still respecting cultural diversity.

Halsey Carr, R & Howard Halsey, A H *Land of a Thousand Hills* Viking, 1999
Rosamond Halsey Carr moved to Rwanda as a young bride in 1949 and has stayed for over 50 years. She watched the decline of colonialism, the problems of independence and the growing violence. When the genocide started she was evacuated by the American Embassy but returned four months later, and began turning an old pyrethrum drying-house on her flower plantation into a home for genocide orphans, which – now relocated near Gisenyi – still functions today. This very readable and moving book chronicles the extraordinary life of an extraordinary woman, in the country she loved and made her home.

Stassen, Jean-Philippe *Déogratias* Aire Libre, Dupuis (Belgium) 2000
If you can read at least some French, this 80-page *bande dessinée* (graphic novel) tells the story of a young Hutu who killed during the genocide and how this, together with drink, destroyed him. With skill and humanity, the creator succeeds in 'telling the untellable' and producing a powerful document.

242

CLAIM YOUR HALF-PRICE BRADT GUIDE!

Order Form

To order your half-price copy of a Bradt guide, and to enter our prize draw to win £100 (see overleaf), please fill in the order form below, complete the questionnaire overleaf, and send it to Bradt Travel Guides by post, fax or email. Post and packing is free to UK addresses.

Please send me one copy of the following guide at half the UK retail price

Title   *Retail price   Half price*

Please send the following additional guides at full UK retail price

No	*Title*	*Retail price*	*Total*
. . .	. . . .	. . . . . .	. . . . . .
. . .	. . . .	. . . . . .	. . . . . .
. . .	. . . .	. . . . . .	. . . . . .

Sub total . . . . . .
Post & packing outside UK . . . . . .
(£2 per book Europe; £3 per book rest of world)
Total . . . . . .

Name . . . .

Address . . . .

Tel. . . . .   Email . . . .

☐ I enclose a cheque for £. . . . . . . made payable to Bradt Travel Guides Ltd

☐ I would like to pay by VISA or MasterCard

   Number . . . .   Expiry date . . . .

☐ Please add my name to your catalogue mailing list.

Send your order on this form, with the completed questionnaire, to:

Bradt Travel Guides/RWA
19 High Street, Chalfont St Peter, Bucks SL9 9QE
Tel: +44 1753 893444 Fax: +44 1753 892333
Email: info@bradt-travelguides.com
www.bradt-travelguides.com

WIN £100 CASH!

READER QUESTIONNAIRE

Win a cash prize of £100 for the first completed questionnaire drawn after May 31 2004.

All respondents may order a Bradt guide at half the UK retail price – please complete the order form overleaf.

(Entries may be posted or faxed to us, or scanned and emailed.)

We are interested in getting feedback from our readers to help us plan future Bradt guides. Please complete this quick questionnaire and return it to us to enter into our draw.

Have you used any other Bradt guides? If so, which titles?.................
....

What other publishers' travel guides do you use regularly? ....
....

Where did you buy this guidebook? ....

What was the main purpose of your trip to Rwanda (or for what other reason did you read our guide)? eg: holiday/business/charity etc. ....
....

What other destinations would you like to see covered by a Bradt guide?
....

Would you like to receive our catalogue/newsletters?

YES / NO (If yes, please complete details on reverse)

If yes – by post or email?...

Age (circle relevant category) 16–25   26–45   46–60   60+

Male/Female (delete as appropriate)

Home country...

Please send us any comments about our guide to Rwanda or other Bradt Travel Guides. ....
....
....
....

Bradt Travel Guides

19 High Street, Chalfont St Peter, Bucks SL9 9QE, UK
Telephone: +44 1753 893444 Fax: +44 1753 892333
Email: info@bradt-travelguides.com
www.bradt-travelguides.com

KEY TO STANDARD SYMBOLS   Bradt

—·—·—	International boundary	⊞	Historic building
------	District boundary	▥	Castle/fortress
-----	National park boundary	✝	Church or cathedral
✈	Airport (international)	♨	Buddhist temple
✈	Airport (other)	♠	Buddhist monastery
✛	Airstrip	♣	Hindu temple
⇝	Helicopter service	Ç	Mosque
▬▬	Railway	⚑	Golf course
·········	Footpath	🏃	Stadium
--🚢--	Car ferry	▲	Summit
--🚢--	Passenger ferry	△	Boundary beacon
⛽	Petrol station or garage	◉	Outpost
🅿	Car park	✕=✕	Border post
🚌	Bus station etc	⌂	Rock shelter
🚲	Cycle hire	□—●—□	Cable car, funicular
M	Underground station	⏝	Mountain pass
⌂	Hotel, inn etc	○	Waterhole
⚠	Campsite	✳	Scenic viewpoint
▮	Hut	✾	Botanical site
♀	Wine bar	♧	Specific woodland feature
✕	Restaurant, café etc	♨	Lighthouse
✉	Post office	≁	Marsh
☏	Telephone	⚐	Mangrove
e	Internet café	➤	Bird nesting site
✚	Hospital, clinic etc	▮	Turtle nesting site
⚱	Museum	～～	Coral reef
🐘	Zoo	➤	Beach
i	Tourist information	∭	Waterfall
$	Bank	⚲	Fishing sites
⚱	Statue or monument		
⁙	Archaeological or historic site		

Other map symbols are sometimes shown in separate key boxes with individual explanations for their meanings.

Index

Page numbers in bold refer to major entries; those in italics indicate maps